SCALE MODEL SAILING SHIPS

SCALE
MODEL
SAILING
SHIPS

Edited by
JOHN BOWEN

MAYFLOWER BOOKS

MAYFLOWER BOOKS, INC.,
575 LEXINGTON AVENUE,
NEW YORK CITY 10022.

Frontispiece. A wide range of sailing ship models competing in a rally for working models at Barrow-in-Furness, Cumbria.

Published in the United States
by Mayflower Books, Inc

ISBN 0-8317-7700-1

Designed by Ray Fishwick

Printed and bound
in the United Kingdom

Foreword

Ship modellers are essentially craftsmen with their hands, for it is only through the manipulative skill of their fingers that tools are made to do the work. But such dexterity is of little avail if the model shipwright is unable to find the information which he requires to pursue his hobby. Thus the aim of this book is not only to provide the beginner, as well as the more advanced worker, with a general guide to information sources and techniques — with particular reference to the galleon, the clipper ship and the fore and aft rigged coaster, which above all other types appear to hold the most attraction for modelmakers — but also to introduce the newcomers to various phases of the building of a ship model, as seen through the eyes of a number of expert modelmakers.

An enormous and bewildering array of prototypes is available to the modeller, but he will soon appreciate that the basic constructional and building techniques, once understood and mastered, can be applied with variations to ship models of all types. Apart from developing a skill in the use of tools, the rest is experience allied to a knowledge of the subject being modelled, and an appreciation of the customs and practices of the period in which the ship sailed.

Some of the contributors cover their particular subject in considerable detail, others range more generally over a broader spectrum, while others again delve into the 'artistic' aspect of the hobby. Backing all this is one of the most comprehensive bibliographies of source material yet to be made available to modellers, plus an extensive glossary of the specialized terminology of sailing ships. Furthermore, particular attention has been paid to the selection and use of the large numbers of photographs, which in themselves will form a valuable pictorial reference.

But whatever the treatment, the underlying theme is to show how to set about the task, and above all where to look for the answers to the many questions which will arise both before and after taking up a hobby whose utter fascination will surely engender a desire, once abilities have progressed beyond the scope of this volume, to acquire a still wider knowledge of the subject. We would like to feel that this book will provide the stimulus for that undertaking.

JOHN BOWEN

Contents

Acknowledgements

Any book is a co-operative venture involving many parties, but this one
more so than most. The publishers would like to thank all those who
helped or advised, and in particular the staffs of the Science Museum
and the National Maritime Museum Draught Room, who were helpful
beyond the call of duty.

Photographs came from many sources, but any that are uncredited
were provided by John Bowen. We are particularly grateful to Alan
Taverner for permission to use his colour photo of his *Bluenose*
model as a jacket illustration.

Making a start

1

by JOHN BOWEN

Although much of the content of the following chapters will relate to models of the three sailing ship types which seem to be of particular interest to modelmakers, nevertheless the information which they contain can be applied to, or used for, a much wider range of vessels. Before going on to talk about such matters as research, and plans and their sources, some points about the three groups will not come amiss.

Nowadays the word 'galleon' is used rather loosely to refer to most ships of the fifteenth and sixteenth centuries. This is a pity, for it was a particularly interesting period in the development of the sailing ship, being that in which the full rigged ship evolved from the single-masted square-sailed vessels of northern and Mediterranean waters. Those who desire further information on this fascinating interplay of hull forms and rigging styles will find much useful material in books such as Landström's *Sailing Ships* and Anderson's *The Sailing Ship*. The origin of the true galleon is somewhat obscure, but it is thought to be a development of the galleas, which in its turn was a descendant of the oared galleys. Some authorities claim that the Spaniards were the first to produce the type, others that it was Henry VIII who introduced it. Be that as it may, the Spaniards continued to use vessels of this kind for many years for their annual voyages to the West Indies and to South America — voyages which have acquired, in the course of time, many imaginary and highly coloured associations. No doubt it is these stories, with their air of romanticism and vivid illustrations, which have done much to establish the galleon — often called, too, the 'Elizabethan Ship' and the 'Period Ship' — as a popular subject for modelmakers, and particularly beginners. The simple

Left. The first of the three main types of ship discussed in this book. This fine sailing model of a galleon, or period ship, the *Elizabeth Jonas*, by A J Lench, shows the decorative nature of these vessels. Much of the decorative work of this period was achieved by the use of paint as distinct from carved work.

sail plan, the striking appearance of the hull with its brilliant paintwork and minimal amount of carved embellishment, all combine to produce a most decorative creation.

As with the galleon the 'clipper' ship has acquired a particular connotation in the minds of the modelmaker, conjuring up visions of the great 'tea clipper races' of the last century. The origin of the word 'clipper' has provided for many years a basis for much discussion and argument, and has produced many 'authentic' conclusions, all varied in content and degree of sophistication. The word itself is used extensively, and inaccurately, in a variety of contexts. The most generally accepted meaning refers to a vessel built essentially for speed, with cargo carrying ability of secondary importance. Contrary to the widely held view, it is not the sole prerogative of the ships engaged in the tea and opium trades of the last century, but is applicable to any type of sailing ship coming within the scope of the above category.

Although the building of clipper ships, both here and in America, extended over a period of thirty-five years from around 1840 onwards, it reached a peak in the early 1850s. Because speed is always news, not unnaturally the exploits and performance of some of these vessels received increasing publicity. This in turn produced, as with the galleon, an atmosphere of romance, the logical end product of which has been to find the better known craft becoming prototypes for models.

The third type of vessel is in complete contrast to the other two. The fore and aft rig was the basic sail plan for many small craft engaged both in coastal trades and for longer voyages to the Baltic, the Continent and the Mediterranean, as well as to American and Canadian waters. Schooners, particularly those engaged in the coastwise trade, make a very good subject for a model. Moreover, the fore and aft rig is eminently suitable for working models, and the enjoyment which can be had from

11

Left. The *Thermopylae* was among the best known of the clipper ships. This beautiful ⅛″ scale model by I Marsh gives a good idea of the lofty rig of these ships and the fine lines of the hull. The perfection of detail is enhanced by the simplicity of its conventional stand mounting and the omission of sails. It is interesting to note that the builder has completed the model with the yards trimmed away from the more customary square athwartships position.
(Photo: Conway Picture Library)

Below. In direct contrast is this action shot of the third type discussed — the fore and aft rigged vessel. This model of the fishing schooner *Bluenose* is about 48″ long. Being a fishing vessel her hull shape and deck layout differ from the coastal trading schooners, but the rig is generally similar. The photograph shows clearly the simple sail plan and the uncomplicated rigging, so it is easy to appreciate why this rig is so popular for working models. The prototypes are of reasonable size, so models can be built to largish scales yet remain of manageable proportions. That they can give much pleasurable sailing is amply shown here.
(Photo: A Taverner)

sailing such a model will be evident to anyone who has been present at one of the many regattas for sailing models held every year in different parts of the world.

These then are the ships. How can information about them be found? The answer lies in research, the key to sound authentic modelling. This is the first step which every modelmaker should undertake once he has decided upon his project: it can take one of two main forms. Original research is one — fundamentally this means delving into old records, trying to contact people with similar interests, and generally casting around in an endeavour to gather all the information possible about your project, not forgetting the historical aspect, so that when pieced

together you can feel sure that what you are about to create will be as authentic as possible. Obviously this is difficult in cases of vessels with obscure origins, or about which little is known or has appeared in print. The second category of research lies more in the field of familiarising yourself with the chosen subject, when this is one which has already been the object of much original work by others. It is then a case of seeking out the appropriate books, and as the majority of these will contain bibliographies and source references, your field is widened automatically. The Public Lending Library service can often be of immeasurable help; once the title is known, it is usually possible for your local branch to obtain a copy, even though it may have to come from a library many miles away. I say 'usually possible' because some books are held in reference libraries, and are not allowed out on loan.

Research naturally involves the question of plans. In the case of the 'galleon' no original plans of these vessels are thought to exist. The earliest known and only scale drawings of English ships of the sixteenth century are those which appear in a manuscript attributed to the contemporary shipwright Matthew Baker, and entitled *Fragments of Ancient English Shipwrightry*. This manuscript is preserved in the Pepysian Library at Magdalene College, Cambridge, England, but reproductions of the essential drawings have appeared in a number of books, such as *The Shipwright's Trade* by Sir Westcott Abell. The plans have been used as the basis both for models of ships of this period, examples of which can be found in many of the leading maritime museums, and for several of the full-size replicas built in recent years.

There are numerous models, and commercial sets of plans for models, of many of the well known vessels of this and earlier and later periods, to be

Below. Several replicas of early ships have been built in recent years to designs based on the Matthew Baker plans mentioned in the text. One of the best examples is this one of the Pilgrim Fathers' ship *Mayflower*. Launched at Brixham, Devon in 1957. (Photo: Conway Picture Library).

found both in this country and elsewhere. In the majority of cases — and I emphasise majority — they have been constructed, or prepared, after much laborious and painstaking research through contemporary records and voyage reports, from a study of paintings, and from such other fragments of documentary evidence which exist concerning sizes, tonnage, armament and so on. Many of these plans can be considered as the nearest possible representation to the original vessel in the light of all available information, but they cannot be considered as authentic in the strict sense of the word.

In contrast to the galleon, a considerable amount of reliable information about the clipper ships has survived both in the UK, in Europe and in America. Copies of the shipbuilders' plans for many of these vessels can be purchased, and there are quite a number of commercial organisations marketing authentic plans — based on the builders' original drawings — prepared specially for the modelmaker. Furthermore, the clipper ship period coincided with the arrival of photography, so a pictorial record of many of these vessels is available. Not unnaturally there are quite a number of excellent books on the subject, and details of these, as well as sources of plans, will be found in the bibliography.

To a certain extent the preceding remarks apply to material for schooners. These vessels were built in small shipyards scattered round the coastline, often with nothing more than a half model as the basis, though plans were used in some yards and a number of excellent examples have survived. The National Maritime Museum at Greenwich has a good collection of plans of traditional British coastal trading craft, including sailing and pulling fishing vessels, collected by the Society for Nautical Research. More plans are to be found in the archives on the Continent (particularly in Scandinavia) and in America. Several vessels have been preserved, and the lines and other details taken from them. Once again, the details of the most useful books, and plan sources, will be found in the bibliography.

As I have indicated, available plans fall into two main categories, shipbuilders' and Museum plans, and commercial plans. Reference has already been made to the collection in the National Maritime Museum. Comprising some half million drawings, this contains not only Admiralty Draughts from 1700 onwards, together with collections from shipbuilders large and small, but also those of some private individuals who by perspicacity, tenacity of purpose, and an abiding interest in their subject, were able to preserve for posterity some small fragment of the thousands of invaluable and irreplaceable records so wantonly destroyed during yard closures and modernisation schemes. Copies of these plans can

usually be purchased, albeit in some cases at considerable cost. The earliest plans in the National Maritime Museum's archives are by Keltridge, dated about 1685; there is no point in asking for plans of galleons or earlier ships, for as I have said already there are none. However, early in the eighteenth century the Admiralty initiated a policy of preserving plans with the result that draughts of almost every type of warship have survived; if those for a particular ship are not available there are usually some of a sister ship, or at least of a similar type of vessel. This collection has been augmented by the many plans made of captured ships, mainly French, Spanish and American. In addition to vessels used as transports, there are drawings of most types of merchant ships ranging from East Indiamen to small coastal vessels. One word of warning. There are not many rigging plans for these vessels, and in a number of instances the amount of detail is minimal: but at least they provide an accurate basis on which to add the results of further research into the subject.

In addition to plans, many museums have collections of the original half models of hulls prepared by shipbuilders — there is a particularly fine collection in the Museum of Transport in Glasgow.

In the case of the eighteenth and nineteenth century ships Admiralty draughts do require some knowledge of the principles of the naval architecture and ship construction methods of the period if they are to be understood fully. Fortunately there are still available books which give the necessary information — some of which have recently been published in the form of facsimile reprints of the original works.

The shipbuilders' plans normally consist of a Rigging Plan, General Arrangement Plan, and Lines Plan, sometimes also a Midship Section Plan. Although the designations are really self-explanatory, this is how they are made up. The Rigging Plan shows the ship in profile, with details of the masts and spars, the position of all standing and running rigging, and perhaps the outline of the sails. Sometimes the amount of detail incorporated is not so comprehensive. The General Arrangement Plan shows, in plan view, the layout of the fittings on the various decks, without necessarily showing every fitting in detail, the shape and position of the deckhouses, hatchways and companionways, and so on; occasionally it includes a sectional profile. The Lines Plan, sometimes referred to as the Sheer Draught, should show a profile of the hull with either the station or frame lines and buttock lines, a half breadth plan showing the waterlines, and a body plan showing the shape of the hull transversely at each of the station or frame lines. The Midship Section is really a constructional plan showing the principal scantlings of the materials to be used in the

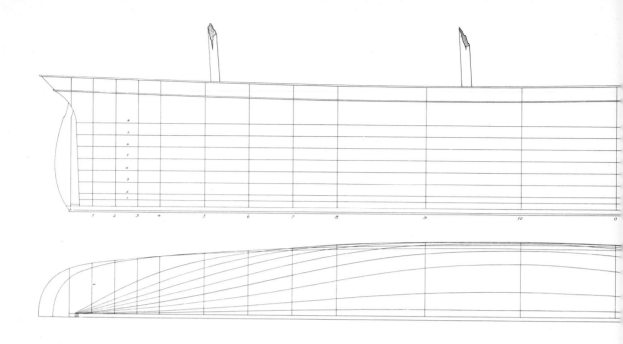

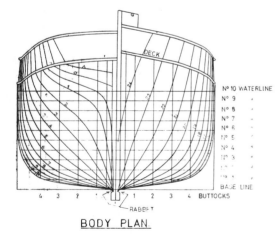

BODY PLAN

N° 10 WATERLINE
N° 9
N° 8
N° 7
N° 6
N° 5
N° 4
N° 3
N° 1
BASE LINE

4 3 2 1   1 2 3 4   BUTTOCKS

RABBET

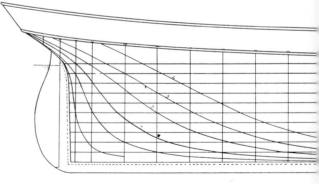

WATERWAY 5½
FLOOR   11

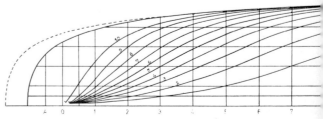

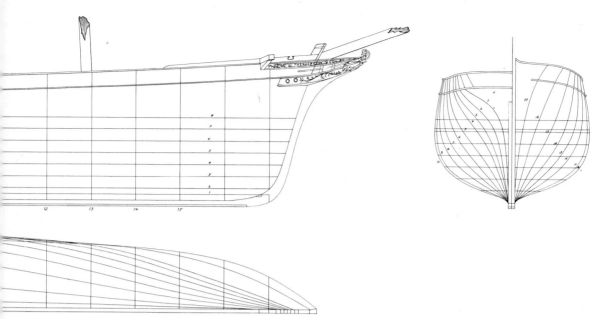

Above and below. Two typical lines plans. The upper one is the clipper *Thermopylae*, whilst the other is a small coasting schooner. Each contains sufficient information to produce an accurate model of the basic hull of the vessel concerned. The one for the coaster is more detailed in that it includes the buttock lines on the elevation and, of course, shows their position on the half breadth plan and the body plan. In each case the sections in the body plan are at arbitrary station lines along the hull, and not positioned at any particular one of the ship's frames.

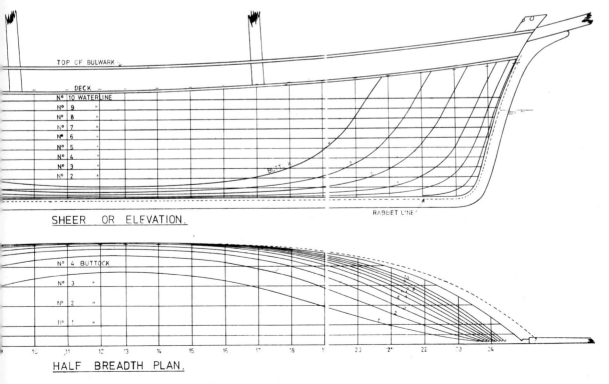

TOP OF BULWARK

DECK
Nº 10 WATERLINE
Nº 9 "
Nº 8 "
Nº 7 "
Nº 6 "
Nº 5 "
Nº 4 "
Nº 3 "
Nº 2

BUTT

RABBET LINE

SHEER OR ELEVATION.

Nº 4 BUTTOCK

Nº 3 "

Nº 2 "

Nº 1 "

10   11   12   13   14   15   16   17   18   19   20   21   22   23   24

HALF BREADTH PLAN.

construction of the hull, and applies more to iron and steel hulls. The point about these plans is that they are shipbuilders plans, not modelmakers plans. Some are well detailed, some less so, and they carry much interior detail of the accommodation. Unfortunately many sets are incomplete, lacking one or more of the basic plans. There is a further complication in that some are the design plans — these were the plans which a shipbuilder prepared when tendering or upon which the order was placed, and they differ, often quite considerably, from the ship as completed. Which brings me once again to the point about researching a subject before starting a model. Always check your information by every possible means.

Modelmakers plans, on the other hand, as marketed by commercial organisations and a number of individual firms, or privately, are plans which have been prepared specially for the modelmaker, and contain, in one set, the information which the modeller requires. In addition to the basic elements referred to above, normally they include detailed drawings of all the various fittings, and in many cases amplification of the rigging details. They should show the ship at a particular date in its life, but here again is something that should be checked as the information is frequently omitted on the drawing. This raises another point. During their lives ships underwent refits or repairs from time to time, when alterations, additions, and removals were carried out, thereby creating differences in their appearance from the 'as built' condition. With the advent of photography this has become much more apparent, so care must always be exercised in this direction when dating a model — and also when making use of photographs. So far as naval vessels are concerned, the Admiralty practice has been to mark these alterations and additions on the original draughts, using a different colour of ink for each major refit. This is all right on the original tracing, but on dyeline or other prints made from these plans they are all the same colour. Trying to sort them out is not easy, and one useful tip is to study the style and so on of the note on the plan giving the date of the refit, and to compare it with the details on the plan — different draughtsmen, different styles and writing.

Leaving aside the General Arrangement and Rigging Plans for the time being, let us have a look at the Lines Plan to see what it is all about. This plan depicts the shape of the hull as seen from three different directions — side, top, and end. The profile, or sheer plan, shows the shape of the hull as seen from the side — that is the outline of the stem and stern, and the sheer of the deck, which is the way it curves up to the bow and stern from amidships. To put it another way it shows the shape of the hull if cut in half vertically along the centre line. Upon this are

superimposed a number of key constuctional lines — the base line, the load waterline (the level at which the ship will float when loaded), a number of equally spaced lines parallel to the base line called waterlines or waterplanes, buttock lines, and along the length of the hull, vertical to the base line, a number of equally spaced lines called stations or section lines. The rules governing the positioning of these lines are complicated and depend upon the practices being employed at the time the ship was built, and the purpose for which they are or were required. On the other hand some plans, particularly many of the Admiralty Draughts, show not the station lines but the position of each frame, often with its corresponding shape on the body plan.

Below the profile is the half breadth plan. The base, or 'key' line here is a horizontal line representing the longitudinal centre line of the ship. Upon this line are erected perpendiculars exactly in line with the station or frame lines on the sheer plan. Also on this plan are a number of horizontal lines parallel to the centre line and equally spaced from it, which are called buttock lines. Finally, to one side, though in some cases it is found superimposed upon the sheer or the half breadth plan, is the Body Plan. On the right hand side of its vertical centre line are a number of curved lines which show the shape of one side of the hull forward of the midship or mid-length point, as if it had been sliced through transversely at each of the station or frame lines forward of midships and is looked at end on. Similarly, on the left hand side of the vertical centre line the curved lines represent the shape of the hull abaft the midship point. You will notice that on this plan are shown horizontal lines parallel to, and equally spaced from, the base line; these are the waterlines. The vertical lines on either side parallel to the centre line are the buttock lines.

Reverting now to the half breadth plan, the series of long curved lines thereon show the shape of the hull, or at least one side of it, when sliced through horizontally at each of the waterlines shown on the sheer, and viewed from above. Similarly, on the sheer plan, the curved lines for and aft within the outline of the hull show the shape of the hull as if sliced vertically from end to end along each of the buttock lines shown on the half breadth plan, and viewed from the side. Here I must make one point quite clear. What I have just described are the lines usually found on a shipbuilder's plan, and basically on those prepared for modelmakers. The principal difference with the latter may lie in the positioning of the station lines, for these may have been put in positions more suited to the requirements of the modelmaker. Of course if you have decided to build a model showing some of the vessel's frames, or on what is called the Navy Board, or Dockyard Model, principle then you

Below. In the text reference is made to the Keltridge plans in the National Maritime Museum. This very fine $\frac{1}{4}''$ scale model by Ewart Freeston of a Sixth Rate of 24 guns was built from a draught by Keltridge (copies of the original draught may be obtained from the Museum). The model is built in what is known as the Dockyard, or Navy Board, or Admiralty style. The distinctive feature of this type of model is that the frames were exposed below the wales, and the decks were only partially planked. Thus the salient features of the proposed vessel were fully visible when the model was submitted to the Navy Board for their approval. There is no doubt that this unplanked form of construction shows up the hull lines to perfection. Sometimes, as in this case, the rigging as well as most of the deck fittings and the carved decorative work was included.

may have to prepare a set of cross sections showing the exact shape of every frame. In some ways this is not as bad as it sounds; provided you have ascertained the position and spacing of the frames, all the necessary information, or dimensions, can be obtained from the lines shown on the above-mentioned sheer and half breadth plans. It is a question of knowing what to measure and how to apply it to draw out each section — but this is really outside the scope of this book. The chapter by Ewart Freeston on Hulls tells you how to make use of the lines plan to shape your hull.

Before leaving the matter of hull lines there are a couple of points which might be mentioned. The first is hull dimensions, and how they are taken, for this is a somewhat more complicated subject than you might

Sixth Rate of 24 guns
from a draught proposed by
William Keltridge 1684

Scale $\frac{1}{4}$ inch 1 foot
Length of gun deck . 93 ft. 6 ins
Breadth . 25 ft 6 ins

Ewart C. Freeston 1971

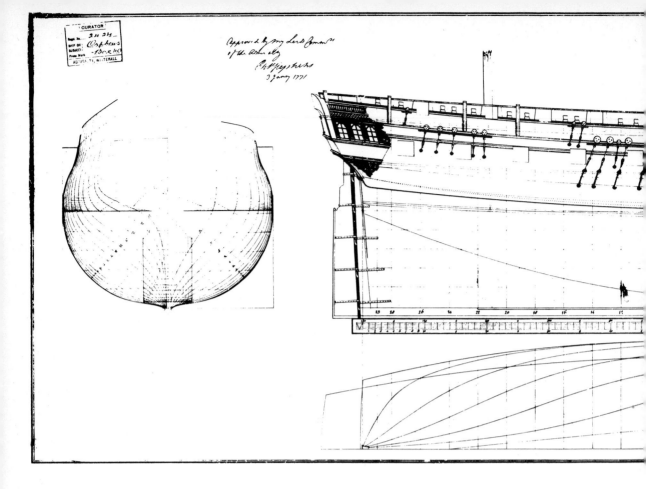

This is a good example of an Admiralty Draught, of 1771. It is the original design draught of the *Orpheus*, 32 guns, launched in 1773, and should be compared with the 'as fitted' draught shown in Chapter 2. Unlike the lines plans shown earlier, this contains details of the vessel's dimensions and a scale, and it embodies certain contemporary constructional lines not found on later ship plans. The explanation of these lines, how they were derived, and their purpose can be found in such books as Rees' *Naval Architecture*.
(Courtesy of the National Maritime Museum).

think. Again it depends upon the period to which the original ship belongs, and the purpose for which they are required. Tonnage, or in the early days 'burthen', has long been the principle measurement of a ship's size. It was calculated from somewhat complicated formulae which require a certain measurements to be taken from a completed ship. Rees's *Naval Architecture* (1819-20) contains some interesting information on the methods of calculating tonnage, while David MacGregor's *Fast Sailing Ships* has a particularly well detailed section on the Rules for Tonnage Measurement and the various amendments made over the years. It is only comparatively recently that certain dimensions of ships have come to the fore as criteria for size. One of the commonest is 'length between perpendiculars', which is really a shipbuilder's term. Unfortunately the positions through which these two perpendiculars — the forward perpendicular (FP) and the after perpendicular (AP) — were erected varies. The AP is at the after side of the sternpost, and the FP is usually at the after side of the stem at upper deck level. Just to complicate matters, on a lines plan which has been prepared for the displacement calculation, the FP is

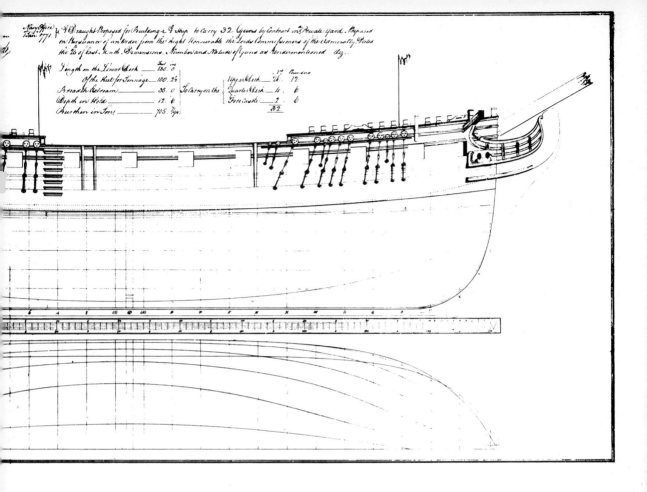

taken through the point where the designed waterline cuts the stem in order to meet the requirements of the appropriate formula. Strictly speaking this line should be referred to as an ordinate and have a number or letter, but more often than not it is labelled FP.

The next dimension is the moulded breadth. This is the greatest breadth inside the outer planking at the widest part of the ship, usually the midship frame, but not always. In iron and steel ships it is to the inside of the shell plating. Lines plans are invariably drawn to the inside of the planking or shell plating.

Depth, sometimes depth moulded, refers to the depth of the hold, and was usually taken from the underside of the upper deck to the top of the ceiling (that is, the bottom of the hold) at the centre line at mid length. Draught, or draft, should not be confused with depth. (It is unfortunate that this is one of the many words in the English language with two totally different meanings, both of which are used when talking about ships). It is the amount of water the ship draws, or in other words the depth of the lowest point of the hull below the waterline at which the ship is floating freely. Obviously this varied in relation to the

amount of cargo, stores, gear, and so on on board the ship at any one time.

The second point to mention is the way of altering or modifying the scale of plans. The accompanying diagram is really self explanatory, but I will outline the way such a scale is prepared. Suppose, for the sake of argument that the length of the ship on your plans is $31\frac{5}{8}''$ between the FP and the AP, and that you want to build a model in which this length will be $23''$. Along one side of a fairly stout piece of paper mark out very accurately a length of $31\frac{5}{8}''$, and draw a short vertical line down from the edge of the paper at each of these two points. Now draw two lines between and extending beyond these two verticals parallel to the edge of the paper, and at distances of $\frac{1}{2}''$ and $1''$ from the edge. Call the points where the lower line cuts the two vertical lines A and B. From A draw a line down across the paper at an angle of, say, $30°$ (though as long as it is less than $45°$ any angle will do, for the precise number of degrees is irrelevant to the exercise), and call this line AC. Now on your model the length between perpendiculars is to be $23''$, so along AC starting at A mark 23 equal spaces, one for each inch of length of the model. This can be done by using a pair of dividers, or a compass, set to an arbitrary distance, or a ruler or draughtsman's scale. It does not matter which method is used so long as the spaces are all of exactly the same length. Call the last (the 23rd) mark D. Join D to B by a straight line. Then draw lines parallel to DB from each of the marked points on AC to the line AB. This must be carried out very accurately to ensure that the points at which these lines cut AB are all at the same distance apart. Where these lines intersect AB erect perpendiculars to the edge of the paper. These spaces along AB each represent one inch on the proposed model. The space at the left hand side can be subdivided to represent, say, twelfths or sixteenths of

This midship section of a typical late nineteenth century iron sailing ship shows all the scantlings of the materials from which the vessel will be built. It gives details of the principal dimensions, of the anchor and cable outfit, deck coverings, frame spacing and so on.

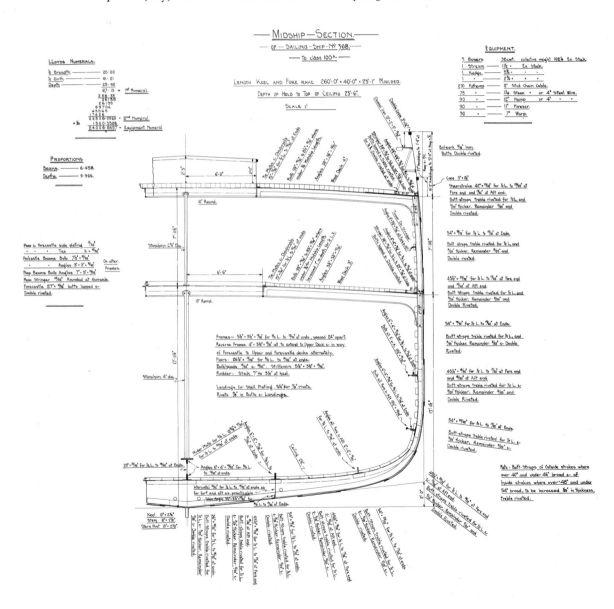

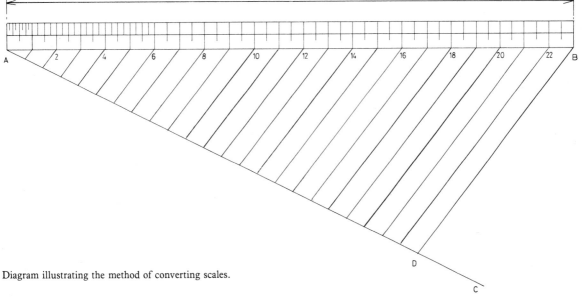

LENGTH FROM PLAN

Diagram illustrating the method of converting scales.

an inch, while the remainder can be subdivided into halves and quarters as so desired, either by measurement, or by applying an extension of the foregoing method. If the scale thus drawn is set against any part of the plan of the ship, its exact size for the model can be read off the scale.

However, to return to the subject of plans. The General Arrangement Plan is really self-explanatory, for it shows, in varying degrees of detail according to the quality of the plan in question, the positions of all the deckhouses and fittings on each deck of the ship. The accompanying elevation of the ship is sometimes a complete external view, sometimes a sectional (internal) one, and sometimes a combination of the two! From the modelmaker's point of view the elevation gives him not only the height of one deck above the other, but the height of fittings, bulwarks, guard rails and so on. If it is an external elevation it normally shows the fittings, portholes and other items on the side of the ship at which you are looking (that is, if the ship is shown with the bow to the right, then all the items on the starboard side are shown). Since the fittings on one side of a ship are not always exactly the same on the opposite side, it is essential that the arrangements shown on the deck plans are checked very carefully with this point in mind.

The Rigging Plan shows the standing and running rigging of the vessel to the best of its ability, and, hopefully, the sizes of the various ropes. When they are not so indicated it means recourse to one of the many appropriate books on masting and rigging listed elsewhere in this volume. The Sail Plan, on the other hand shows the masts, spars and outlines of the sails, sometimes with the major items of rigging added.

The Rigging Plans prepared for modelmakers are a combination of these two plans.

The point to remember about a General Arrangement Plan, shipyard type, is that is what it is. If the fittings shown on it are depicted in considerable detail then that is an added bonus. Whereas the modelmakers plans will carry detailed scale drawings of all the various houses and fittings, if you are using shipbuilder's plans, it may require some research to obtain all the information which you require. The National Maritime Museum has many plans of ships' fittings covering a considerable period of years, and you will find other useful sources listed at the end of the book in the bibliography.

Moving on from plans, the next consideration is tools and materials and so far as the latter are concerned, the authors of the various chapters have given guidance on this matter. Where timber is being acquired, always try and make sure that it is dry, seasoned and free from knots and shakes. Keep a lookout for odds and ends; it is surprising what use can be made of all those odd bits and pieces encountered in the course of our daily lives. But where tools are concerned the question is not so easy to answer, for those used in ship model building can be many and varied, and depend upon a number of factors, the type of model being built and the materials being used for its construction, the skill and ability of the modelmaker — some can produce work of a very high calibre with amazingly few tools whilst others seem able to function only when surrounded by an elaborate and well-equipped workshop — and the working facilities available, to say nothing of the depth of his pocket where money is concerned. For

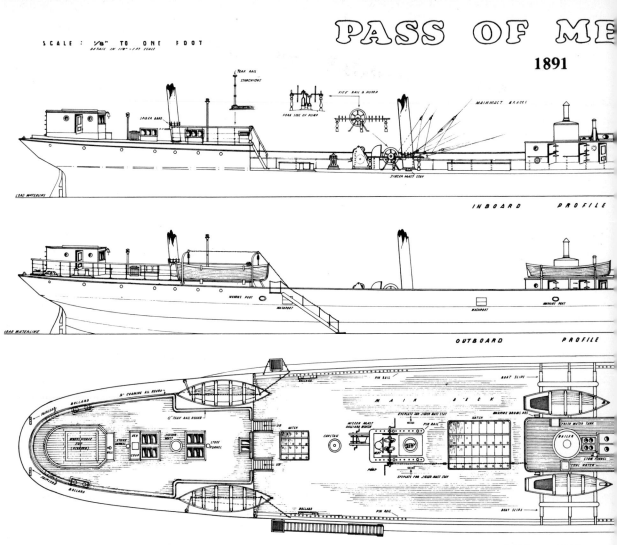

INBOARD PROFILE

OUTBOARD PROFILE

DECK PLAN

Pass of Melfort. A typical example of a plan prepared for modelmakers from a shipbuilder's original plan. As well as containing (elsewhere on the sheet) the hull lines and body plan, there are several cross sections, and the deck fittings are shown in detail. The rigging plan is on a separate sheet. (Copies of these plans may be obtained from the *Model Shipwright* Plan Service.)

Overleaf. The sail plan of the steel ship *Formby* is a good example of the type of plan to be found in the older technical books — in this case Rankine's *Shipbuilding* of 1866.

those working mainly in wood, and after all that was the principal material used in the construction of these three types of vessel, the following tools come to mind: tenon saw, fretsaw, chisels of various sizes and types, spokeshave, rasps and files, hammer, set square, pliers, hand drill and drill bits, X-Acto blades and tools, vice, oilstone, rule or scale. I cannot stress too strongly that these are only suggestions — they form a good basis, but it is not a pre-requisite that all must be on hand before starting work on a model. Many, no doubt, will be in the average household tool kit in these days of 'do-it-yourself'. Later on such items as gouges, a coping saw, clamps, pinchucks, a soldering iron, calipers, small archimedean drill, and so on may be considered.

As work progresses, or as the beginner becomes more skilled, it happens frequently that either the need arises for a special tool, or he realises that a particular job could be made much easier if he had a tool of a certain type. More often than not he sets about designing and making one from whatever materials are to hand. Invariably these tools are of the small hand variety, though there are modelmakers who have built small powered saw benches capable of cutting timber to incredibly fine tolerances. Very narrow chisels can be made by grinding down and sharpening the ends of old needle files, or old darning needles. Pieces of broken hacksaw blades can be used for a variety of purposes — in fact the uses to which

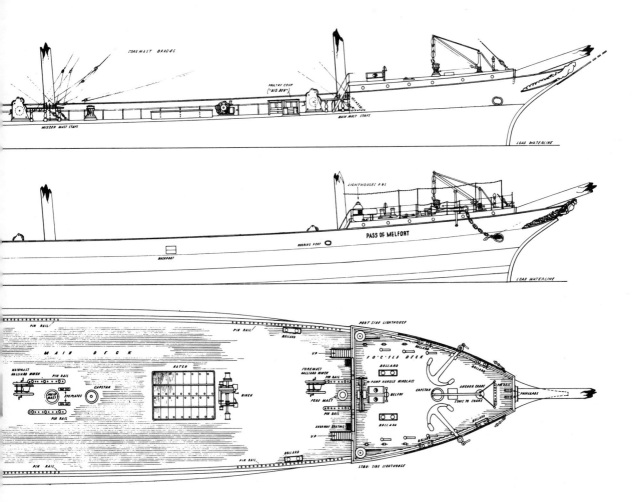

they can be put, with a certain amount of ingenuity and skill, are quite amazing — knives, tweezers, gouges, grooving saws, nail or dowel holders, to mention but a few. You can make useful light clamps from those wood spring-type clothes pegs just by shaping the ends to suit the job in hand. Crochet hooks are invaluable when rigging a model, as are the small spring-type hair clips. Razor blades are always useful, and there is a small plane on the market which uses the standard double edged razor blade as its cutter. The recently introduced bonded type of blade produces a flexible steel cutting tool when the plastic material is removed. The dental and surgical professions are another good source of precision tools, for here you find scalpels, tweezers, clamps, probes, and drills (burrs) which are of considerable use, and not only to the builders of miniature and small scale scenic models. The watchmaking trade, of course, is also a place to find small precision tools and instruments of the highest quality.

Power tools are nice to have, and there is no doubt that items such as a Unimat lathe, or a jewellers'/watchmakers' lathe, a power saw, an electric drill, or a motorised fretsaw do make the work easier, if you know how to use them to their fullest potential. Many a modelmaker has done all the turning he requires using nothing more than an ordinary hand drill held in a vice. However, if you are involved in work which calls for a great deal of fine drilling, such as dowels in a plank-on-frame model, then there is little doubt that one of the small battery operated hand drills — which are not really very expensive — would be a good purchase. Not only will it speed up your work by making the drilling of accurate holes much easier, but you will be much less likely to cause damage to your model.

B

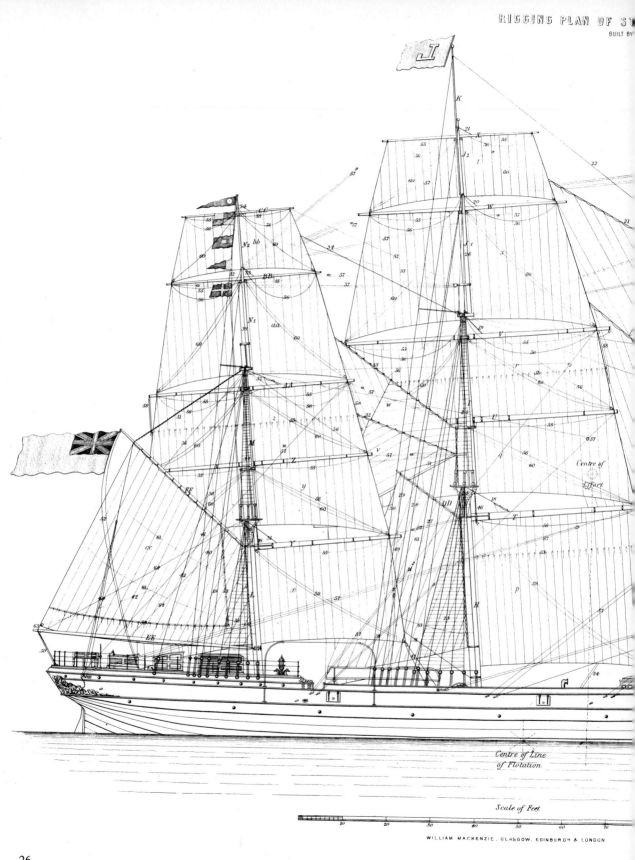

Centre of
Effort

Centre of Line
of Flotation

Scale of Feet

WILLIAM MACKENZIE, GLASGOW, EDINBURGH & LONDON.

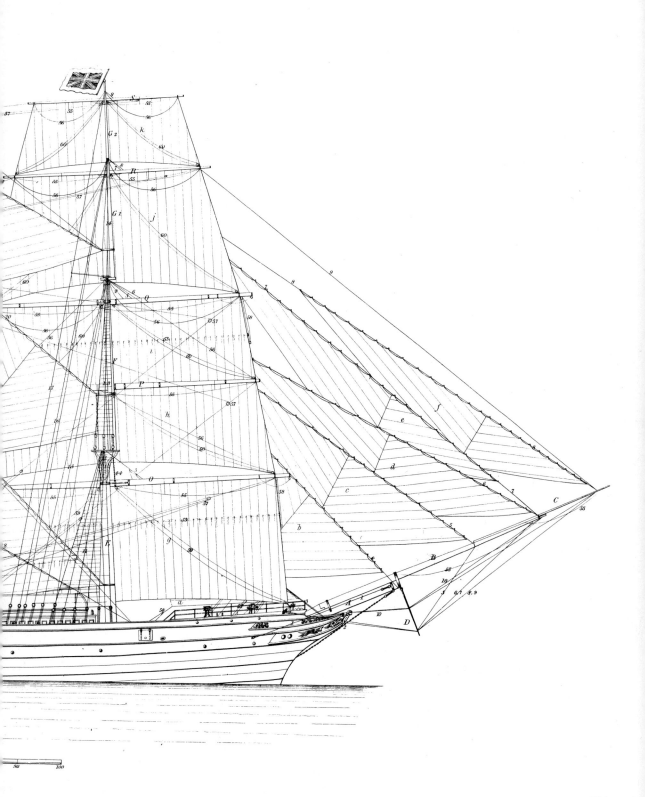

Hulls and decks

2

by EWART C FREESTON

There are two basic methods of making the hull for a ship model in wood; one is by carving it to shape from a block, the other is by building it up on a framework. In the first case the block can be one piece of wood, or made up to the required size by glueing several planks together, popularly known as the Bread and Butter method, the bread being the wood and the butter the glue. In the second case the hull is built up in a similar fashion to that of a real ship by fixing planks horizontally to frames erected vertically on a keel, or by adapting that method to make it more suitable for modelmaking purposes. There is a third method however, which is, in effect, a combination of these two, and that is by making the hull solid up to the waterline, or thereabouts, and then building up the topsides on parts of frames fixed to the lower, solid half. These methods will be described in some detail in the following pages, but it is advisable to have a clear picture in your mind of these basic ways.

It is not possible to say which is the best method to adopt because it all depends on the type of model that is being built, and therefore, what is best for one model may be unsuitable or even impractical for another. For instance, if you are building a small scenic model with the ship floating in a sea, then the best way is to carve the hull from a solid block. Similarly, if you are building a model of a Thames barge or a Humber keel, both of which are flat bottomed with flat sides, and where the accent from a modelmaker's point of view is on the sails, the rigging, and the fitting out then carving from the solid is probably best; on the other hand if you are building a full hull model of a ship of the *Victory* type with guns and gunports and wish to show the construction of such a vessel to scale and to a high standard of work, then the built-up method is best, but this requires exceptional skill which it must be admitted is acquired only by experience.

So whatever you do, one piece of advice may not be out of place; if you have little or no experience — and this is not to disparage anybody's skill — do not for a first attempt start making a large model of a four-masted sailing ship or a 100 gun ship of the line, for not only may it be quite beyond your capabilities, but you might easily get discouraged and give up in disgust. Far better start on a fairly simple yet interesting type such as a Galleon, an eighteenth century brig or cutter, a nineteenth century smack or trawler, or a sailing coaster. Any of these and similar vessels will give you plenty of scope to develop your skill and inspire you to greater efforts.

TIMBER

But before describing how to make a hull it is necessary to say something about the sort of wood which will be required; to use any old piece of floor board or joist is to court disaster, make the work unnecessarily difficult, and the result unsatisfactory. It is worth spending a little extra cash on good timber, of which there are now bewildering varieties, some of which are not suitable for modelmaking. Therefore it is impossible to say that this or that timber is the best under all circumstances, since the requirements for a solid hull model are different from those in which the wood has to be sawn into thin planks and bent to shape.

But the basic requirements of a timber for making ship models can be summarized as follows: (1) The wood should be stable and not liable to split or warp when being worked; (2) it should be reasonably easy to carve but hard enough to retain sharp edges and a smooth finish; (3) it should be able to be bent without fracturing if reduced to small scantlings; (4) the grain should not be open or too pronounced, which would make a good finish difficult to obtain; (5) the colour should be neutral, or at least unobtrusive if it has to be stained or polished; (6) it should accept glue or paint readily, otherwise the finish may be unsatisfactory and defects become apparent in course of time.

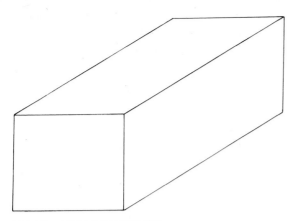

HULLS - (1) BLOCK METHOD

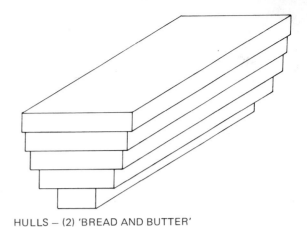

HULLS — (2) 'BREAD AND BUTTER'

It must be said that very, very few timbers measure up to this ideal or in fact need to do so, as some of the virtues mentioned may not be vital in certain cases. However, there are several timbers which can be eliminated as unsatisfactory for worthwhile ship model hulls, or which it would be best to avoid. At the head of the list I would put balsa, for it is impossible to work accurately to scale in a wood such as this which can be dented by pressure of the fingers, which will not give a smooth finish, which cannot be sawn or cut cleanly and which will not retain sharp

HULLS — (3) FRAMED CONSTRUCTION

29

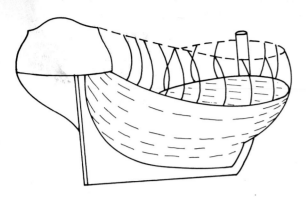

HULLS — (4) SEMI-FRAMED

edges. It may be suitable for some purposes but it cannot be recommended for a first class ship model. Others to be avoided are the Baltic firs sold under the names of red deal, yellow deal or pitch pine, and those which are of a gummy and resinous nature. Usually they have many knots which can constitute a weakness, a grain which is alternately hard and soft making a smooth finish difficult, and they exude resin which can make staining patchy and painting a risk. However, if you are making a solid core which will be covered subsequently with planking, or used as a former which will be discarded after constructing a hull of gummed paper strip, tinplate, or GRP, there is no valid objection to their use; the fact that such timbers are amongst the cheapest, and may be purchased as off-cuts, makes their use positively attractive.

Also to be avoided are the furniture timbers such as oak, mahogany, walnut, teak and suchlike. These are undoubtedly beautiful woods for the right purpose but for ship models they should be used with discretion. Oak usually has an open and much too pronounced grain for a scale model, and it does not accept paint satisfactorily, which tends to flake off in time. Mahogany and woods sold under that name, such as sapele, need to have the grain filled when used, as they frequently are with beautiful results, to plank the hull of a racing yacht, which is then finished by varnishing. Walnut is the least objectionable if you can obtain a piece with a fine grain. Teak is of little use for not only has it an open grain but it has the disadvantage of an oily or greasy texture. This makes glueing and painting something of a problem as the natural oil in the timber will not allow the glue or paint to penetrate the surface, and this may lead to trouble at some future date. Beech may be used for block hulls but it is very hard, not easily worked, and if reduced to small scantlings is liable to collapse when being bent because of the presence of hard and soft areas. This applies also to ash, which has a rather pronounced grain.

For constructing a hull by the bread and butter method many of the pines are suitable, though parana pine, which has the attraction of being obtainable in wide planks, should be carefully selected; it is liable to split in use, and the large red streaks which are often to be seen in it can be a hazard. The best of the pines is probably British Columbia pine which is a straight-grained timber usually free from knots; yellow pine (real name white pine) if you can get it, is light in weight, rather soft, easily worked and glues and paints well; Canadian hemlock is a trifle heavy but worth consideration; obechi, which is readily obtainable in a variety of widths and lengths, may need the grain filling, and you will certainly need to keep your chisels and planes sharpened, for the high content of grit in this wood plays havoc with cutting tools — though I have used it on many solid hulls with satisfactory results; jelutong is a nice timber, not easily obtainable, and much used by pattern makers, but look out for the latex sacs which are sometimes to be found and may be awkwardly placed; satin walnut (real name red gum) is a handy timber to use as a baseboard as, of course, are some of those already mentioned.

All these timbers are principally recommended for large solid hulls, but for the maker of small scale models, popularly known as miniatures, many timbers suggest themselves which are normally not to be found in large sections. Among these are holly, a very hard wood which takes a beautiful finish and is almost white in colour; hornbeam, obtainable in larger scantlings and which is a lovely stable wood and is an excellent substitute for box where the colour of that wood might be an objection; and sycamore which is also a hard, white and stable wood.

But the best and finest timber the ship modelmaker could ask for is lime, and this is the timber I would select if I had only one choice. It has all the virtues which have been listed and, in a well selected and seasoned specimen, no vices. It is of a creamy colour, is fairly hard but can be planed, sawn or carved with ease; it is quite stable with an unobtrusive and attractive grain. It can be obtained in wide boards of any thickness or length and I cannot praise it too highly. It can be sawn as thin as .0040" without sign of collapse, and small boats made of it can be hollowed out almost to paper thickness without distorting. It can be stained and polished to represent any other wood without tedious preparations. But it is expensive and therefore its cost would be prohibitive and wasteful for a large solid hull. For small waterline or similar models, or when converted into planks for making the frames for a built-up model, or sawn into thinner planks for the sheathing of such a hull and for the laying of decks, it is well worth the cost in view of its admirable qualities.

The man-made timbers such as plywood and hardboard have their uses and should not be disregarded. The multi-plys are ideal for building-boards, and prime quality resin-bonded three- or five-ply can be used for solid frames or bulkheads if care is taken when fastening into the edges to avoid separating the plys. Hardboard is also useful for making templets as it will remain flat and keep its shape, and so is better than flimsy cardboard for this purpose.

The last item is bamboo which is actually a grass. When fixing wood parts together, whether planks or small fittings, avoid as far as possible the use of screws or nails, except as temporary holds, if you value your chisels, gouges or planes. Replace any metal fastenings with wood dowels, or for very small work bamboo dowels, glued in. If you draw split bamboo through a series of diminishing holes drilled in a piece of tinplate, you can obtain dowels as thin as a needle. If these are dipped in glue and tapped into corresponding holes in the work, the fastenings are then as good as the wood itself and are practically invisible when glasspapered, stained, polished or painted, and will not play havoc with edge tools if you cut through them either accidentally or on purpose.

ADHESIVES

As I have already mentioned glueing, it might not be out of place here to add some words of advice in view of the many types of adhesives now available. The days of the glue pot on the fire are long since gone, at least as far as we are concerned; there are many more convenient ones that can be used. Tubes or tins of the fish glue type still have their uses for fixing small parts, but for larger areas probably the best to use is one of the white resin glues such as Evo-stick Resin W. This and other similar types, made especially for woodworkers, are used cold, are ready for immediate use, and allow plenty of time for precise adjustment before clamping together. Any surplus must be wiped off with a damp cloth otherwise the adhesive dries so hard it can turn the edge of a chisel. The joint it makes is waterproof and practically everlasting, being unaffected by change of temperature. There are other waterproof glues in powder form of the resin type, and also of the casein type sold under various trade names, to which water is added to make a paste which can be used after a short waiting period for the mixture to mature; unfortunately some of these latter glues have a tendency to leave a dark stain if any oozes out on to a clean surface and it is not removed at once. Impact adhesives of the one liquid type are inconvenient to use since they allow no time at all for adjustment — once contact is made the parts cannot be moved. Those of the two liquid type do allow a little time for clamping the parts together, but there is

little advantage in them. There are two liquids to deal with, one of which is applied to one part and the other, thicker, liquid to the second part, after which the two parts are clamped together as soon as possible for the chemical reaction to take place; it must be admitted the resulting joint is excellent.

But it is the Evo-stik Resin W or similar types that I would recommend as they are so clean and convenient to use. I have used them successfully on both large and small areas. It is always a sound policy to fit the joint dry first to make sure the parts fit; if two planks are to be glued together, the facing surfaces should not only be planed, but also glasspapered. A plane tends to close up the pores of the wood so that glue is unable to penetrate; in fact it is best to wait a minute or two to allow this to happen as, if the two parts are clamped together immediately the glue is applied, there is a risk of the joint being starved of glue if too much pressure is applied. Make sure there are no air spaces between the planks, for you cannot make a good joint by expecting the glue to fill up cracks or holes in badly fitting parts.

CARVING FROM SOLID

The principle of carving a ship model from the solid is to prepare the wood block slightly larger than the scale dimensions of the prototype, and to draw on the top face the shape of the plan view of the vessel and on the sides the profile. Then cut away as much waste as possible, and finally by the use of planes, chisels, gouges and glass-paper, and aided by templets, to remove the excess wood until the shape of the vessel is reproduced. For an example of a ship model hull let us consider the lines of a typical Thames Estuary smack measuring about 46′ 0″ x 13′ 0″ x 9′ 0″. At $\frac{1}{4}$″ = 1′ 0″ scale a block of straight-grained wood sized 12″ x $3\frac{1}{4}$″ x $2\frac{1}{4}$″ would be required. When the block has been planed to size mark a centre line on it lengthways all round, and across it all round the station lines 1-9. Make a tracing of the plan view and carefully transfer this on to the top face. Similarly trace the profile, excluding the stem, keel and rudder, on to both sides of the block. The first step is to saw away the waste below the overhanging stern and at the same time cut away the stem so as to reduce the block to the shape of the profile. Now saw vertically round the shape of the plan view drawn on the top face; this will of course remove the station lines drawn on the sides, so these will have to be redrawn now, and whenever they are removed as carving proceeds, so that a correct shape will be produced.

Next make a series of templets in stiff white card of the vertical shape of the hull at each station as shown on the body plan, then with sharp chisels and gouges pare away the outside of the block, and as you proceed offer up the templets at their respective positions to

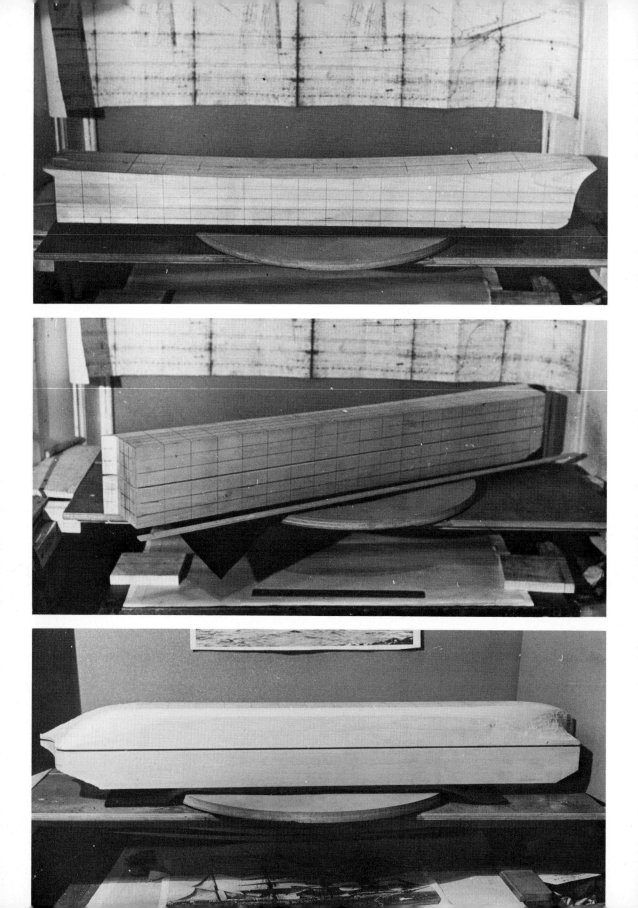

Opposite top. An early stage in carving a block hull. The station lines have been marked in along the side, the stem and stern profiles cut, and the sheer cut.
(Photo: Harry Boyd)

Opposite centre. The block turned on one side to show the slot cut out for the keel strip. Note that the station lines have been carried across the bottom.
(Photo: Harry Boyd)

Opposite bottom. The hull partly roughed out. The station lines on the bottom have disappeared following the shaping of the rise of bottom to the curve of the bilge, which has also been cut.
(Photo: Harry Boyd)

Below. With the shaping of the hull well advanced, the rebate is cut along the side to accommodate the strip of wood which will form the bulwark.
(Photo: Harry Boyd)

check the gradual development of the shape. Finish off with glasspaper and plane a flat where the stem, keel and sternpost will go; make these parts of some harder wood and glue and dowel them into position after cutting them to exact width and thickness and making neat joints where they meet. If the stem piece is of the type which has an extended knee carrying a figurehead, as in a clipper ship or a nineteenth century warship, it is probably best to cut a groove in the hull and glue and dowel the stem into this; this will make a stronger joint, for there is a considerable

strain on the head from the fittings attached to it and from the pull of the rigging.

BREAD AND BUTTER CONSTRUCTION

During the above procedure you will soon have realised that cutting away the surplus wood involved quite a lot of hard work. Much of this hard work could have been avoided by glueing together a few planks to make up the required thickness, in the following way. Referring to the draught, you will see on the body plan four horizontal parallel lines ABCD; these can represent four planks, and on the half breadth plan you will see four curved lines also marked ABCD which show the shape of the hull at these levels. Now if you saw four planks to these shapes and then glue and dowel them together, it is clear that there will be less carving to do since most of the surplus wood has already been sawn away. Of course, the number and thickness of the planks depends, to a large extent, on the particular vessel being modelled, the size of your model, and the timber available; plank thicknesses ranging from $\frac{1}{2}''$ to $1''$ will be found generally adequate, and preferable to very thick planks; the shape of the hull at any level can always be determined from the body plan and station lines by interpolation.

You will need to exercise a certain amount of care when assembling the planks and the best way to do

this is to draw on each plank the longitudinal centre line all round, and at least one station line, say the midship line No 5, all round. Glue two planks together, never more at one operation, making sure the guide lines are in register, and either securely clamp them together while the glue dries, or temporarily screw them together for the same purpose. When the glue is dry, glue on a third plank in the same way after removing any screws and replacing them with wood dowels; proceed thus until all the planks are assembled. The top plank should have all the station lines and the centre line marked on it, and then you can proceed to carve the hull to shape as before, checking the shape with the templets.

All these hulls so far described will have flat top surfaces and be of a shape corresponding to the plan and profile as shown on the draught. The top face will have been cut to the longitudinal curve of the ship's side and this, which is called the sheer line, adds grace and beauty to the appearance of any vessel. The deck is, of course, lower than the top edge, and its level is shown as a dotted line. So to represent the deck, the top plank must be hollowed out to a scale depth of about 18″, leaving the bulwarks as a thin rim around the top. This is not easy to do in a fairly large model but is a perfectly feasible and satisfactory way in a small scale or miniature scenic model; in a larger

model it would be better to hollow out the top plank to a greater depth than 18″ and to secure several curved beams to the interior and to lay a separate deck.

The reason for the beams being curved is that a deck is higher in the middle than at the sides, the purpose being to drain off water as on a road; this is called the camber of the deck, and will be more fully described when we come to true scale models, since the camber was made to certain proportions according to the width of the deck. Another and perhaps still better way is to make the solid hull lower by the measurement of the height of the bulwarks, to camber the top surface and then to add the bulwarks separately by bending a thin strip of wood around the edge, fixing it by glueing and dowelling it into position, and covering the join by a flat or semi-circular rubbing strake; this produces a very neat and authentic finish if carefully done and makes laying the deck an easier task.

If the project involves a very large hull, possibly one measuring a few feet in length, the weight of the

Forming the camber of the deck, a job made simpler on the larger models by the use of this tool with a means of adjusting the curvature of the blade.
(Photo: Harry Boyd)

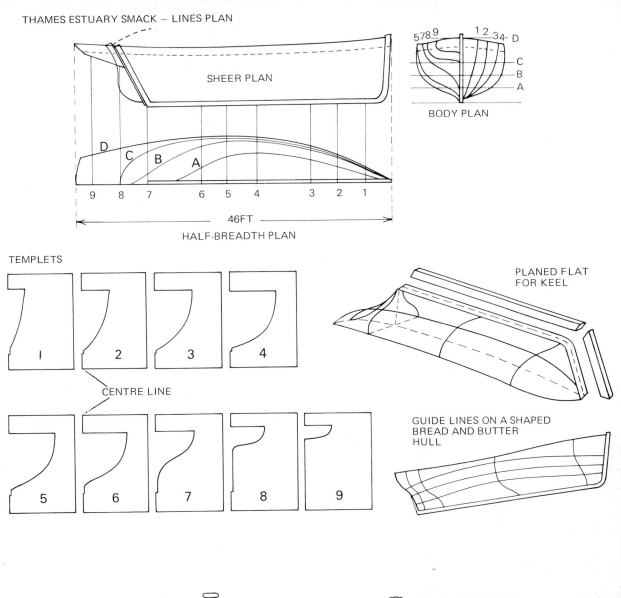

THAMES ESTUARY SMACK — LINES PLAN

SHEER PLAN

BODY PLAN

HALF-BREADTH PLAN

46FT

TEMPLETS

1 2 3 4

CENTRE LINE

5 6 7 8 9

PLANED FLAT
FOR KEEL

GUIDE LINES ON A SHAPED
BREAD AND BUTTER
HULL

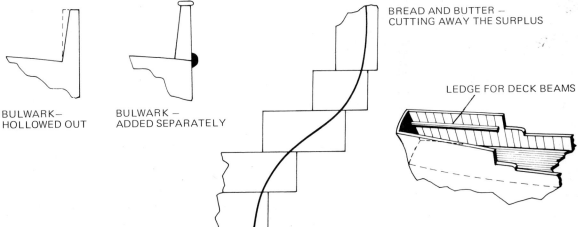

BULWARK—
HOLLOWED OUT

BULWARK —
ADDED SEPARATELY

BREAD AND BUTTER —
CUTTING AWAY THE SURPLUS

LEDGE FOR DECK BEAMS

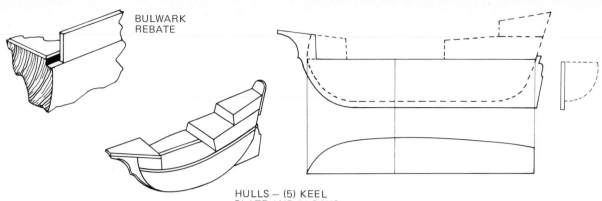

BULWARK
REBATE

HULLS — (5) KEEL
PLATE AND BLOCKS

BULWARKS

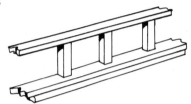

(1) OPEN RAIL

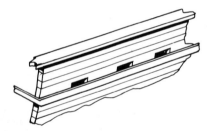

(2) PLANKED

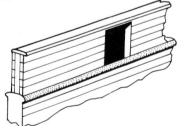

(3) WITH WASHPORTS

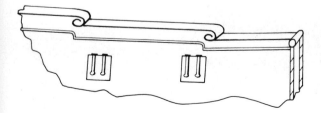

(4) NAVAL STYLE

wood makes the hull unnecessarily heavy; so in addition to sawing the planks to an outside shape, a large part of the centre of each plank can also be cut out, which not only saves weight but may be more economical, for sometimes the piece removed from the top planks may be large enough to use for the bottom planks; but be careful that you do not undercut the next lower plank, since the inside cutting line must be drawn using the lower level as a guide.

When the outside of a hull made in this fashion has been finished off to your satisfaction with fine glasspaper, the interior can remain as a series of steps on which the beams to support the deck can be fixed. There is no need to hollow out the inside to make a thin shell unless you are building a working model of a sailing ship or yacht, though if you intend to show a lower deck as well as the weather (top) deck it will be necessary not only to reduce the thickness of the sides to that of bulwarks but also to extend down below the line of lower deck, as shown on the draught in order to incorporate a ledge on which beams can be laid to support the upper decks.

An improvement on the solid block hull is to sandwich a keel plate between two outside blocks. This way is very suitable for a galleon or an Elizabethan type of ship which has a high forecastle and high stern works. Saw a central keel plate out of thin wood or three-ply wood to the shape of the profile which should include the stem, keel and rudder. Two blocks are now required for the port and starboard sides of the hull up to the main deck. These are screwed temporarily one each side of the keel plate, the station lines drawn on them, then removed and each one carved separately; they can be finished off when permanently in place, but make sure the one is the mirror pattern of the other, for it is easy to carve two port sides instead of one port and one starboard block, so mark them distinctly before starting to work.

When shaped to the pattern of the templets glue and dowel them in position, one each side of the keel plate, and when dry build up the forecastle and the sterncastle by blocks of wood of the required thickness, glueing and dowelling them to the lower block. Cut a shallow rebate around the main hull to take the bulwarks, reducing the widths of the upper blocks by an equivalent amount. The bulwarks themselves can be made of thin three-ply wood cut to shape and glued and pinned to the blocks. Make as close a joint as you possibly can though this may not be easy; a good idea is to make a pattern in cardboard from which to obtain the exact shape required. I am not an advocate of filling bad joints with plastic wood but, in a difficult fitting job like this, it may be possible to arrange the joint where an external strengthening wale is subsequently to be fastened.

This derelict hull (photographed near Bideford in 1949) is interesting in that it shows the shape of the hull of a small wooden coaster, the arrangement of the hatch coamings, the timbers for the bulwarks, the waterway, and the position of the hawse pipe.
(Photo: John Bowen)

Finish off the outside surface with fine glasspaper to a nice smooth finish in preparation for painting.

BULWARKS

Of course, in most ships the bulwarks were part of the structure of the vessel and something more than thin three ply wood is required to represent them since they were part of the hull and were fixed to the tops of the frame timbers which extended above deck level and served for protection of the seamen and for use in connection with the belaying points for the rigging.

But taking the simplest example first; in a few small coasting vessels the bulwarks were merely stanchions and a top rail, forming an open structure. In others the stanchions were planked over giving more protection, and in a model, if the bulwarks are made of ply wood, small square strips of wood may be glued to the inside to represent the top timbers of the frames. In the bulwarks themselves scupper holes were cut, at deck level, for the discharge of water from the decks. In larger nineteenth century vessels the bulwarks were thick enough to accommodate a hinged washport, about 2' 0" square, which opened by water pressure from the inside and closed by gravity; this type can be seen in the *Cutty Sark*.

In still larger naval and merchant ships the bulwarks were planked on the insides as well as the

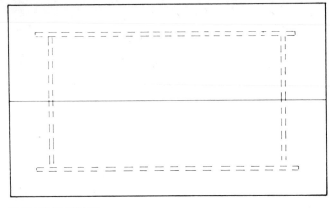

BUILDING BOARD

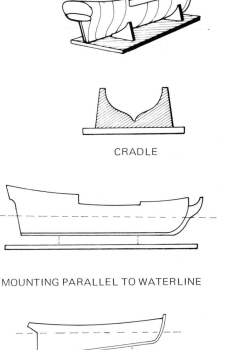

CRADLE

MOUNTING PARALLEL TO WATERLINE

outsides forming a substantial barricade from the enemy when in action. In them were cut gunports for the deck guns, and to them were fixed the belaying pin rails, swivel guns and cleats; and on top was the topgallant rail which not only made a neat finish but was often elaborately decorated where the decks changed height with what were called hancing pieces — these could be scrolls, reclining mermaids or sleeping dogs. In the seventeenth and eighteenth centuries the top timbers of the frames were extended so that they pierced the forecastle bulwark topgallant rail and were then used as belaying points. In clipper ships at the bow and stern the topgallant rail often carried an extra open rail or low iron stanchions and chains.

FRAMED HULLS

The second of the basic methods of making a model of the hull of a ship is by building it up on a framework, based on the way in which wooden ships used to be built. Fundamentally it consists in laying a keel, fixing frames vertically to it and then covering them with thin strips of wood to represent the hull planking. Building ship models in this way demands a strict attention to scale and so it is absolutely necessary to be careful in this respect, otherwise the various parts will not fit and the finished model could not be described truthfully as a scale model.

Modelmakers have evolved many ingenious variations of this method of construction, some of which I shall describe, but just as a real ship is built on a launching way so the model has to be erected on a building board. This should be a piece of multi-ply wood or blockboard, $\frac{1}{2}''$ or so thick. Do not use soft insulation board or inferior chip board but select a nice clean board and make sure it is perfectly flat; some boards can be slightly twisted which could affect the symmetry of the model. In size it should be

longer than the extreme length of the model and wider than the extreme breadth. As well as being flat the edges should be square, the sides parallel and the corners right angles. Screw four battens to the underside, making sure the screws do not go right through. This will counteract any tendency for the board to twist out of true and enable you to get your fingers underneath easily when it becomes necessary to move the model. Clean up the top surface and draw a line with a hard, sharp pencil down the centre of it lengthwise and a similar line across the board at the position of the midship frame. Go over these lines with a scriber, making sure each line is perfectly straight and does not wander along the grain; this will give you a permanent record, which cannot be removed, readily available as a datum line from which measurements can be taken.

THE KEEL

The first parts to be made are the keel, the stem with its figurehead if any, and the sternpost and rudder. The first step is to lay the keel, which should be a perfectly straight strip of some hard, close grained wood the length and size of which is taken from the

Below left. Looking forward on the author's seventeenth century Dockyard model. This gives a good idea of the treatment of the decks in this style of model construction, with the beams exposed, but the deck fittings in place. Note the belfry at the after end of the forecastle and also the elaborate cathead.

Below right. Another view of the same model, showing the construction of the bulwarks and the fittings thereon, including the 'sleeping dog' hancing pieces on top of the capping of the bulwarks.

Bottom. In contrast to the Dockyard style of construction, this illustration shows a model framed the same as the original vessel. Note particularly the futtock frame construction, and the cant frames at bow and stern. The gunport openings have been lined, and this photograph shows clearly how they are square, with the bottom edge parallel to the keel. The tops of the timbers have yet to be trimmed off to the correct height. (Photo: Bob Lightley)

draught; to this the stem and sternpost are fixed by housing joints, and at the intersection of these joints wedge shaped pieces of wood called the deadwoods are fitted, and the whole assembly bolted down on to the baseboard along the scribed centre line by means of two bolts at carefully selected positions. The holes drilled for these bolts can eventually be incorporated in the supports used for mounting the finished model in its case. Assemble all the parts dry, check that the measurements and angles are correct, and that the stem and sternpost are in alignment when viewed from either end, then glue and dowel them together. Allow several hours to elapse before any clamps are removed and the structure bolted down.

I have always found it more convenient to carve the figurehead, if there is one, before actually fixing the stem to the keel since it is definitely easier to do so if you can hold the work in your hands and turn it this way and that as becomes necessary. The type of figure depends, of course, on the particular vessel, but the method of carving any figurehead is basically the same, and the figure should always merge with the sweep of the stem and should not appear to be just

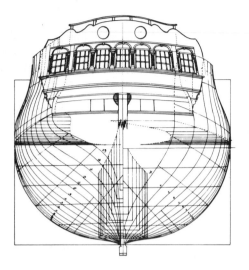

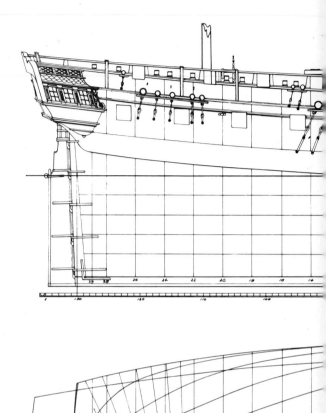

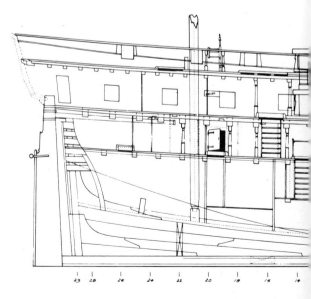

A sheer draught (top) and profile for the frigate *Orpheus*, 32 guns, of 1773. These were redrawn from Admiralty originals held in the National Maritime Museum and represent the ship 'as fitted'. As such the plans show some differences from the design draught printed in Chapter 1, and when using a set of official plans it is always wise to determine whether all the draughts being used represent the same stage of the ship's career. Unfortunately with the Admiralty Collection most draughts show only the design stage and so are not very detailed: however there was an Admiralty Order in force from 1773 until the early 1780s that draughts of all ships *as built* should be deposited with the Admiralty after completion. These often show the decorative work — and as with *Orpheus* — include more than usually detailed profile and deck plans. (Note that this redrawn plan does not have the conventional midship frame symbol mentioned by the author, but this can be seen in the design draught.)

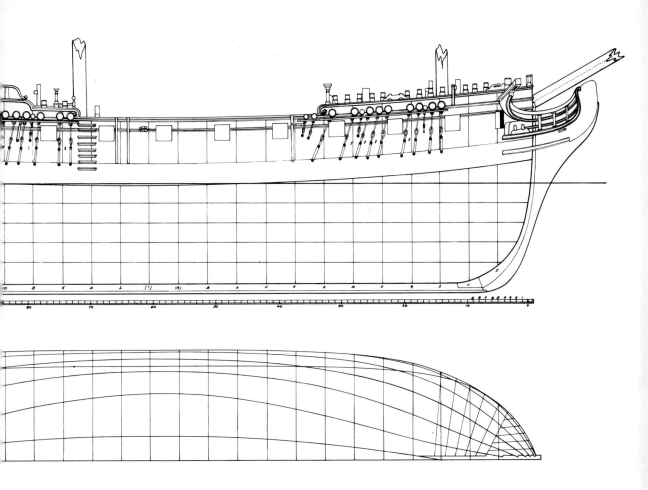

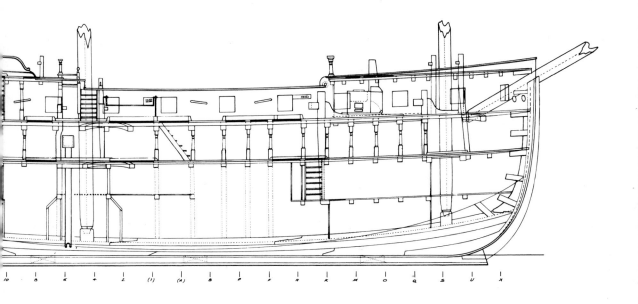

stuck on the end. Make a sketch of the figure and cut two pieces of wood to this shape and of suitable thickness. Glue one piece to each side of the top of the cutwater so giving you the figure in profile. Then carve the figure as seen from head on by the use of a very sharp, slim knife and small gouges. The general shape should be settled before finer details are attempted, but a smooth finish is not essential.

A less satisfactory way is to build up the figure with the use of modelling paste, of which there are several sorts on the market. Whether this is entirely successful in the long run I do not know, since these materials may have the habit of developing cracks due to shrinkage; I prefer to carve the figure as described using the modelling paste for adding finer details or for correcting mistakes!

Similarly it is much easier to hang the rudder before fixing the sternpost to the keel. Rudders were hung on several pintles working in gudgeons fixed to the the sternpost to make a hinge. In small scales the straps can be made of hard white card, but it is better to use metal for a working rudder. Copper or nickel

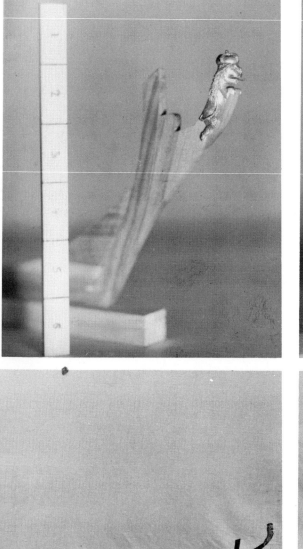

silver is better than brass, but note that the straps are at right angles to the post and not parallel to the keel, otherwise the rudder will not turn on its pintles. Obtain some small bore copper tube and solder a small piece vertically on to the strap at the centre of the sternpost edge. The rudder straps are similarly dealt with, but in addition these must have a piece of copper wire soldered into the tube so that it protrudes and engages in the tube on the post. Rivet the straps in their respective positions on the post and rudder so that the rudder swings easily.

Top left. The author's method of carving the figurehead as an integral part of the stem at a very early stage in the construction of the model.

Top centre. The sternpost and deadwood. Here again, at an early stage, the rudder has been completed and hung, to take advantage of the clear access to the sternpost for fitting the gudgeons.

Bottom left. The keel, with stem, sternpost and deadwoods in place.

Bottom centre. The midship frame in place, and showing very clearly its construction.

Above. The rudder of the *Cutty Sark* showing the gudgeons and pintles, and how the whole blade is coppered, as well as the hull of the vessel.
(Photo: John Bowen)

To keep the keel assembly vertical while the model is being made it is advisable to make two split brackets. Screw these down on to the baseboard in suitable positions so that the stem and stern are held rigidly, and if the slots of the brackets are lined with felt no damage will be done to the model.

FRAMING

The frames have now to be erected on the keel, and if you examine the draught, you will see the position of the midship frame is marked ⚹, and forward and aft of this line other vertical lines, which mark the positions of the aft side of the forward frames, and the forward side of the aft frames. The shapes of the frames are drawn on the body plan and these lines show the actual shape of alternate frames, that is, they exclude the outside planking; so if your draught is drawn to the scale to which you are working it is necessary only to trace off on to suitable timber.

It may not be necessary to make every frame unless you intended to leave off some of the planking to show the interior; but if you are planking the hull, you must insert enough frames to ensure that the hull planking lies in a gentle curve — if the frames are too far apart the planking will lie in a series of flats.

Frames in a real ship were built in pairs made up of a number of sections called floors, futtocks and top timbers; the floor goes right across the keel, the futtocks make up the sides of the frames and the top timbers form the stanchions of the bulwarks and are extensions of the last futtock.

A simple way to make a frame is to saw it out of a piece of resin bonded five-ply wood, the top being sawn out so that the deck may be laid and the stanchions formed. To hold the frames in place as they are being erected it is necessary to make a jig, which is supported at each end at the correct height. Make the jig of hardboard or three-ply wood and cut in it a hole which should be of the shape of the hull contour at the gun deck level or the top of the bulwarks or other convenient height. To fix each frame on to the keel it is better to make the keel a little deeper than shown on the draught and to cut a slot in the frame which can then be glued on to the keel and secured with a dowel put in askew. When all the frames are erected, fair them up with coarse glasspaper to the proper curves and make up the stern which is built up on top of the sternpost, either from a solid block of wood or formed by frames erected on the wing transom, a massive baulk of timber fixed to the sternpost and which supported the whole of the transom.

PLANKING

The frames have now to be planked, but before this can be done some careful measuring is called for. It is

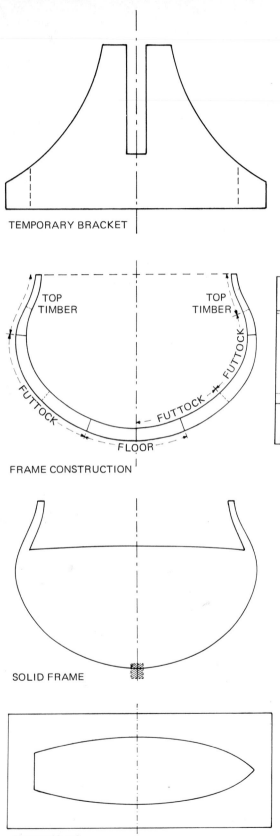

TEMPORARY BRACKET

FRAME CONSTRUCTION

TOP TIMBER

TOP TIMBER

FUTTOCK

FUTTOCK

FUTTOCK

FUTTOCK

FLOOR

SOLID FRAME

FRAMING JIG

obvious that the girth of the vessel amidships is greater than at the bow or stern so each frame has to be divided into parts according to the number of planks there are on the hull sides, and thus finding the width of the plank on each frame. Narrow planks are easier to lay than wide ones and if you make the planks about 1′ 0″ wide not only will they look right but they will bend easily. Prepare sufficient timber for the planking no thicker than about 1/16″. Measure the girth of the midship frame — this is best done with a strip of paper laid against its edge; divide this length into the required number of spaces and transfer them to the edge of the frame carefully marking them as you do so. Short planks are easier to lay than long ones, and of course look more like the real thing since planks were rarely longer than about 24′ 0″, and if you make them this size they will be about right; make sure the butts meet on a frame and that the butts are staggered.

Because of the difference in the girth measurements of each frame it is obvious that generally speaking a plank will be wide in the middle and taper towards its bow and stern ends. In the majority of hulls the taper will not be excessive but if the girth amidships is very great as in a vessel with a broad beam the planks would be such that their ends would taper off almost to a point, in which case it is necessary to introduce stealers, or parts of extra planks to cover the midship part of the hull. Above the water line the run of the planking will more or less follow the sheer; it is below this that the stealers are introduced and they can be worked in, allowing the planks to follow the curves of the hull naturally without forcing them into place. Sometimes because of the fanning out effect of the planking as it approached the sternpost below the counter the reverse takes place and the planks widen so that it becomes necessary to introduce an extra plank there, either between two planks, or into one plank, in order to avoid a very wide end which would look unsightly. It is possible to make an expanded drawing of the hull surface and to lay out the shape of each plank on paper, but probably the better way in a model is to fit the planks and introduce the stealers as it becomes advisable. It is also better to plank both sides of the hull simultaneously so that they match and are equal.

At the bow and stern where the hull planking takes on a sharp bend some difficulty may be experienced in getting the planks to lie nicely on to the frames without fracturing. If the planking is of thin wood it is an advantage since the planks will bend easily, but if the timber used does not respond, the trouble may be overcome by heat in one form or another. Soaking or boiling in hot water has been suggested but this has the great disadvantage of swelling the wood excessively and also of raising the grain. Steaming is better either by holding the plank in the spout of a kettle and forming the curve between the fingers, or by rigging up a tube through which steam is passed after packing the tube with several of the planks which are to be used. Another method is by dry heat and can be done by holding a round steel bar or a copper tube in a vice, heating the metal at one end to dull red, and then by working the strip of wood backwards and forwards quickly over the bar it can be made to assume the correct curvature permanently. This method has the advantage that no distortion takes place, but be careful not to scorch the wood by too much heat or by not keeping the wood on the move.

Some modelmakers start from the garboard strake (the lowest strake on the hull and the one rabetted into the keel) and work upwards, others advise starting at the bulwarks and working downwards; I prefer the former way, so lay the garboard strake, taking the widths from the marks on the frame edges, and start at the bow end where the plank should fit neatly against the stem into which it was actually rabetted. Secure the planks with glue and hold them in place while the glue is setting with either pins or spring clothes pegs, which make excellent clamps for holding parts together. When the glue is dry the clamps can be removed and replaced with wood dowels.

Lay the second strake close up against the first taking care that the butts do not lie on the same frame unless at least three strakes separate them. Continue thus until the bulwarks are reached when, if you have followed the marks correctly the top strake will fit exactly. The inside of the bulwarks is lined in the same way, but it is better to do this after the deck is laid as it is then easier to make a neat join where the bulwarks meet the deck. When the planking is finished, go over the surface with glasspaper to remove any irregularities there may be in the joins of the planking.

This method of planking can be used to cover a solid wood hull, and in this way simulate a plank on frame model. It can give a good appearance if carefully done and is one of the ways in which the bone ship models were made by prisoners of the Napoleonic wars. A solid core was made of wood and then thin strips of bone were nailed to it to represent the planking.

SEMI-FRAMED HULLS

Mention was made at the beginning of this chapter of making the hull partly solid and partly built up on frames. To do this carve the hull from the solid wood up to say the gun deck, or to be more accurate to the thickness of the deck beams (say 1′ 0″) below. Now saw out the tops of the frames from fairly stout

plywood. The lower part will form the beam to support the deck, the upper cross piece is there for strength while the hull is being planked, and it is then cut away when the time comes to plank the inside of the bulwarks.

If you are making a hull with the frames exposed, then each frame must be built up in pieces with floors and futtocks. In a large ship there would be many more pieces than these, the object being to have the grain of the wood follow the curves of the frame as far as possible. As will be seen in the sketch, the moulded dimension (the width athwartships) of the frame would be about 12″ to 18″ at the keel and taper upwards until at the top timber it would be about 4″ to 6″.

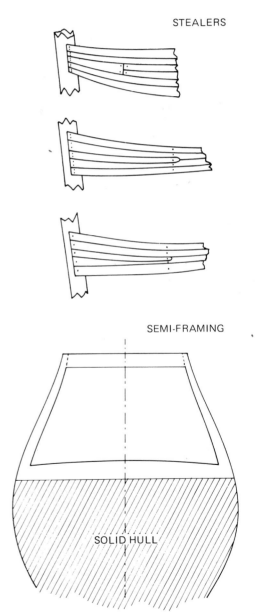

STEALERS

SEMI-FRAMING

SOLID HULL

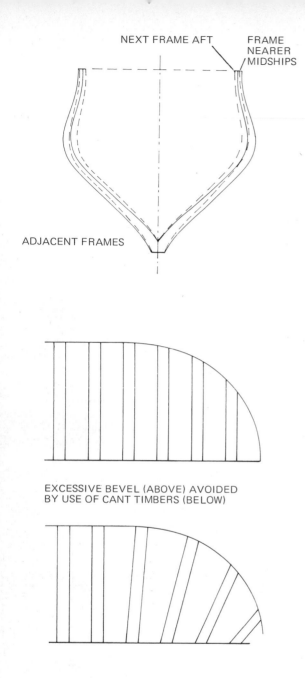

NEXT FRAME AFT   FRAME NEARER MIDSHIPS

ADJACENT FRAMES

EXCESSIVE BEVEL (ABOVE) AVOIDED
BY USE OF CANT TIMBERS (BELOW)

It will be evident that as the frames approach the bow or stern they become smaller so each frame has to be bevelled to some extent, consequently when making the tracing from the draught both sides of the frame must be shown, and one side of the frame must be drawn to one frame, the other side to the next frame further from the midship position. With care the bevel can be partly cut with a sharp chisel before the frame is glued in place and finished off with glasspaper when all the frames are fixed. However, right forward in the bows it is obvious that the bevelling becomes excessive if the frames are fixed square to the keel. Therefore the last few frames are set at an angle and these are called the cant frames; some bevelling is required, of course, but not so much. These cant frames, because they butt against the deadwoods and stem, are half frames, and their shapes can be arrived at by carefully preparing a drawing from the draught; but if this is found too difficult, the only other way is by trial and error. Frankly it is a difficult part of the framing and if you find it impossible, solid blocks shaped to the correct sections offer an easier way out.

DOCKYARD MODELS

Some of the Navy Board or Admiralty Dockyard models, as they are variously called, of the seventeenth and eighteenth centuries were made in a manner which is peculiar to them alone. Alternate floors and futtocks were omitted but all the frames were fastened close together giving the appearance of two or more solid bands of timber running the length of the hull. To build a model in this fashion calls for an extremely high degree of skill, but briefly, two frames are made as a unit and when the units are finished they are erected on a keel and each unit is glued to its neighbour until all are assembled, in the following manner.

After sawing out of suitable timber the various pieces that make up the frame, the floor and top timbers are temporarily glued to a tracing of the frame, and the futtocks of the next frame are glued and dowelled on to them which will bind all together as a unit. As each pair is made the tracing paper is discarded and the frame is fixed to the keel and glued to the previous pair. The first unit to be made is comprised of the three frames amidships, and then the next frames fore and aft are made simultaneously until the stem and stern are reached when, if your measurements have been correct they will all fit exactly. Accuracy in measuring is essential, and strict adherence to scale is necessary otherwise a small error in the thickness of each frame can accumulate to a large error when there are 100 or more frames to be joined together.

It is therefore necessary to make a copy on thick tracing paper of each frame, to saw out the floors and futtocks separately and to assemble them on the tracing paper, glueing the parts together carefully and placing them while they dry under weights on a perfectly flat surface; a sheet of plate glass is admirable for this purpose. When dry they can be trimmed up and fixed to the keel by drilling a hole for a dowel through the floor timber into the keel.

DECKS

Before the hull can be said to be completely finished there are many more details which have to be added, one of which is the laying of the deck, which in the vast majority of ships consists of planks of wood laid longitudinally and of an average width of about 6″, though ships of early periods could be 9″ or more; but if you make them 6″ they will look right. The length varied according to the timber available and as with the hull planking, the butts were stepped so that

Below. The author's seventeenth century Dockyard model, showing the essential feature of this style of framing.

Bottom. Four stages in the framing of a Dockyard type model. Note the jig for keeping the keel assembly vertical, and the sliding square to ensure that the frames are in correct alignment both vertically and transversely. The photograph, bottom right, shows the cambered deck beams.

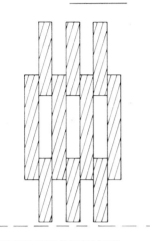

'DOCKYARD' STYLE FRAMING

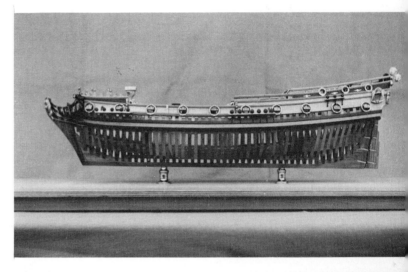

47

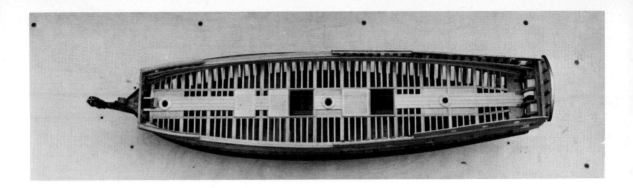

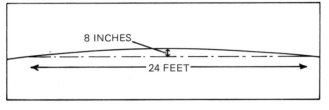

DECK CAMBER

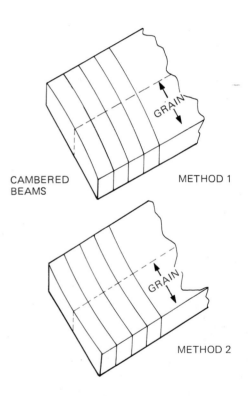

CAMBERED BEAMS

METHOD 1

METHOD 2

several planks separated butts meeting on the same beam. Decks were cambered to throw off water, and the round up of the camber was about 1″ for every 3′ 0″ of width; so if a deck were 24′ 0″ wide, the round up amidships would be 8″. The curve of the camber is an arc of a circle and to draw a pattern of it is quite easy. Set out the curve as the arc of a circle using the three points to lie on the circumference of a circle. It is very useful to keep a templet to this pattern because it will be frequently used. Paper or cardboard would soon be useless so make it of three-ply wood, and from a single square you can make with one saw cut, an inside and an outside curve to use whenever you require a convex or concave templet.

The decks were supported on beams which themselves were supported at their ends on clamps fastened to the inside of the hull, and the beams were sawn out to the shape of the camber. There are two ways in which the beams may be made, one of which is to obtain a piece of wood of suitable thickness, with the grain across the width, and after marking the centre line to shape the top face to the curve of the templet, slices being sawn off the plank to the required width of the beam. The other way, which is probably better as being more like the real thing is to use a piece of wood, again with the grain across the surface, but of a thickness equal to the width of the beams. Mark the centre line, then with the templet draw across the surface curved parallel lines separated by the depth of the beams. Every saw cut will now

give you a correctly shaped and sized beam, and if you saw carefully very little cleaning up will be necessary. If you are making a model with the deck beams exposed, then the draught will show how many are needed and their spacing; if a deck is being laid it may not be necessary to fix so many, but there must be sufficient to give adequate support to the length of the deck, and care should be taken to place them so that they are not in the way of masts or hatches, or other fittings which penetrate the deck.

If you study a deck of wood planks it will be seen that all around the edge is a wider plank variously

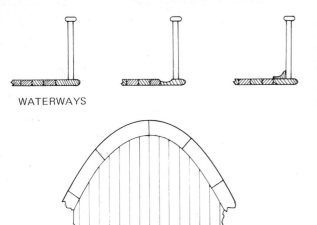

WATERWAYS

WATERWAYS – MADE IN SECTIONS
AT BOW

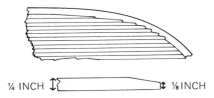

¼ INCH ⬍ ⬍ ⅛ INCH

JOGGLING OF PLANKS

Opposite. Taken before the forecastle beams, etc, were added, this illustration gives a good idea of the deck beams, and the timbering of the decks for dockyard type construction.

Below. The *Cutty Sark,* showing how the deck planking is joggled into the margin plank. Note the variation in the length of the snapes.
(Photo: John Bowen)

called the 'waterway', the 'covering board' or the 'margin plank'. It was very often merely a board wider than the ordinary deck plank, though in the *Cutty Sark* it is the same thickness but about twice the width of the ordinary planks and is hollowed out to form a gutter; this type was used in other clipper ships. In some vessels, notably of those of the Navy or in the East Indiamen, it was much thicker than the deck planks and finished with a curved section which can easily be represented by adding a strip of quarter round moulding.

The plank is glued and dowelled hard up against the bulwarks on to the deck beams and can be as long as may be convenient. As there is only a gentle curve for most of the length of the deck little difficulty will be encountered in fixing it, but at the bow and stern where the curves are much more pronounced and sometimes almost semi-circular, it will be necessary to build up the waterway in pieces cut with a fretsaw to correspond with the shape.

The deck planks are laid from the middle outwards in perfectly straight lines and their ends butt against the margin plank. Though to be absolutely correct some are butted and some are let in, or joggled into, the plank according to a set of rules which say that a plank must be joggled if the snipe (that is, the diagonal cut) is more than twice the width of the plank, and the square end is then made half its width. So if a plank is $\frac{1}{4}''$ wide, and the diagonal cut more than $\frac{1}{2}''$, then it is joggled, making the square end which is let into the margin plank $\frac{1}{8}''$. If the run of the deck planking is interrupted by the fittings such as deckhouses, hatches or masts, then a mitred surround is formed by planks a little wider than the deck planks so making a neat finish. The holes for the masts should be a trifle larger than their diameters so as to allow for adjustment of the rake by the insertion of small wedges which are then covered by the mast coating around the base to prevent ingress of water.

49

Below. The bow of the Dockyard model showing the beakhead, head rails and catheads — note the decoration on the end of the cathead.

Bottom. The stern of the same model, showing the transom and taffrail. Again much of the detail work has been completed at an early stage of the construction of the model, showing the necessity for careful planning of building sequences.

Opposite. This close up of the completed stern of this model gives a good indication of the amount and intricacy of the carved work. Note also the detail on the stern windows, and the hinges on the two gunports.

DECK PLANKING

Now the deck has to be laid, and one way of doing this is to tack and glue a single sheet of three-ply wood to the beams. The deck planking is simulated by scribing parallel lines with a sharp knife or steel scriber held firmly against a steel rule; run a hard sharp pencil into the groove and finish with fine glasspaper. If carefully done this method can be made to look passable, but nothing is better than a properly laid deck. This is how it is done. Fix a sheet of thin three-ply wood to the beams and scribe the centre line longitudinally and mark in the position of the various deck openings. Prepare the wood for the deck which should be about 1/16″ thick and of a scale width of 6″. Lay a straight edge against the centre line and proceed to lay the deck in strips glueing and pinning each plank of about 24′ 0″ long against the straight edge. Having laid the first line of planks, you can continue to lay the remainder of the planks in lines, but separate them with a strip of black paper glued to the edges. The openings in the deck must be framed with a margin plank generally of similar size to the deck planking, and the deck planks made to butt against it. When the planking is finished replace the pins with wood dowels glued in and go over the whole deck with varying grades of glasspaper to a smooth finish when it will appear as a properly planked and caulked deck as on a real ship.

THE BOW AND STERN

The stern above the rudder, which was called the transom, provided light, through the windows cut into it, for the captain's and officer's cabins which were situated in this part of the vessel. In ships of the seventeenth century the sterns were elaborately decorated with painted and gilded figures and other carvings of all descriptions, over and around the windows. In later centuries the decoration was less elaborate but still plentiful. At each side of the transom stern galleries were built out and served, among other things, as officers' lavatories.

To provide the detail for these parts, a very good job can be done by building up the panelling or the balustrades with bristol board on to a solid block of wood built on to the stern, but use a sharp knife so that no fuzzy edges are left on the panelling. The fancy scroll work can be effectively done with similar material but keep a look out for the embossed gold paper from greetings cards, cake frills, cigarette boxes and such like for you can find plenty of strips and shapes which if carefully cut out will provide mouldings, crests, shields and imitation rope patterns. If you are expert in these matters the cherubs, knights in armour or sea monsters can be carved from wood as with the figurehead, or built up with modelling paste. The painting needs to be

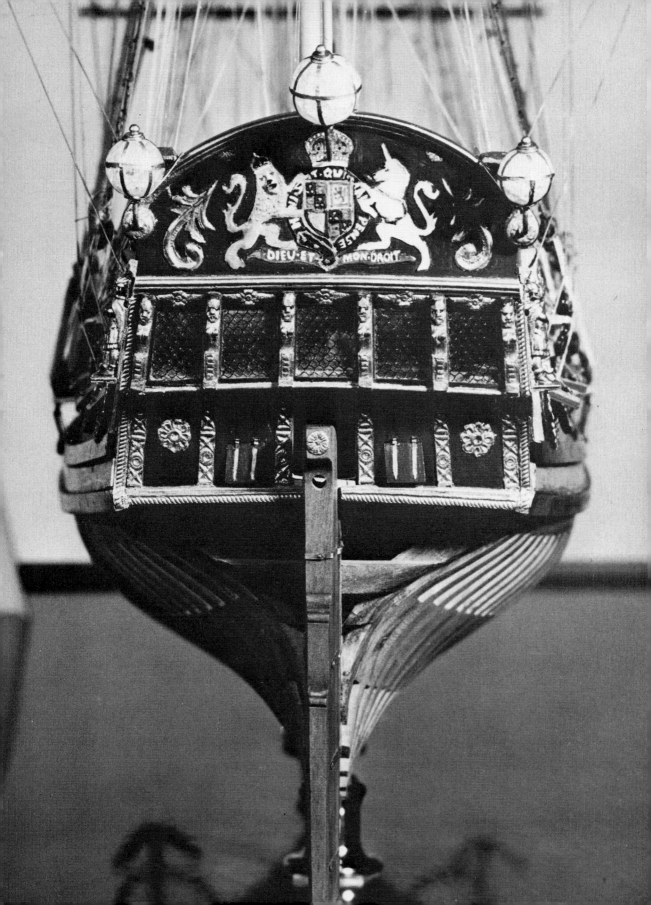

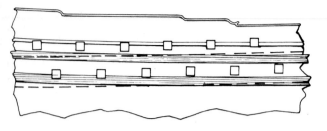

THE RUN OF THE WALES

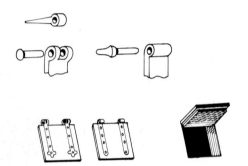

GUNPORT LIDS AND FITTINGS

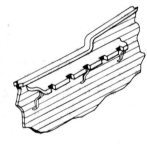

CHANNELS

CHAINS

PLATES

carefully done so as not to look crude but use the best gold paint you can buy for it will then keep its colour.

The same technique is adopted for the cheek knees, hair rails and trail boards; these are the parts which make up the head timbers and give support to the stem head. Build up the various parts with wood, and if you first cut pieces of cardboard to the shapes required and use them as patterns it will prove an easier way to do the job for the curves, though at first sight quite complicated, if reduced to the component parts are not so difficult as they appear. The head rails, for instance, are in fact straight when looking down on them and are curved only as they pass from the figurehead to the hull as viewed from the side.

TOPSIDES

The wales, that is the strengthening bands of timber which were fixed to the sides of the hull can quite easily be made of bristol board of suitable thickness, or thin wood glued and pinned to the surface. The wales normally ran parallel to the sheer and in early ships did actually strengthen the hull, but in later centuries this was not their prime function and there were fewer of them, but they form an attractive feature as they accentuate the line of the sheer. The gunports, on the other hand, ran parallel with the line of the decks and not with the sheer; and their lower edges, called the cills, were all about 2′ 6″ above it so that the gun barrels were all the same height above the deck; consequently sometimes the gun ports crossed over the line of the wales. It is important to note that gun ports are rectangular; that is, the sides are vertical and top and bottom horizontal. If this is not observed the ports would not open on their hinges. Carefully mark out the positions of the ports which, on solid hulls, can be cut out with a sharp chisel of suitable width. An alternative method is to drill a hole just smaller than the port and then to enlarge it with the chisel, but keep the edges clean and finish off with a flat file. Leave the port lids glued on partly opened and with dummy guns protruding from the ports. If you are making a scale model it is not too difficult to make the port lids to open and shut. Make the straps of thin copper strip and after rivetting them to the lids bend the tops over into a loop so that they work in a pin inserted in the hull sides.

Also fixed to the hull sides are the channels, a contracted form of the original 'chain wales'; these were timbers fixed along the sides in the appropriate position, and to these were fixed the chain plates which held the deadeyes to which the shrouds were led from the mast head, so clearing the upper sides of the hull and spreading the shrouds which supported the mast. Originally the chain plates were actually chains, but later on, about the mid-nineteenth century they became plates. The deadeyes attached to the chains were stropped and rivetted or looped to them and are best turned from black or dark brown ebonite or plastic rod, in preference to wood which may split. They vary in size according to the shroud to which they are lashed, the largest being about 12″ to 15″ in diameter, and are drilled with three holes for the lanyards connecting them to the upper deadeyes at the ends of the shrouds; but take particular notice of the position of the middle hole — it is lowest at the chains but highest at the shroud.

At this stage you are ready to proceed to the deck detail or the masts and spars of your model.

Below. The wales completed and fitted with their mouldings. Note how the gunports, in order to keep their correct alignment, cut into the wales. The gunport lids have been fitted, and their decorative wreaths added. The channels, with lower deadeyes, are in place, the spacing of the shrouds being such as to clear the gunport. 'Sleeping dog' hancing pieces have been fitted at the ends of the topgallant bulwark rail.

Bottom. With the hull completed, the bowsprit and lower masts have been stepped and a start made on fitting the standing rigging.
(All uncredited photos: the author)

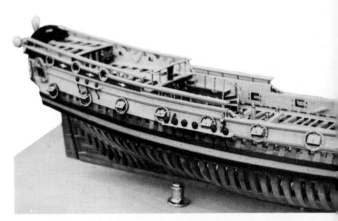

Deck fittings

by ROGER GLEN

Although bad workmanship or technical errors in any part of a model can mar its perfection, there is little doubt that the one place above all others where these are most likely to be found is among the deck fittings. Unfortunately this is also the area where their very number and variety make it impossible to include them all in one chapter. What follows, therefore, is a selection of typical examples of the deck fittings to be found on the types of vessel previously mentioned. In some instances constructional notes have been included; these can be applied, in one way or another, to other examples of such fittings. Most modelmakers plans include details of the deck fittings, but in addition many books, of which full details will be found in the bibliography, contain much useful information.

Above. The coaster *M A James* typifies the deck layout of many of these vessels.

FIFE RAILS *(right)*

Fife rails were fitted at the foot of the masts and in addition to carrying belaying pins, were also so made that they could be used as bitts. These have the stanchions set in cast iron sockets, but they were also constructed with the stanchions carried through the deck and secured to the lower deck beams. The belaying pins, of hardwood, and later iron, were about 16″ long by 1½″ diameter with the top part shaped like a handle. Pin rails were also fitted, where appropriate, along the inside of the bulwarks, as in the photograph of the bollard. Sheaves, either single, double or treble, were often fitted in the base of the stanchions.

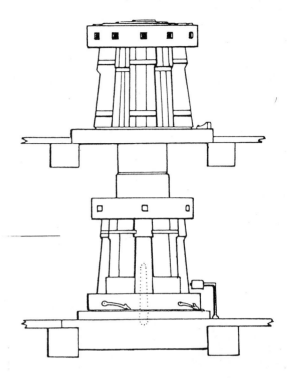

CAPSTAN *(above)*

A typical iron capstan of the clipper ship era. Note the four pawls at the base, and the rectangular sockets for the capstan bars. When not in use the latter were stowed adjacent to the capstan, but in a position where they would not be washed overboard.

NAVAL CAPSTAN

Not only was the ground tackle of a warship heavier than that of a merchantman, but men-of-war's men

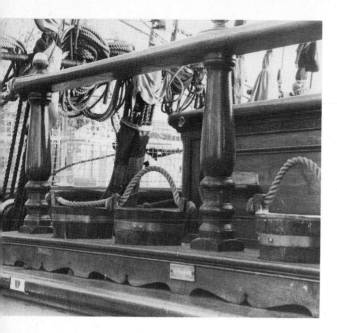

were expected to perform many tasks like hoisting in guns and getting up spars, that involved moving very heavy weights. The large crew of a warship transmitted their combined effort through blocks, tackle and large capstans. The capstan was more powerful than the windlass because more men could apply their strength to it at any one time, and navies developed an even more powerful double-capstan — illustrated — that consisted of two drums on separate decks, connected by a common barrel. They could operate singly or as one.

The deep whelps of the example shown is a British feature, the French Navy preferring a more cylindrical shape, while the Dutch at the end of the eighteenth century developed a smooth drum where — in effect — the space between the whelps had been completely filled in.

BUCKETS *(left)*
Here the teak firebuckets are set in a rack built into the base of the ship's poop rails. The buckets, about

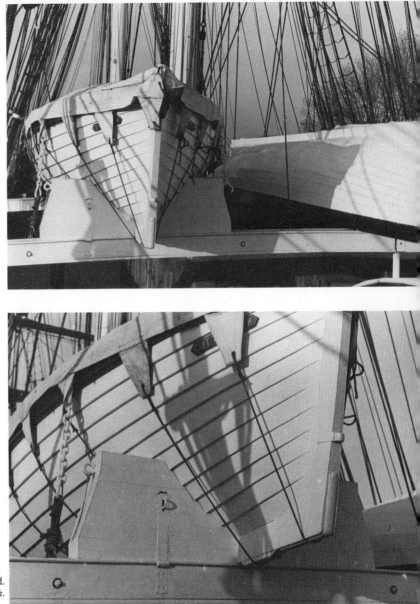

Above. An iron crutch supporting a boat skid.
Above right. Boat stowage on the *Cutty Sark*.
Right. Close-up of a lifeboat chock.

15″ high, were built up of staves, in the same way as a barrel, with two brass bands; two staves were of increased length to accommodate the rope handles.

LIFEBOATS AND DAVITS

The construction of lifeboats requires as much attention to detail as does the model on which they are fitted; unfortunately too often they appear to have been added as a hurried afterthought. The plans for modelmakers usually show the size of the various boats, even though they may be deficient in detail. As boats more often than not were carried either stowed upside down or else were fitted with a canvas cover,

the lack of information about interior fittings is not always a disaster. So far as the exterior is concerned, the constructional methods described in *Model Open Boats*, and in the article in *Model Shipwright* No 19 entitled 'Building a Model Whaleboat' can be used or adapted for the construction of the model's boats.

Whereas the boat carried on coasters was either carried under a simple type of radial davit, or more usually stowed on deck or on the hatch, the larger size and number of boats carried by the clipper ships required more substantial stowage arrangements. The general practice was for the boats to be carried on skids, that is, heavy beams fitted across the ship,

57

usually above a deckhouse. The outboard ends of the skids were supported by strong iron crutches. The boats were either stowed upside down or else on chocks secured to the skids, when they were protected from the elements by strong canvas covers. Radial type davits were fitted adjacent to the ends of the skids for launching the boats. These are quite simple to construct. The main point to remember is that they tapered from the centre to either end, and that the upper end terminated in a form of ball to accommodate the swivel eye to which the upper block of the lowering tackle was attached.

WARSHIPS' BOATS

In the sixteenth century large royal ships carried at least 3 boats — a 'great boat', a 'cok' or 'cock', and a 'jollywatt'. By the beginning of the following century they are known as 'longboat', 'pinnace' and 'skiff' although it is not certain they were exactly the same types. The longboat was usually towed at sea and could be anything up to 52 feet in length. Unfortunately little more than the dimensions is known about these craft and the 'barges' and 'shallops' that also crop up in documents and books of

the period, and it is not until the eighteenth century that official plans exist. There is a set dated 1706 held in the National Maritime Museum at Greenwich: Sir Clowdisley Shovell's boat is included, but apart from the 'yawls' all the other boats are only differentiated by the number of oars.

Illustrated are a selection of naval boats of the 1780-1800 period to a constant $\frac{1}{8}'' = 1' \ 0''$ (1/96) scale for comparative purposes.

The *longboat* was the ships' workboat and carried a davit and a windlass for handling the anchor and various other heavy duties. These were replaced during the 1780s by *launches* which were originally dockyard service craft and tended to be more flat-bottomed and better rowing craft than longboats. Both were usually rowed 'double-banked', that is with pairs of rowers on the same thwart one pulling the starboard oar and the other the port: in 'single-banked' boats the rowers sat on alternate thwarts. Under sail longboats and launches were rigged as sloops.

Pinnaces were narrower and sharper, primarily an officers' boat which was swift under oars but handier under sail than the rather larger *barge*, which it

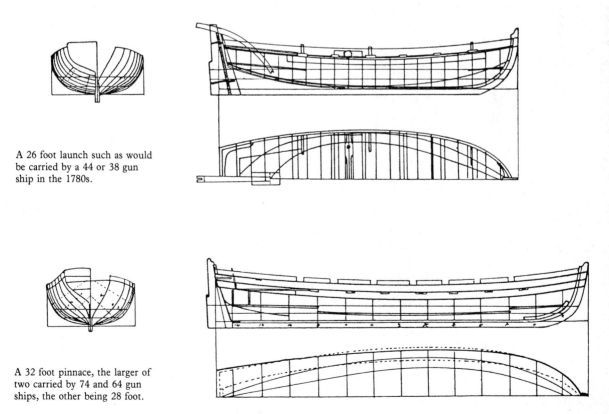

A 26 foot launch such as would be carried by a 44 or 38 gun ship in the 1780s.

A 32 foot pinnace, the larger of two carried by 74 and 64 gun ships, the other being 28 foot.

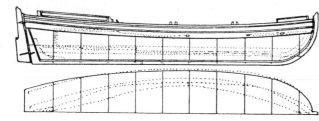

A 26 foot yawl was carried by many third rates until replaced with cutters in the 1770s and 1780s.

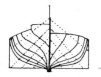

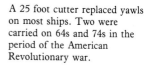

A 25 foot cutter replaced yawls on most ships. Two were carried on 64s and 74s in the period of the American Revolutionary war.

An 18 foot cutter was carried by every naval vessel from sloops upwards from 1781. They were often referred to as 'jolly boats'.

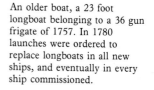

An older boat, a 23 foot longboat belonging to a 36 gun frigate of 1757. In 1780 launches were ordered to replace longboats in all new ships, and eventually in every ship commissioned.

tended to replace. From the mid-eighteenth century there was a tendency for the lighter and more robust clinker-built *cutters* to oust both the barge and the pinnace. Eventually, cutters also superceded *yawls* which were the original clinker-built small boats with an emphasis on sailing qualities. Cutters carried a ketch rig with a lug foresail and a sprit mizzen but the others sailed under a two-masted spritsail rig.

When the dominance of the cutter was complete sea officers took to the use of very light rowing *gigs* (after about 1800) and the smallest cutter became known as the *jolly boat* from about 1780. Later the double-ended *whaleboat* was introduced and was used in any duties that required extreme seaworthiness.

Boats were stowed on the booms until about 1790 when a pair of davits for the lighter boats — usually cutters — began to be fitted to the quarters of some ships, but others had only a single set to carry a seaboat across the stern. The Admiralty disapproved of quarter davits in vessels smaller than sloops but by the 1820s this prohibition had fallen into disuse. At first davits were simple baulks of timber, but in the later 1820s curved iron davits were being fitted.

CATHEADS

These were heavy beams, either bolted to the deck, or to the inside of the bulwark on some smaller vessels, and extending over the ship's side. At the outboard end were fitted two or three sheaves to form the upper part of a tackle. Their purpose was to provide a means of hoisting the anchor, after it was weighed, into a position where it was accessible for stowing.

Below. The outboard end of the *Cutty Sark's* cathead, showing the sheaves.
Top right. The inboard end of the cathead.
Bottom right. The standard 'round crown', iron-stocked Admiralty pattern anchor. This is *not* the usual stowage.

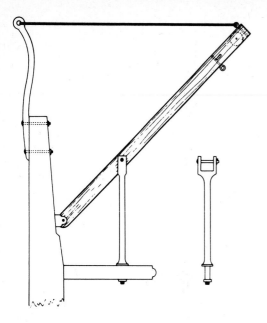

Left. A naval quarter davit from the end of the Napoleonic wars. This is an experimental version of the standard type which did not have the supporting crutch but relied entirely on the topping lift.

ANCHORS

Whereas most fittings vary enormously, depending on ship type and period, until the nineteenth century there is little difference between merchant and naval anchors, except size.

The most common form of anchor from at least the fourteenth century was the 'round crown' type whose arms were arcs of a circle. However, from 1702 until 1825 the Royal Navy (and, indeed, most navies during this period) used an 'angled crown' version with straight arms. However, following enquiries into ship losses caused by the arms breaking off, an Admiralty round crown was introduced, and this became so widely used that it was called the 'common stocked' anchor.

Although a ship's outfit of anchors would be all of the same shape they differed in weight and hence size, and were known by the functions they performed. Thus there were 'bower' anchors, a 'stream' anchor, and a 'kedge'. In warships and large merchantmen like East Indiamen, there would be a 'best bower' or 'first bower'; a 'small' or 'second bower'; and two other bowers called a 'sheet' and a 'spare'; a smaller 'stream'; and a 'kedge'. Oddly enough the four bowers were the same size, two being catted forward, with the other two in the fore chains. The smaller anchors were stowed in the hold or in the boats on the booms.

For naval vessels actual dimensions can be found easily by consulting Falconer (See Bibliography) and less easily for merchantships by looking up Lloyd's Classification Rules for various periods. However certain basic proportions apply to anchors for most of the sailing ship era, as follows.

The arms equal $\frac{3}{8}$ of the shank and form, or are contained within, an arc of a circle whose centre is $\frac{3}{8}$ of the length of the shank from the crown. The flukes are $\frac{1}{2}$ the length of the arms, and $\frac{2}{5}$ of the arm broad. The circumference at the throat is $\frac{1}{5}$ of the shank's length. The stock is the same length as the shank plus half the diameter of the ring, the breadth and diameter being $\frac{1}{12}$ the length. The upper plane is straight, but only the centre $\frac{1}{6}$ of the lower side is parallel to it, the remainder tapering upwards to $\frac{1}{24}$ the length. The stock usually has two or more iron bands on each arm.

Some documentary sources may give the weight of the anchors only. By taking the weight in tons and multiplying it by 1160 and then finding the cube root, the answer will be a reasonable approximation of the length of the shank, from which the proportions can be obtained by the above rules.

Iron stocks were used on small anchors (12 or 13 cwt) in the Royal Navy from about 1780 but much larger iron stocked anchors came into service in the early part of the nineteenth century. In the early- and mid-nineteenth century American stocks were often made circular or octagonal in section. Following trials in the 1850s the Admiralty also favoured Trotman's patent anchor which had pivoting arms. This was widely used in the merchant navy, but was only one of a large number of nineteenth century 'patent' types of ground tackle utilized, before the modern 'stockless' anchor took over.

When constructing model anchors always remember that in order to function at all the arms and the stock have to be in different planes — if the arms are seen in side view then the stock should be end on.

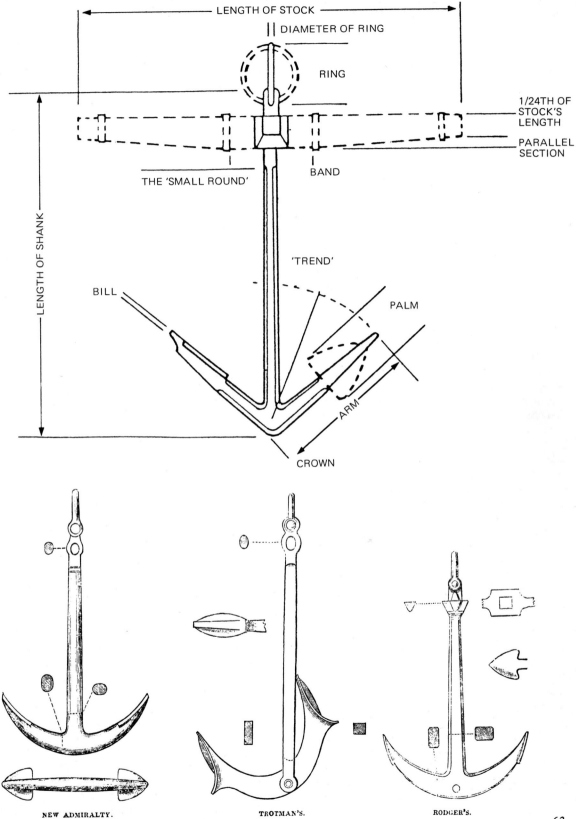

ADMIRALTY 'ANGLED CROWN' ANCHOR

LENGTH OF STOCK

DIAMETER OF RING

RING

1/24TH OF STOCK'S LENGTH

PARALLEL SECTION

BAND

THE 'SMALL ROUND'

LENGTH OF SHANK

'TREND'

BILL

PALM

ARM

CROWN

NEW ADMIRALTY.

TROTMAN'S.

RODGER'S.

63

PUMPS

There were many different patterns of pumps fitted to sailing ships. Most were operated by 'Armstrong Patent', there being no other source of power other than men. But in the latter years of sail, where a vessel had a donkey boiler on deck, they were sometimes capable of being driven by a messenger chain from the steam winch. In such cases a gypsy wheel was fitted to the crank shaft of the pump.

The simplest type of hand pump is probably the single bucket type worked by a lever. These can be made up quite easily from scraps of brass. Start with a base plate, marked out on a piece of flat brass. Drill holes for the pump barrel and for the lever stanchion, then cut the base plate to shape. The barrel of the pump can be made from a small piece of brass rod shouldered to fit into the base plate and drilled out for the plunger (which of course is not fitted). A rim can be formed from a piece of brass wire silver soldered to the top edge with a lip filed in it. The stanchion is formed from brass rod with a reduced end to fit into the base plate and a fork end at the top with a small hole through it. The operating handle is made of brass or copper, filed and beaten to shape. The stirrup and connecting rod are made from brass wire. When finished and painted the whole unit should be fitted to a small wooden pad slightly larger than the base plate, then fixed to the deck with pins and adhesive.

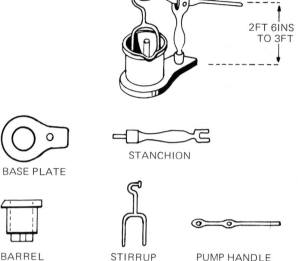

SIMPLE DECK PUMP

2FT 6INS TO 3FT

BASE PLATE

STANCHION

BARREL

STIRRUP

PUMP HANDLE

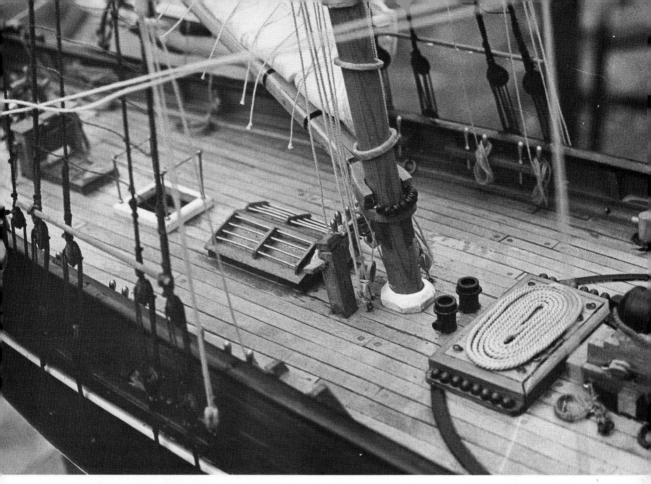

Opposite. The author's model of *Albatross:* a small hand pump is visible abreast the main mast.
Left. Another version of the small hand pump. In this instance the handle is sustained by a fulcrum pin bolted to the deckhouse.
Above. John Mayger's naval brigantine *Dolphin.* Pump barrels are visible before the mast but handles are unshipped.

DOWNTON TYPE PUMP

This type of pump is constructed in much the same way as those already described except that in this case the bucket rods are connected to a crankshaft which runs in a centre bearing mounted on a stanchion. The two end bearings are mounted on the fife rails. These are simply cut from the solid and the centre bearing is a hole in the end of a flattened piece of wire. A rather more complicated bearing can be made by drilling a small brass block and soldering it to the top of the stanchion. The crankshaft is a piece of brass rod annealed, bent to shape and cut to length. However remember to place the centre bearing and stanchion in position before forming the second crank. The cranks can be either at 90° or 180° relative to each other. The two flywheels can be made from a

DOWNTON TYPE DOUBLE CRANK PUMP MOUNTED ON FIFE RAILS
(SCALE ¼IN = 1FT)

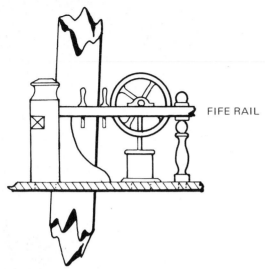

FIFE RAIL

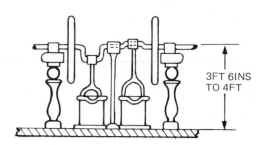

3FT 6INS
TO 4FT

Below. Downton type pump abaft the main mast of the author's model of the *Vincent A White.*
Right. A three barrelled version of the Downton pump, aboard the *Cutty Sark.*
Far right. A twin-barrelled pump is visible forward of the main mast in this model of the brigantine *Raven.*

matching pair of watch gear wheels with the teeth filed off in the lathe. Round section rims can be formed from the outer plastic casing of small diameter electric wire from which the wire has been withdrawn. The piece of plastic is then split along its length on one side only with a razor blade and wrapped around the outside diameter of the wheel. It is scraped where the two ends meet and fixed with adhesive. Once painted they look quite realistic and can be fixed to the shaft with a touch of solder. The ends of the bucket rods can be flattened and annealed and bent around the crank pins to form bearings. This completes this pump.

TWIN BARRELLED DECK PUMP

This pump is made in a similar manner to the first pump described except that it has two barrels in which the buckets work up and down. The bucket, relative to the pump on deck, is almost at the bottom of the hold. The barrels of the pump, no matter which type, extended right down into the space between the outer planking and the inner ceiling of the hold. They were usually reduced in diameter for about 2' 0" at their bottom ends. In this reduced part a simple foot or non-return valve was fitted. As the bucket was pulled up to the full extent of its stroke, the bilge water was drawn into the main cylinder and could not return because of the foot valve. On the down stroke the water was forced through another valve or valves in the bucket and so transferred to the top of the bucket and could not return past those valves. With continuous strokes the pump barrel was filled and the water eventually overflowed onto the deck, to run away overboard through the scuppers. The bucket was made watertight by having a recessed portion on its outer diameter into which a number of turns of rope about $\frac{1}{2}$" to $\frac{3}{4}$" in diameter were tightly wound and secured. These were then liberally coated with tallow. Water made the rope swell and so ensured a good fit in the cylinder.

To make a replica of this pump, as can be seen from the sketch, is a fairly simple job. The base plate is first marked out on $\frac{1}{16}$" brass plate and cut to shape with two - $\frac{1}{4}$" holes for the spigots of the pump barrels. It is a good idea to countersink these holes slightly on the underside of the plate to allow soft solder to be run into the joint when fixing the pump barrels. A centre hole should be drilled for the pump lever stanchion, together with four or six holding down bolt holes around the edge of the plate. Clean up the plate with emery cloth to remove all burrs and at the same time form a slight chamfer around the top edge. Next turn up the two barrels, forming a rim on the top edge and a spigot on the bottom (to fit the holes in the the base plate). Then drill out the barrels about $\frac{1}{4}$" deep, but do *not* drill right through. Leave about $\frac{3}{16}$" of solid metal at the bottom and then drill a $\frac{1}{16}$" hole right through that. File lips in the top and the two barrels are complete. The centre (fulcrum) stanchion was often decoratively shaped — typical of the Victorian period. Having turned up the stanchion and with a slot cut in the top section, a $\frac{3}{64}$" hole should be drilled right through for the fulcrum pin. Actually this is best done before the slot is cut. The pump lever should be made from $\frac{1}{16}$" brass plate, with a centre hole for the fulcrum pin and two lugs, at

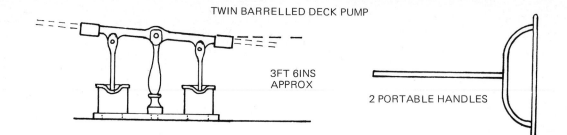

TWIN BARRELLED DECK PUMP

3FT 6INS
APPROX

2 PORTABLE HANDLES

the same centres, for the barrels. Two small pieces of brass tube about $\frac{3}{32}''$ bore should be soldered to each end of the lever to form sockets for the extension handles. The two bucket rods are made from $\frac{1}{16}''$ brass rod with a small fork end turned up, cut drilled and soldered to each rod.

The whole job can now be assembled. The two barrels and the centre stanchions are soldered into the base plate, making sure that the slot in the top of the stanchion is lined up with the long centre line and that the lips in the barrels both face the same way. Next rivet or solder the two bucket rod pins into the lugs on the lever. Then by inserting the two rods into

the small holes in the bottoms of the barrels which are left protruding about $\frac{3}{8}''$ below the base plate, the fulcrum pin can then be inserted and either riveted or soldered into position. A small wooden pad about $\frac{1}{32}''-\frac{1}{16}''$ thick is made to fit under the pump and finally two extension handles are made from $\frac{1}{16}''$ brass wire as shown in the sketch. The handles would of course only be fitted to the pump whilst the pump is in use, otherwise they would be stowed in a suitable rack, either against the inside of the bulwark or against a bulkhead at some convenient position in such a way that they would not be too exposed to seas coming on board in heavy weather.

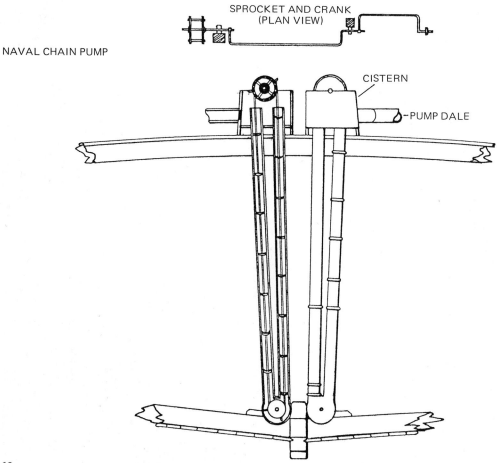

SPROCKET AND CRANK
(PLAN VIEW)

NAVAL CHAIN PUMP

CISTERN

PUMP DALE

CHAIN PUMPS

Sir Walter Raleigh is credited with the invention of chain pumps, but we do not know what these devices looked like. Although the endless chain mechanism is quite complex it need not bother modelmakers since it is usually only the cistern and pump-dale (discharge pipe) that is visible on a model, although the long cranks that provided the motive power will also need to be rigged.

The cistern was simply a wooden tank into which the water filled before being emptied down the pump-dale. This dale was sometimes carried to the ship's side in vessels like 74s where the pumps were on the lower gun deck (and so near to the waterline) but most vessels' pumps seem to have discharged through a short dale onto the leeward side of the deck and the water allowed to run out through the scuppers. In some cases the cistern was open-topped, so that some representation must be made of the sprocket wheel and the chain of 'buckets' (actually discs) that it turned.

Chain pumps were powerful machines: with 8 men turning the cranks a ton of water per minute could be discharged. Therefore it is a mystery that they were not much used in merchantmen (except East Indiamen) nor in other European navies. Certainly, since the water was never under pressure, they could not be used for fire-fighting or hosing down, and British warships carried separate 'engine-pumps' which worked on the usual vacuum principle.

HAND OR 'DOLLY' WINCH
(SCALE ¼ IN = 1FT)

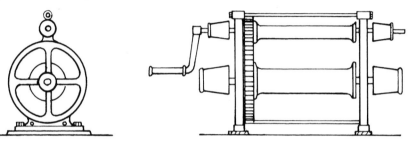

WOOD PAD UNDER CHEEKS

HAND OR DOLLY WINCH

A simple general purpose winch found in many sailing vessels. The framework was of cast iron, as were the mechanical parts, but the drums and warping ends were of wood. On a model this ironwork can be made from brass sheet, with the gearwheels from old clock parts.

LADDERS

The photograph shows the short wooden ladder leading to the poop of the *Cutty Sark*. Although this example has the stringers (sides) shaped, the straight sided ladders are built in the same way. Note the two through bolts, and the protective nosing on the treads.

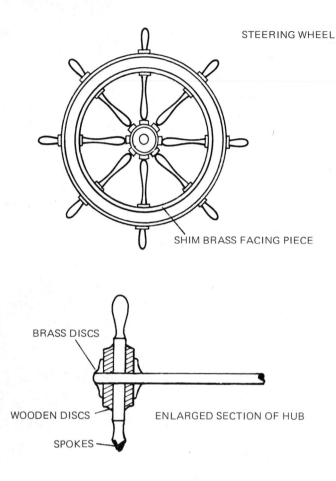

STEERING WHEEL

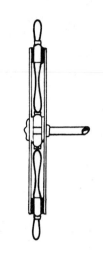

SHIM BRASS FACING PIECE

BRASS DISCS

WOODEN DISCS   ENLARGED SECTION OF HUB

SPOKES

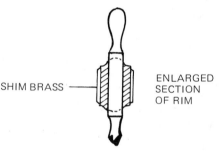

SHIM BRASS   ENLARGED SECTION OF RIM

STEERING WHEEL

The steering wheel can be quite an exciting problem for any modelmaker. My own method is as follows:

First draw out the wheel on paper at about double the actual size intended for the model. Then accurately draw the shape of one spoke. Centre lines will suffice for the remainder. Let us say we have to make an eight-spoked wheel. Turn up eight spokes out of boxwood, most of the work being done with a file and sand paper. In the real thing the base of the spokes are square as is the portion which passes through the rim. In fact on a full sized wheel the rim is made up of shaped section *between* the spokes. However, in a model wheel the rim is made in one piece. Mount a suitable piece of box wood on a *mandrill* (actually a small bolt about 2″ by $\frac{1}{8}$″ with two nuts and two washers and the head cut off). Place the boxwood disc, roughly cut to shape, in the centre of the bolt and put a nut and washer on from each side. Tighten up against the disc, mount the mandrill in the lathe, and turn down the outside diameter of the disc to that required.

Below and right. Three versions of steering gear in a clipper, a coaster (the *Vincent A White)* and a naval vessel *(Dolphin).*

Next shape one side of the rim and slightly undercut it to form the width of the rim, but be careful not to cut right through. Sand up this face and then remove the work from the lathe chuck. Turn the disc and repeat the process on the other side. When both faces of the wheel rim have been turned, sanded and undercut, carefully cut right through on the inner line and the rim will come away cleanly leaving just a little sanding to do on the inside surface. Paste a piece of white paper on the face of a spare piece of flat timber, then with a compass mark out the rim of the wheel. Mark the centre, and the eight spoke lines. Drill a *vertical* hole through the centre mark, and press into this hole a piece of brass rod for the wheel spindle. Place the rim of the wheel on the drawing and from that mark the position of each spoke hole on the outside edge of the rim. The rim should then be drilled in all eight places and the spokes inserted through them. Next turn up two small brass discs or use brass washers, and two boxwood discs with centre holes the same size as the spindle.

Before assembling the wheel, clean up and polish the shaft. Then replace it in the block of wood with the paper facing, having first countersunk a suitable

sized recess in way of the hole for the face of the disc to drop into. Place a brass disc onto the spindle with the shaped profile facing downwards and soft solder the disc to the spindle, next place a wooden disc on the shaft and with epoxy adhesive glue it to the brass disc. Having adjusted the length of the spokes in the wheel rim, place rim and spokes over the spindle. With the aid of the rim and spoke outline on the paper face of the block, adjust the concentricity of the wheel and secure the ends of the spokes to the spindle with epoxy glue. Place the second wooden disc in position and finally add the second brass disc. Secure this brass disc with a touch of soft solder taking care not to burn the wood discs. Leave until the glue is hard, then remove wheel and spindle from the block. Cut off the surplus length of spindle and varnish. Your wheel is complete.

The brass facing rings for the rim of the steering wheel can be made from very thin brass shim, say 0.002″; the rings are marked out with a pair of sharp dividers and cut out with scissors and then glued to the face of the wheel with an epoxy adhesive after polishing.

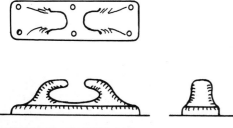

TYPICAL PLAIN FAIRLEAD

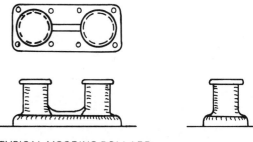

TYPICAL MOORING BOLLARD

FAIRLEADS

Fairleads can also vary in size considerably according to the vessel to which they are fitted; in practice they are made of cast iron and like the bollards are well rounded off and smoothly finished to prevent any chafe to the ropes which pass through them.

Model fittings can be made either of brass or hardwood. Take a piece of material of suitable thickness and mark out the profile of the fairlead, then drill out the internal shape between the jaws and finish with a file and emery cloth or sand paper, finally mark the securing holes and drill these, two or three coats of paint and the fairlead is ready for fitting.

BOLLARDS

Bollards, which are simply convenient posts placed in pairs to secure mooring ropes, come in various sizes according to the size of the vessel to which they are fitted. They are usually made from cast iron, with all corners radiused, and no sharp edges or projections on which ropes can catch or chafe.

These fittings can be modelled from brass: first a base plate is prepared with two holes for the posts drilled on the centre line of the plate and the correct distance apart. These holes should be slightly smaller than the diameter of the post, which is also turned from brass with a spigot to fit into the base plate and a rounded rim at the top. Alternatively they can be

made from close grained hardwood in exactly the same way. Bollards are an important fitting on board ship, yet they are often dismissed by modelmakers as of no consequence. Many otherwise good models are spoiled because their builders have taken the easy way out and purchased 'a bollard', without considering whether it is the right size or correct shape or style for the vessel in question. Purchased bollards stand out like the proverbial sore thumb on a model.

Top right. A typical bollard. This one has a hardwood pad between the base and deck planking.
Bottom right. Forecastle companionway on a small coasting schooner. In this example the top is fixed.

FORECASTLE COMPANIONWAY

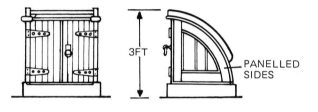

3FT

PANELLED SIDES

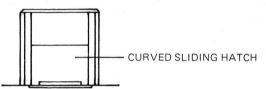

CURVED SLIDING HATCH

DECK ERECTIONS

The sketch shows a typical forecastle companionway which would probably have been built of mahogany or teak, or for that matter good quality soft wood such as pitch pine, yellow pine or douglas fir. This type of companionway would have been built very solidly with panelled sides and narrow, tongued and grooved boards forming the doors which would have been at least $1\frac{3}{4}''$ thick and through bolted edge to edge, with horizontal internal stiffeners. The top curved sliding hatch would have been formed of thick timbers laid thwartships with curved rails at each side, tongued or morticed to the thwartship boards and running in slotted guides at each side.

To make a model of this fitting, simply prepare a suitable block of wood with a curved back and top and having squared, shaped and sanded it, secure thin strips of wood onto it with a waterproof adhesive to form the panels, hatch, doors and coamings. The doors can be formed from one piece suitably scored to

DOORS OPEN
OUTWARDS

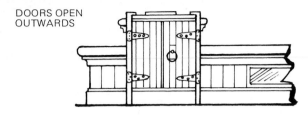

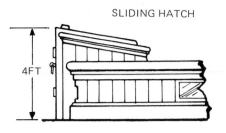

4FT

represent planks, or the planks can be laid individually. The hinges are simply strips of shim brass cut to shape and secured with adhesive. Depending on the size, the knob and ring handle can quite easily be made from brass wire, the knob shaped up in the lathe with a small hole drilled in it. The rings can be made from smaller diameter wire shaped on a mandrill or with round nosed pliers, inserted in the hole and soldered with either soft or silver solder, the shank of the knob then being pressed into a small hole drilled in the face of the doors. In the other sketch a similar type of hatch is shown except that it is built in straight lines with no curved top and back. This can be built in the same way as the first example but superimposed on the block or frame which forms the trunk cabin, this type of trunk cabin and companionway being typical of American built wooden vessels especially the big schooners.

Deckhouse styles and variations are almost as numerous as those for companionways. Though strongly built to withstand heavy seas, nevertheless they were fine examples of the joiners' and shipwrights' craft. Points to observe are the panelling, moulding along the top edge, and the construction along the base of the house.

Below and right. Contrasts in deck arrangements and details between the steel-hulled *Cymric* (below), the ketch *Emma Louise* (top right) and the *Maud Mary*.

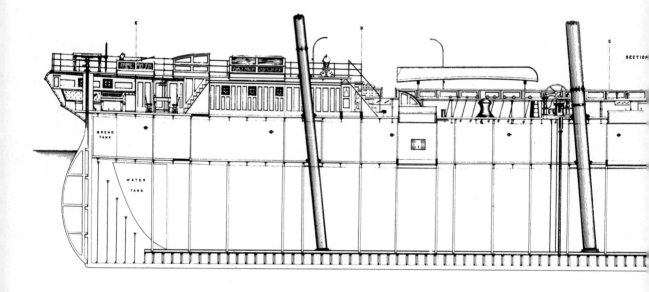

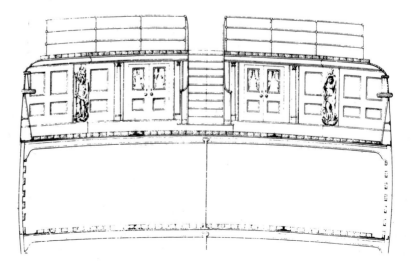

Above. Profile drawing of the steel ship *Formby,* demonstrating typical deck erections for later ships in the prestige 'clipper' trades.
Right. Bulkhead decoration for this ship shows that the change to steel did not mean the end of elaborate finishing to deckhouses.

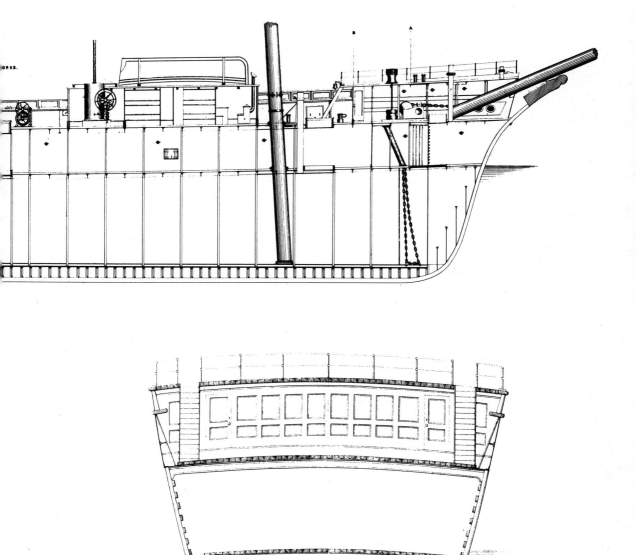

ORKS.

Opposite. The *Raven* (top) and Alastair Brown's ketch *Clara May*. Note how the deckhouse finish reflects the period — with her cut down rig the ketch represents the last period of commercial sail, when no frills or fancywork was possible.

Above left. A deckhouse on the *Cutty Sark*. In many ways tea clippers were the prestige ships of the merchant marine, but this deckhouse is not untypical of larger vessels before the advent of iron and steel.

Above right. The monkey poop of the same ship. Note the fine panelling.

Below. A wooden windlass on a small coaster.

WINDLASS

The wooden windlass was operated by two long rocker arms mounted on top of the 'Pawl Bitt', which in turn were connected to the ratchet and pawl wheel by big steel or wrought iron links. The material used in their construction was nearly all wood, with a small amount of wrought iron, steel and some cast iron. The two outboard ratchet wheels were operated by the rocker gear pawls alternately, when heaving in the anchor. The centre wheel took a pawl secured to the after side of the pawl bitt to prevent the barrel turning back with the weight of the anchor and cable.

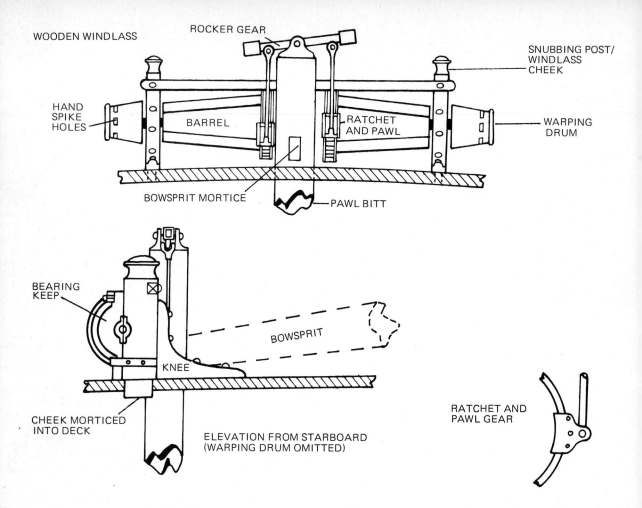

WOODEN WINDLASS

ROCKER GEAR

SNUBBING POST/ WINDLASS CHEEK

HAND SPIKE HOLES

BARREL

RATCHET AND PAWL

WARPING DRUM

BOWSPRIT MORTICE

PAWL BITT

BEARING KEEP

BOWSPRIT

KNEE

CHEEK MORTICED INTO DECK

ELEVATION FROM STARBOARD (WARPING DRUM OMITTED)

RATCHET AND PAWL GEAR

The barrel of the windlass can be turned from suitable close grained hardwood — box, sycamore, or beech. The positions of the three ratchet wheels in the centre of the barrel can be grooved deep enough to accommodate a plastic strip which has teeth on it similar to a ratchet wheel. Such plastic strips, made in various sizes, are used by electricians for bunching electric cables together, and when glued in place provide a good representation of a ratchet. Be sure that they are laid in the grooves correctly facing the right way, that is, the two outboard ones with the teeth facing down on the after side of the barrel and the centre one the opposite way round.

The rocker gear fitted to the top of the pawl bitt can be made from small pieces of brass and copper. With very small scale pieces like this an easy way to fit the pins is to place the pin in the hole and just touch each end with a small soldering iron, tipped with soft solder, to secure it. The link arms can be made from brass wire but if the pawl gear is too small to make, a hole drilled in the ratchet wheel and the end of the pawl link bent at 90° and inserted into the hole will be quite sufficient.

Right. Naval vessels usually carried capstans but smaller ships, without the deck space or the large crews capstans required, shipped a windlass instead. Two views of John Mayger's brigantine *Dolphin*.

The cheeks in full-sized practice pass right through the deck and are secured either to a 'tween deck beam or the lower part of a frame. On a model they can be shouldered and fitted into a mortice in the deck planking. The cheeks are usually finished off at the top as a snubbing post. This can be achieved quite easily with a small round file and piece of sand paper. Care should be taken not to rub away the corners under the cap when sanding. The spreader bar is let into the after side of the pawl bitt and can be secured with ordinary sewing pins (these give a good impression of a snap head bolt or spike in a 1/48 model). Similarly where the brackets are fitted to the cheeks they can be secured in the same way. The strap securing the lower part of the bearing keep can be made from a strip of copper or brass bent around the keep and cheek. This is held in place with small pins or adhesive.

Windlasses were usually painted in a dark colour, red, green, or black — after all a muddy anchor cable can make an awful mess as it comes in. Where the windlass was fitted under a topgallant forecastle the rocker gear was mounted seperately on this deck, with long iron rods extending down to connect with the ratchet gear. A similar type of windlass was used on the small wooden coasting vessels. Operating space was often somewhat limited!

Right. A windlass rocker 'box' on a topgallant forecastle: the rods connect with ratchet gear below.
Below. A wooden windlass, showing ratchet and pawl.
Bottom. The windlass of the author's *Raven* model.

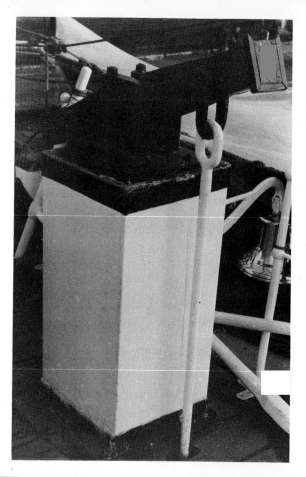

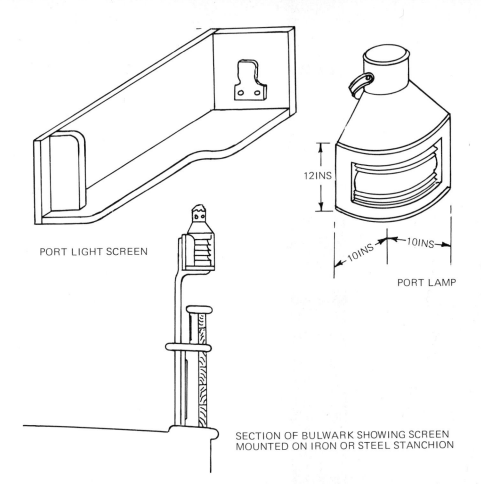

PORT LIGHT SCREEN

12INS

10INS 10INS

PORT LAMP

SECTION OF BULWARK SHOWING SCREEN
MOUNTED ON IRON OR STEEL STANCHION

NAVIGATION LIGHT SCREENS

These were simple structures constructed of timber at least $1\frac{1}{4}''$ thick and mounted either on stanchions passing through the rail, as indicated in the sketch, or lashed to the shrouds of the foremast, or indeed at any other convenient point close to the extreme width of the vessel. Care was taken to ensure that the sails would not obstruct the light beam of the lamp. The chock at the forward end of the screen is there to ensure that the beam of light shines ahead at the correct angle. The lamp is made with the lens so arranged that the beam of light is visible through an arc of $112\frac{1}{2}°$. According to regulations the light should be visible $2\frac{1}{2}$ points, or $22\frac{1}{2}°$ abaft the beam. The paraffin lamp, made of copper or galvanized steel sheet, was secured in its screen on a large brass or steel clip called a tongue.

In a model the screen can be constructed from timber, either hardwood or plywood, and should be painted internally — green for the starboard lantern or red for the port lantern. The lamp itself can be made from a piece of copper or brass rod, turned in the lathe to form the cone and chimney. The back is then filed to 90°.

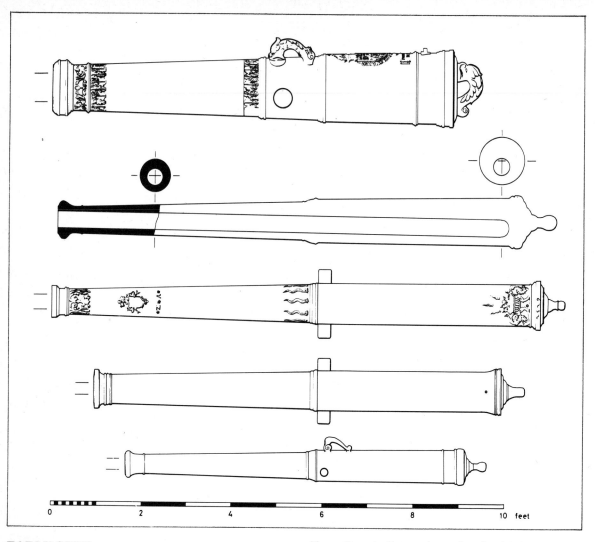

0   2   4   6   8   10 feet

EARLY GUNS

Of all fittings guns probably cause the unsuspecting modelmaker more problems than any others. By the time of the Armada (1588) cannon were of the cast type that with relatively minor external alterations lasted until the nineteenth century. Hence it is particularly difficult to generalise, and, rather than mislead with simplifications, the reader is directed to the bibliography.

The main work is still Michael Lewis's *Armada Guns* but this can now be supplemented with the evidence from underwater archaeology. The accompanying drawings of Armada, and later, guns are of actual examples found in recent archaeological work around the coasts of the United Kingdom.

LATER GUNS

From about 1700 guns lost their historic, and rather picturesque names, such as 'culverin' and 'saker' and became denominated simply by the weight of shot

Above. Recently discovered guns from Spanish Armada wrecks. Top to bottom, they are a 50 pounder from *La Trinidad Valencera;* a bronze demi-culverin from *El Gran Grifon* (muzzle only) restored to demonstrate the off-centre bore. (However in the summer of 1977 the rest of this gun was found and it proved to be longer — a full 12 feet in fact so our knowledge of early guns is constantly improving); a long 6 pounder from the *Trinidad;* a 4 pounder from the same ship; and a 3 pounder demi-saker from the *Grifon.*

Opposite top. A composite bronze and wrought iron swivel gun from *La Trinidad Valencera.*
Opposite below. Bronze swivel gun and breech blocks from the *Girona.*
(All early gun drawings by courtesy of Colin Martin, St Andrews Institute of Maritime Archaeology).

they fired, as an '18 pounder' for example. The shape also became more uniform and while this is an advantage to modellers who do not require precisely accurate guns it is a considerable problem to those of more exacting standards. The references in the

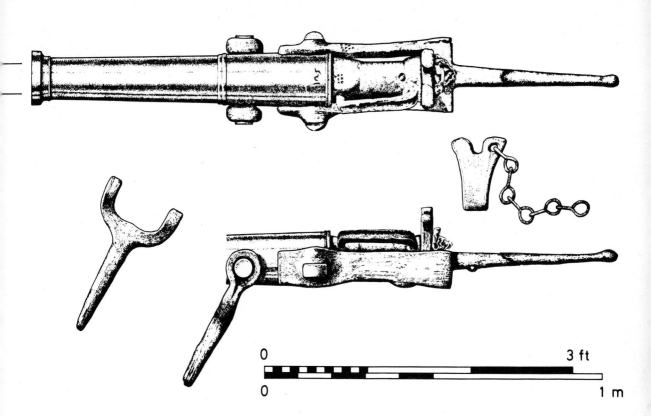

0   3 ft

0   1 m

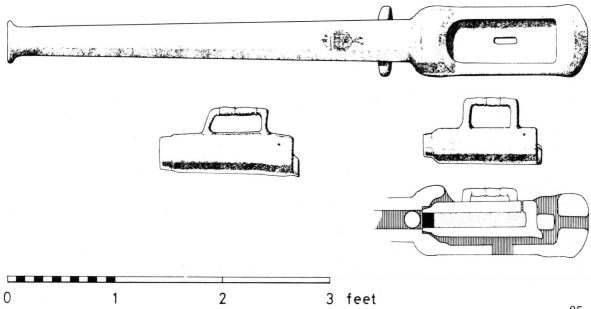

0   1   2   3   feet

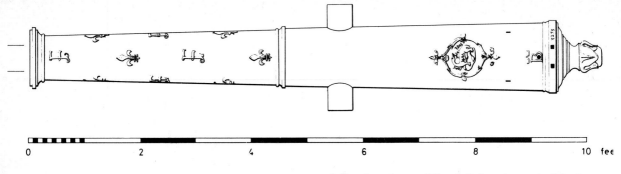

A French royal gun, of Francis I, from the wreck of the *San Juan de Sicilia*. Raised from Tobermory Bay in 1740, the gun is now in Inverary Castle.

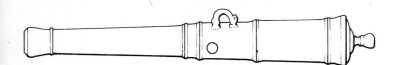

12-pdr

6-pdr (bronze)

Cast gun types from the Dutch *Adelaar*.

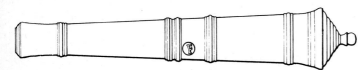

6-pdr(iron)

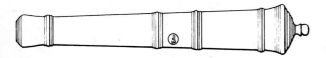

3-pdr

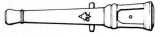

swivel

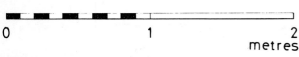

0   1   2
metres

bibliography will give the right dimensions for guns on particular rates of ships at particular times, but often only the length and the bore diameter is quoted. Thus it is necessary to have a working formula to reconstruct the proportions of the gun, and the following is reasonably accurate for the end of the eighteenth century.

The circumference at the base ring is eleven times the bore, at the trunnions it is nine times, and at the muzzle ring it is seven times the bore. Different lengths would produce a different taper to the barrel, since the bore of all guns of the same calibre is the same, of course.

The trunnions were usually placed about 3/7 of the distance from the base ring to the muzzle, and some weapons — usually the smaller calibres — had the trunnions below the longitudinal axis of the gun.

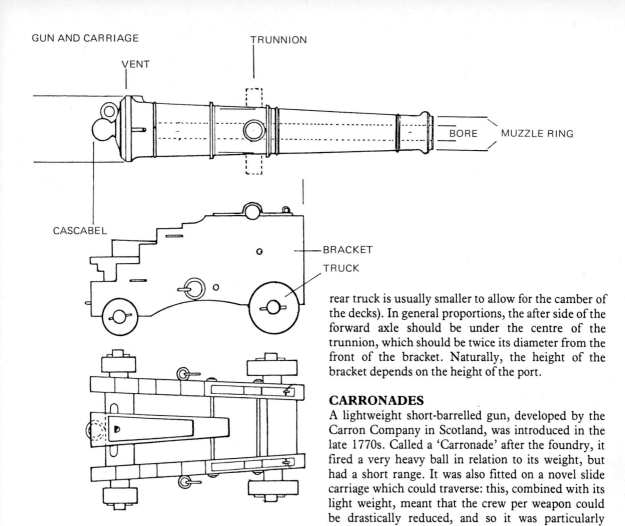

GUN AND CARRIAGE

VENT

TRUNNION

CASCABEL

BORE   MUZZLE RING

BRACKET

TRUCK

rear truck is usually smaller to allow for the camber of the decks). In general proportions, the after side of the forward axle should be under the centre of the trunnion, which should be twice its diameter from the front of the bracket. Naturally, the height of the bracket depends on the height of the port.

CARRONADES

A lightweight short-barrelled gun, developed by the Carron Company in Scotland, was introduced in the late 1770s. Called a 'Carronade' after the foundry, it fired a very heavy ball in relation to its weight, but had a short range. It was also fitted on a novel slide carriage which could traverse: this, combined with its light weight, meant that the crew per weapon could be drastically reduced, and so it was particularly popular with merchant ships.

Rather than proper trunnions the carronade had a lug underneath the barrel to which short 'trunnions' attached. The barrel and the bed recoiled along the slide, which was pivoted from a heavy timber inside the gunport.

Once the principal dimensions of the gun are established it is relatively easy to build a suitable carriage, bearing in mind that when mounted horizontally the gun barrel should be slightly below the centre of the gunport. There were various 'rules' for carriage proportions but they all vary considerably, and can only be regarded as guide-lines. However, the following is contemporary with the above gun proportions.

The length of the brackets (cheek pieces) equals the distance from the centre of the trunnion to the end of the cascabel plus twice the trunnion diameter. The thickness of the brackets, and the diameter of the axle trees, equals the bore diameter. The diameter of the trucks (wheels) is three times the trunnions (but the

CARRONADE

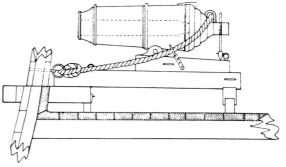

This model is of a ship of the *Mayflower's* period and size. Built by L Pritchard to plans prepared after lengthy research by Dr R C Anderson, it can be considered as an authentic representation of a vessel of that era. Apart from the hull and fittings it is particularly instructive for the features which it shows of early masting and rigging practices. As has been mentioned earlier in the book, there is only a limited amount of information available for vessels of this period, thus models of this calibre are well worth studying in order to grasp some of the fundamentals of their rigging and masting. At this time the tops were still circular, though shallower, and the deadeyes were still triangular, but with three holes for the lanyards. The courses were still sails of considerable size, but the topsails retained the tall narrow shape. Note the heavy mainstay with its associated rigging at its lower, or forward, end, and the considerable use of double, or sister blocks.
(Photo: Conway Picture Library)

Masting and rigging

by BILL SHOULDER

With the hull of a model completed, the builder begins to see in his mind's eye the finished effort, the tall masts with their yards, and the intricate tracery of the rigging, all of which to the beginner may appear a bit daunting. In fact, the whole system is a combination of a number of relatively simple elements combined into an (apparently) complicated whole, so let us deal firstly with the masts and spars.

The dimensions of these you will of course obtain from the drawings or plans from which you are working, but in some cases, as for early merchant ships and a great number of Admiralty draughts, these are not available, so a little research is called for. In the case of naval ships, a number of more or less complicated rules exist for determining the dimensions, based on fractions of the sum of the length and breadth of the ship, and proportions thereof. Similar rules exist for merchant ships, although probably not so rigidly adhered to. Reference to the bibliography will give the reader some idea of where to look for information, which once obtained, should be committed to paper in the form of drawings and notes.

MASTS

It is essential that the timber used for these is well seasoned, straight grained and free from knots or other blemishes. The grain should be unobtrusive and the wood easily worked. The traditional wood for the purpose is lancewood (once used for the shafts of carriages and for billiard cues) although its modern substitute, degame is excellent; however, any straight grained timber may be used providing the colour is right and the other criteria met. The writer has used parana pine with good effect, and in spite of warnings, it has not twisted in some years, but resinous soft woods should be avoided, at small scales anyway.

To ensure that the grain runs the full length of the spar, it is necessary to split lengths off the plank with a knife or axe. Plane the exposed edge square, and set off from this edge a parallel line just over the maximum diameter of the mast, and plane down to

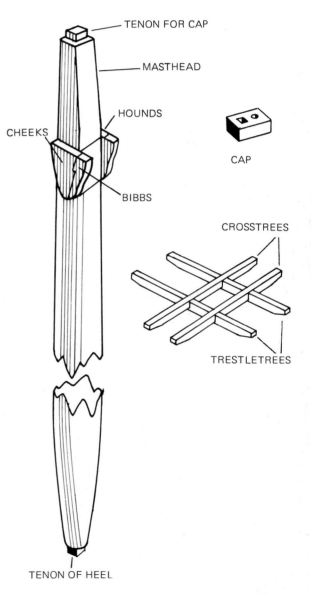

TENON FOR CAP

MASTHEAD

HOUNDS

CHEEKS

CAP

BIBBS

CROSSTREES

TRESTLETREES

TENON OF HEEL

Below and opposite. Late seventeenth and late eighteenth practice. The seventeenth century First Rate (below) retains the flat circular tops, the rather heavy standing rigging, and the spritsail topmast, and crosses a lateen yard on the mizzen. The sail plan is still on the narrow side, with very deep topsails and light topgallants. On the other hand the sloop *Atalanta* (opposite) built in 1775 shows flat rectangular tops, and the rigging has lost much of its 'heavy' appearance. The lateen on the mizzen has been replaced with a driver with boom and gaff, but the deep single topsails, surmounted by light topgallants, are still evident.
(Photos: Atalanta by courtesy of J P Dickmann; First Rate — Conway Picture Library)

this line. Reduce the other side to the same dimension to produce a square section timber, and cut off to the required length plus an inch or so extra.

Mark a centre line down each face of the spar, and mark off each end by squaring a line all round, and mark off the masthead position. On opposite sides, set out the taper, and remove the wood to this line with a small plane. Re-mark the centre line and taper, and plane the other two sides to this, thus producing a square-sectioned, tapered mast. It should be noted that the tapered sides are not straight , but very gently curved outwards. In the full size vessel, this curve is arrived at by a set of rules, but in the small scale model, it is sufficient to ensure that the mast finishes with a slight convex curve to its profile. Anyone

making a very large scale model is referred to Steel or Rees (see Bibliography) for the formula.

The square section now has the corners planed off, resulting in an octagonal section, and again these corners are removed until the section is nearly round, when the mast may be finished with glasspaper, finishing with the finest grade along the length of the mast. Those with access to a lathe may prefer to use it to shape the mast, and the writer has used an electric drill held in the bench vice to do the job, the mast being held in the chuck. This needs some care to avoid making the mast hollow in the middle, and in any case, final finishing must be by hand in the long direction.

The lower masts, which in the larger ships had to be made from a number of baulks of timber fitted together by a complicated system of joints, were additionally strengthened by pairs of iron hoops fitted over the mast, the space between the hoops being occupied by 12 — 13 turns of rope called 'wooldings'. These are easily made by suitable whippings round the mast, the hoops being represented by a few turns of gummed paper strips, painted black. Of course, masts that carried a fore and aft sail set on hoops were not so fitted, as the wooldings would interfere with the proper setting of the sail.

With a few exceptions, mastheads are square in section, the junction between the masthead and mast being known as the *hounds*, and the masthead should now be reduced to this section as far as the hounds. Immediately below the hounds, on each side, the mast is flattened for a short distance to take the *cheeks* to which are attached brackets called *bibs*, all of which form a support for the *trestletrees*. The cheeks and bibs in most models are made in one piece of hardwood with the grain running vertically, the lower end of the cheeks fairing into the mast so as to appear to grow from it.

The point at which the mast meets the deck is called the *partners*, and the maximum diameter of the mast is here. Above, the mast tapers towards the hounds as described, and below, a rather sharper taper is made towards the tenon of the heel, where the mast is stepped. Mast lengths are often given as 'hounded' or 'headed', and this is explained as follows: The 'headed' or given length of the mast is the distance from the bottom of the tenon of the heel, to the top of the tenon on the masthead, ie the total length of the mast. The 'hounded' length is from the bottom of the tenon of the heel to the hounds, the difference between the headed and hounded lengths being therefore, the length of the masthead.

The trestletrees are strips of hardwood lying in a fore and aft direction on top of the cheeks at the hounds, and these are notched to receive the *crosstrees*, similar strips lying across the trestletrees.

These must be securely fixed in position with glue and pins, as they take considerable strain from the rigging. The structure thus framed supports a platform of planks (lower masts only) called the *top*, the shape and construction of which vary with the period and between the Royal and merchant navies. Broadly, the tops in the Tudor and Stuart navies were round, becoming rectangular in form, with only the front edge rounded in the eighteenth century.

Round tops, for those with lathe facilities, can be turned, or cut from thin plywood with a fretsaw, a disc for the base with a ring or rings of plywood superimposed to make up the thickness. For the later style tops, it is best to make use of a simple jig. The shape A in the appropriate drawing is made of 3-4mm

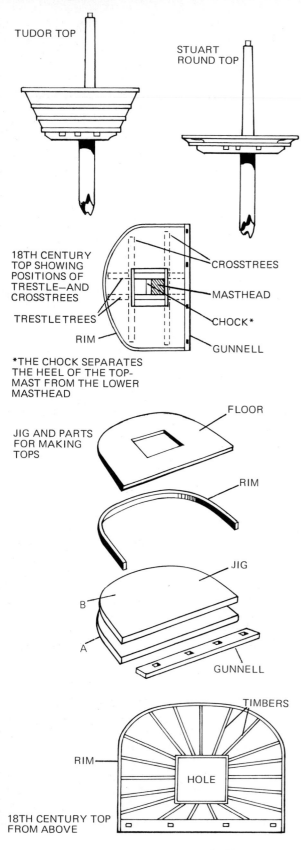

TUDOR TOP

STUART ROUND TOP

18TH CENTURY TOP SHOWING POSITIONS OF TRESTLE—AND CROSSTREES

CROSSTREES

MASTHEAD

TRESTLETREES

CHOCK*

RIM

GUNNELL

*THE CHOCK SEPARATES THE HEEL OF THE TOP-MAST FROM THE LOWER MASTHEAD

FLOOR

JIG AND PARTS FOR MAKING TOPS

RIM

JIG

B

A

GUNNELL

TIMBERS

RIM

HOLE

18TH CENTURY TOP FROM ABOVE

GUNNELL

ply to the outside form of the top, the upper section B, the same thickness as the depth of the rim, and smaller than A by the width of the rim all round, except the back edge. This is glued on to A to leave a rebate all round, and the rim, of hardwood rendered pliable by steaming for a short while, is bent into this rebate, and held there with elastic bands until the wood dries out and the shape is retained. The floor may be of 1-2mm plywood, with the hole cut into it for the mast position. It is glued to the rim while the latter is still in the jig, taking care not to glue it to the same; when dry, sand off the outside edge to a good finish and remove it from the jig. The straight rear edge, or 'gunnell' as Steel calls it can now be glued into place: it is wider than the rim, and pierced for four or five stanchions. The holes for the futtock plates, and any other holes required to facilitate the lead down of the rigging from aloft should now be made, the timbers fitted and after painting (usually black) the top can be fixed firmly in place on the trestle and crosstrees. If fine brass pins are used for this — $\frac{5}{8}''$ brass Lill pins from dressmaker's suppliers are fine — they can be left overlength, the protruding ends being turned over into small eyes under the trees to take blocks.

The masthead has a tenon cut into the upper end to take the *cap,* a block of timber lying in a fore and aft direction, with a hole through the forward part to take the *topmast.* Topmasts are made in a similar manner to the lower masts, and often have sheaves in them for the passage of ropes. The square heels have the corners chamfered off, and are made of such a size as to be an easy fit into the square opening formed in front of the lower masthead by the trestletrees and crosstrees. The upper end has a masthead, with cheeks at the hounds to support trestle- and crosstrees, but a platform top is seldom fitted. The trees on the upper masts are invariably called, collectively, the crosstrees, and the overlap of masts at the tops and upper crosstrees is sometimes called the 'doubling'.

SPARS

The spars consist of the yards, booms, gaffs etc, and are made in a similar manner to the masts, being tapered and rounded in the same way. *Yards* are divided into two parts at the centre, called the *slings,* each half being further divided into four parts called the *quarters.* The middle two quarters are kept parallel, and often, especially in the lower yards,

made octagonal in cross section. The taper is worked from the junction of the first and second quarters to the yardarm or outer end on each side, and is round in cross section.

Provision has to be made for a number of cleats of various types on the spar, whose function is to retain the lashings of blocks and so on in positon. These are best made by morticing thin strips of hardwood into the spar, shaping them afterwards with small files. Where cleats are diametrically opposite each other, the wooden slip may be morticed right through the spar, so that it projects on both sides, but in any case, the grain of the cleats should run in the same direction as that of the spar.

Gaffs, which spread the head of a fore and aft sail, and *booms,* which spread the foot, are usually given jaws, which partially encircle the mast and are made as shown in the appropriate drawing. To retain the jaws close up to the mast, a chain of wooden beads on rope is slung between the jaws and round the mast — this is called a *parral,* and appears in rather more complicated form to retain the yards close to the masts. Sometimes the boom was held to the mast by a *gooseneck,* a metal hook on the boom engaging an eye on the mast, allowing free movement all round. The

Below left, below right, bottom. Two views of the *Cutty Sark's* topmast trestletrees, crosstrees and spreaders. Note the cleats on the spreaders for the upper backstays, and the shrouds on the crosstrees with the futtock shrouds below. In the illustration on the right, of the mizzen topmast trestletrees, note the chain tye for the upper topsail yard passing over the sheave in the mast, and the chain shackled to an eye on the crosstrees and leading to the spanker gaff to take the weight off the gooseneck. The bottom photograph shows some of the rigging of the *Cutty Sark's* bowsprit. Three chain martingales are secured to the dolphin striker and thence run aft to points near the cathead. Fixed to the after side of the cathead is the whisker, its purpose being, as can be seen, to spread the jibboom guys.

parral beads, or *trucks* to give them their proper name are usually made of lignum vitae on the prototype, but small glass beads, dark brown or black can often be made to serve as substitutes on the model. The parrals on the yards, already mentioned, consist of two or three rows of trucks, depending on the size of the yard, the trucks being separated vertically by wooden strips, or *ribs*. On later ships of the clipper era a different kind of parral was fitted, where a leather lined stirrup was fitted to the after side of the yard, a similarly lined metal strap confining it to the mast.

Once the masts and spars have been made, it is important that all fittings such as footropes, blocks etc are secured to them in their proper positions before attempting to commence the rigging.

Opposite. A contrast in bowsprit fittings: top circa 1580, bottom circa 1830. On the *Elizabeth Jonas* (top) there is the minimal amount of rigging, but the gammoning can just be se just where the lower edge of the forecourse crosses the bowsprit. The lower photograph — of the brigantine *Dolphin* shows clearly the cap at the end of the bowsprit for the jibboom, with the dolphin striker fitted separately immediatel abaft it, and the run of the martingales. Of particular interest the way the forestay is secured to the bowsprit, with the preventer stays below led back to the stem, and the fore topmast stay bridled and coming down on either side of the bowsprit and back to setting up tackles.

Right. The lower yard truss of the *Cutty Sark,* so constructed that the yard can be cockbilled as well as trimmed. The U-shaped truss is secured at either end to iron bands round the yard, while the centre of the U can swivel on the pin, which in turn can pivot on a pin set vertically through the mast band. Note the short length of chain from the mast to a shackle on top of the yard, to take the weight.

Below. The *Cutty Sark's* spanker boom, showing how it is secured to the mizzen mast, to allow it to move both horizontally and vertically.

Opposite top. In contrast the gaff and boom shown here are those for a small wooden coaster. The boom fitting is similar to that of the *Cutty Sark,* but the gaff is of the sliding type, and so is fitted with wooden jaws with a parral passed round the foreside of the mast from jaw to jaw.

Opposite bottom. The yards of the *Queen Margaret,* a four mast barque built in 1893. There is a wealth of rigging detail on this fine model of a beautiful vessel. The rigging of the stunsail booms is particularly clear, and it is a good example of late nineteenth rigging practices.
(Photo: Conway Picture Library)

RIGGING

The character of a sailing ship model depends very considerably upon well made and well proportioned masts and spars, and no less upon well made and proportioned rigging, of the right colour. Not so very long ago, the modeller had a fairly wide choice of fishing lines and surgical silk lines from which to make his rigging. While the latter are to some degree available, with the advent of man-made fibres and monofilament lines, the old made-up lines of the angler have virtually disappeared. Fortunately for the modeller, it is not very difficult to make up one's own rope, using dressmakers' threads and sewing cottons. A simple rope making machine can be made from Meccano parts with no great effort, and the end result is better than the use of purchased rope, as it can be made very close to any scale size required, and exactly the colour of one's choice. The one thing that should never be used for rigging is hairy string, yet this is still seen at some exhibitions, and thoroughly spoils an otherwise well made model.

As has been said, ordinary sewing cottons can be used for the rope, and can be purchased in the right shades of colour. If cotton thread is used, the rope made from it should be well stretched, and rubbed through a block of beeswax before use, the latter process settles any slight hairiness and seals the rope against atmospheric moisture, which even on a small model can shrink the rope alarmingly after it has been rigged, pulling the masts and spars out of alignment and in extreme cases causing breakage. The writer prefers to use a commercial terylene thread known as 'Trylco' for making rope, which reacts minimally to humidity, and produces a pliable rope with a certain amount of stretch, or elasticity. It is therefore unnecessary to stretch it before use, although a rub with wax will be required to remove any fluffiness. Nylon threads are unsuitable for rope making, as the result is too stiff and springy.

96

THE PARTS OF THE ARM

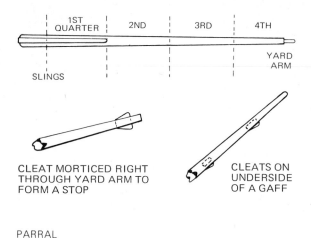

SLINGS

1ST QUARTER · 2ND · 3RD · 4TH

YARD ARM

CLEAT MORTICED RIGHT THROUGH YARD ARM TO FORM A STOP

CLEATS ON UNDERSIDE OF A GAFF

PARRAL

GAFF JAWS. NOTE THE ANGLE FORMED INSIDE THE JAWS — SIMILAR ON A BOOM BUT MADE WITHOUT THE ANGLE

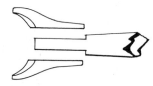

CONSTRUCTIONAL PARTS

GOOSENECK

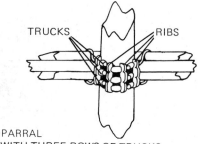

TRUCKS

RIBS

PARRAL WITH THREE ROWS OF TRUCKS

Above. The *Cutty Sark's* stunsail boom yardarm fitting — the end of the curved bar was secured to a cap which fitted over the end of the yard.
Opposite. A general view of the rigging of Roger Glen's working model three mast schooner *Vincent A White*.

Regarding the size of the rope to be used, a number of tables of rope sizes are available (see the Bibliography) and the rope should be scaled down from these. Remember that, in Britain anyway, the rope size is designated by its circumference, so the diameter is roughly $\frac{1}{3}$ of this. Thus, a 3″ rope is approximately 1″ in diameter. Those with the necessary equipment and skills will use a micrometer for measuring the diameters, but a simple way is to wrap several close turns round a dowel for say, $\frac{1}{2}$″. Assuming that it takes 16 turns to the $\frac{1}{2}$″, then the diameter of the scale rope is $\frac{1}{32}$″. At 1/48 scale, this represents $1\frac{1}{2}$″ diameter, or a $4\frac{1}{2}$″ rope — other scales proportionately.

Ship's rigging may be classified in two ways: the standing rigging and the running rigging. The former is composed mainly of heavier rope than the latter, and is more or less permanently in position, serving to support the masts and to stay them against the pressures of the wind and weather. The running rigging, as its name implies is freely mobile, being used to haul the yards and sails aloft and into position for sailing. In this it is assisted by a number of blocks, which are metal pulleys, or *sheaves,* enclosed in a wooden box, surrounded by a rope (sometimes iron) strap — to give it its nautical name, *strop* — by which the block is attached to any required firm fixture on the ship. The blocks allow for the alteration of direction of the running rigging, and, when two or more blocks are used in combination, form *tackles,* which give a mechanical advantage to those hauling on the ropes.

The standing rigging was usually tarred to protect it against the elements, and this is best represented in the model as either black, or very dark brown of a

rather cold hue. The running rigging was not so treated, with the result that the colour varies from that of new rope, a sort of fawn or beige, to old rope, which is darker in colour and attains a silvery sheen from the bleaching action of the sea and sun. The running rigging, then, is generally lighter in colour than the standing rigging, but it should not be so much lighter that the contrast becomes rather jarring. It is on the judicious choice of colours, both for rigging and other elements of the model that distinguishes it and makes it a 'ship in miniature' rather than a model of a ship, and every opportunity should be taken to observe the real thing, taking photographs, sketches and notes, thus building up a fund of infomation for future reference.

Rope consists basically of threads, or yarns, which, twisted together, form strands, the size of the strands determining the ultimate size of rope made from them. Three strands twisted together form a *hawser-laid* rope, and this is usually laid up right-handed, ie if the rope is held in the palm of the hand, pointing it away from the body, the twist turns away and to the right. Three hawser laid ropes twisted together form a *cable,* and it follows, that as the basic hawsers are right-handed, the resulting cable is left-handed. Some ropes, such as the shrouds, heavy ropes which support the masts laterally, are made of four strands laid up left-handed round a central 'heart'. For model purposes, the heart may be dispensed with, and in fact a three-strand rope laid up left-handed looks correct.

Mention must be made of *worming, parcelling* and *serving,* practices designed to protect the rope from wear in areas subject to chafing. Worming is the practice of running a thin line into the spiral grooves of a larger rope, sealing the heart of the rope against moisture and subsequent rot. It is usually carried out on the larger ropes, such as the anchor cable, giving it a distinctive appearance, and should be done on any

model of any size. It is a tedious process, and some means of turning the rope between rotating hooks must be devised. If the line is the same colour as the rope, it is difficult to see, but if a line of a contrasting colour is used it is easier to apply, and can be stained to match the rope afterwards.

Parcelling consists of wrapping the rope with old canvas, and is rarely applied to models. It precedes the practice of serving, in which the rope, with its parcelling, is *served* for the whole or part of its length with close turns of spunyarn, or very thin line. Serving should always be carried out where indicated — it gives character and authenticity to the model. Where lengths of rope require serving, such as the foremost shrouds, the rope should be suspended between two hooks, geared together in such a way as to rotate together and at the same speed, the hooks, and the rope being turned slowly while the line is fed on to it by hand. Other items, as the pendants of tackles, slings of yards, strops of blocks etc, being smaller, are best served by hand using a needle and thread. Serving was usually tarred over, so is made with black thread.

Various eye-splices, knots and hitches of all types will be required, and it is essential that they are secure and not liable to work loose with the passage of time. Splicing, except on very large ropes, is not really possible, and indeed, uneccessary, a firm eye-splice for example, can be made by forming an eye of the required size at the end of a rope, securing it with a couple of half-hitches of black thread, leaving about an inch of the short end spare. Separate the strands of this short end, and lay them evenly down the side of the rope with a little thin glue, then apply a whipping over the top of black thread, glueing the turns as you go along, finally cutting off the surplus ends of the stranded short end. An eye-splice made in this way is quite secure, the use of glue preventing any unravelling, but of course, where the size of the rope, or scale of the work permits, more orthodox methods of rope working should be used. Always seal off knots, rope ends or whippings with a dab of glue, allowing it to dry before cutting off any surplus. The best glue to use is a water soluble one — 'Seccotine' is my own preference, but avoid the use of the quick-drying 'balsa' cements which leave nasty shiny blobs everywhere. Occasionally it is necessary to undo some part of the rigging, either to adjust, or to correct an error, and the application of a little warm water to the knot with a fine brush allows it to be picked apart without wholesale removal of rigging.

It pays to spend a fair amount of time planning the sequence of rigging on a model, remembering that some of the inboard gear becomes almost inaccessible once the standing rigging is in place. The yards and other spars should have all necessary blocks etc fitted

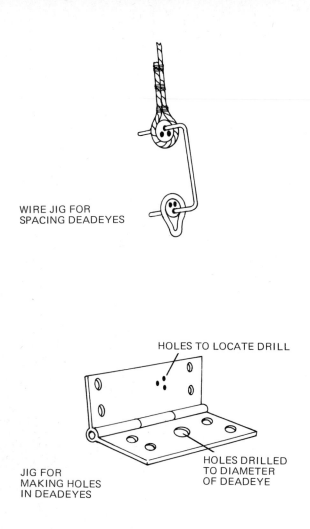

WIRE JIG FOR
SPACING DEADEYES

HOLES TO LOCATE DRILL

JIG FOR
MAKING HOLES
IN DEADEYES

HOLES DRILLED
TO DIAMETER
OF DEADEYE

With the lower masts stepped, and all the shrouds set up, (it is best to leave the ratlines until later) the lower yards can be hoisted into position; a dab of glue on the end of the running line will enable it to be more easily rove through the blocks. Some of the running rigging from the yards can be secured at this stage, but some will have to be left until later — the builder will have to decide, depending upon accessibility. The caps can then be fixed in position, after which the topmasts can be hoisted and rigged as the lower masts. Generally, the rule for rigging is to work from forward to aft, from below upwards, and from within outwards.

The ratlines can now be fitted, and this can be a bit trying on the eyes, so cut a length of thin white card to fit behind the shrouds under the tops and behind the deadeyes. Draw horizontal lines on this a scale 15" apart, and use it as a guide for the ratlines, which should be attached by clove-hitches to the shrouds, and secured with a dab of glue to prevent them slipping. If the scale is large enough, then the ratlines should end in eye-splices which are attached to the outer shrouds by lashings of thin line.

Running rigging can be a tedious job, and a good light is necessary — I prefer to do mine in daylight, but artificial light, if used, should be well diffused, as the shadows produced by unidirectional light can be very confusing. Some long, fine forceps or tweezers, fine sharp pointed scissors and a small crochet hook are among the most useful tools to have by you, and the kind of latchet hook that is used on knitting machines is of help too, particularly when mounted in a short length of dowel for a handle. The running rigging should be brought down to its belaying point, and secured there with a couple of half-hitches and a dab of glue to make it safe. The end can then be cut off close, and the offcut used to make a loose coil which is then hung over the belay, giving a very 'shippy' appearance. Finally, go carefully over all the rigging and check for parts that might come adrift, and finish by trimming off any loose ends with sharp pointed scissors.

One cannot leave the subject of rigging without some reference to blocks and their manufacture. It is surprising how many of these will be required, even in a single-masted vessel, and on a three- or four-master the number can run into hundreds. They are of course, obtainable commercially, of varying quality and finish, and the would-be purchaser is advised to shop around. The same may be said of deadeyes. Those with access to a small lathe should have no difficulty in making them, but quite effective ones can be made without one. Materials range from hardwoods — box, holly, apple etc — to plastic rod of various diameters, knitting needles also providing a useful source. A material known as 'Tufnol' is also

to them, and it may be expedient to reeve some of the running rigging through them at this stage, leaving the free ends trailing, to be secured later. Generally, it is best to follow full size practice and commence rigging at the bowsprit, working aft. Ship the bowsprit, complete with blocks, travellers etc, and secure it by its standing rigging, then step the lower masts in succession from fore to aft, placing shrouds, swifters or backstays and stays over the masthead in that order. Shrouds are put over in pairs, the first pair to starboard side forward, second pair port side forward, and so on alternately working aft. Ensure that all the standing rigging put over the masthead is well pressed down on to the hounds before securing the lower ends. Assuming that the lower deadeyes are already in place on the channels, a simple wire jig will ensure that the deadeyes seized into the shrouds are evenly spaced and level with the rail.

obtainable in rod form and of a turning quality. The colour of deadeyes is very dark brown, nearly black, and this colour should be matched if possible, otherwise use black. If hardwoods are used, they can of course be stained, but will have to be shaped into dowels of suitable diameter first. In the absence of a lathe, short lengths of the rod can be held in a drill chuck (hand or power), and the peripheral groove put in with a rat-tailed file, after which the exposed end can be rounded off at the edges, leaving the centre part flat. After parting off with a fine saw, the three holes can be made, using a simple jig made from a 3″ butt hinge as in the drawing, suitable drills being made from sewing needles with the eyes broken off, and the point rendered three-square on an oilstone. Finish by rounding off the edges on the other side. In setting up the tackles, which are such a feature in the rigging of sailing ships, be careful to avoid foul lines, which would not be tolerated on the full-sized craft, and this latter dictum applies to the rigging as a whole. Exact belaying points are often difficult to establish, and the builder must rely upon common sense to tell him where the belay is most likely to be for any particular rope. A belay is certainly wrong if it fouls another rope, and should be shifted accordingly. Finally, do see that all the yards are trimmed square to the masts and that they are hoisted to their correct heights in relation to each other.

Top. *Cutty Sark.* The problem of belaying — the pin rail at the base of the foremast.
Bottom. Roger Glen's working model of the brigantine *Raven* (to Underhill plans), showing the foremast bitts with (incorrectly) coiled ropes on the pin rails.

Working model sailing ships   5

by MAX DAVEY

Opposite. The author's ¼″ = 1′ 0″ (1/48) scale working model of the brig *Marie Sophie,* built to Underhill plans, makes few if any concessions in detail or accuracy. Superbly detailed, such small modifications to the rigging as were required to meet Max Davey's method of controlling the sails are not apparent.
Right. Under way. *Marie Sophie* was a notable performer with a most realistic and authentic appearance on the water.
Below. The excellence of the detail and the high standard of the craftsmanship are clearly to be seen here, in the hull, deck fittings, masts and rigging.

To see your very own miniature sailing ship claw her way off a lee shore and beat away to windward, especially in heavy weather gives a deep feeling of personal achievement and fulfilment. This skill is not difficult to attain but it does need specialised knowledge. I hope that my experience will help others to share in the pleasure of building and sailing real working scale models.

CHOOSING A MODEL
Firstly the size: I have found that it is not possible to achieve true course sailing with a model much under 36″ hull length. Even on a smallish pond, huge scale waves will force the model's head off to leeward and it

is difficult to steer a definite course. Another objection to a small hull is that in anything but a flat calm it bobs up and down on the water like a toy. The advantages of the 36″ hull are that the (detachable) lead keel need not weigh more than 15 to 20 pounds and the ship sails realistically on the water. In addition it is reasonably easy to transport to rallies and exhibitions. Next it is an advantage to start with a comparatively large model of a small ship. That is say a ketch at $\frac{1}{2}$″ = 1′ 0″ (1/24) scale or a schooner at $\frac{3}{8}$″ = 1′ 0″ (1/36) scale. The rapid adjustment of gear at the waterside, sometimes under heavy weather, is much easier at the larger scales. My brig *Marie Sophie* (now in the National Maritime Museum at Greenwich) at $\frac{1}{4}$″ = 1′ 0″ (1/48) scale was a very good sailer, but I felt that this was the smallest practical working scale if all details of the rig were to be preserved and the gear shifting was not to become too fiddly.

Because of the scale effect of reducing displacement, certain ships are not suitable for our purpose. For example the revenue cutter had steep floors and little displacement with a cloud of lofty canvas. Another would be the 'J' class racers. Models of these could be likely to sail on their ears in anything but a gentle breeze. At the other extreme there is the Thames barge with massive beam and displacement and well able to stand up to her scale canvas. My model of the topsail schooner *Little*

Mystery (also at the National Maritime) was a very good sailer as her floors are flat and the centre section is full for cargo carrying. The scale of $\frac{3}{8}$″ produced a hull about 36″ long and the rig was robust and easily adjusted. The *Marie Sophie* hull is also full amidships giving ample displacement. In view of the above I cannot recommend small models of large ships such as four masted barques.

I do strongly wish to assure prospective builders that there is no need to make masts, spars and rigging overscale, merely because the model is going to sail. So often one sees models with topmasts twice scale thickness with huge trucks to match and royal yards two feet thick. I have proved that yards $\frac{1}{8}$″ thick will stand up to all usual sailing usage. Care must of course be taken with mast tops when entering or leaving cars and houses, but this applies to any scale model. With fast models sailing on lakes with concrete edges there is always the danger of ramming the bank. This can quickly happen on the run if there is a sudden broach-to in a squall. Models of earlier ships or square riggers are safer in this respect because the bowsprit was steeved up at an angle. The worst offenders are ships with horizontal bowsprits. In the case of my trawler the spar is made to slide in and out: on the real ship it was hauled out between the bitts by a heel rope and on the model the rope is replaced by a brown rubber band running from one bitt to the other

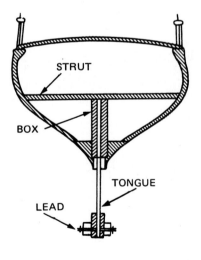

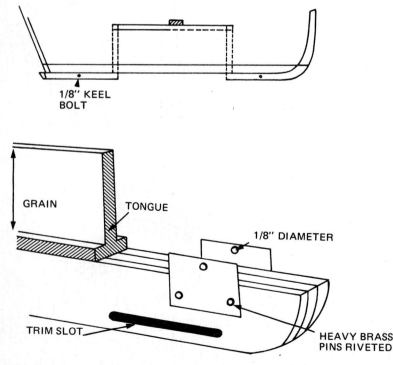

via the slot cut in the heel of the spar. In the event of a collision the bowsprit will slip back an inch or two and can be saved. Needless to say it needs to be made of some hard wood such as beech or greenheart. I always make my jibbooms of greenheart from the tops of old fishing rods, although these are becoming difficult to find. Models of earlier ships should be quite stable as they were generally beamy and rigs prior to the clipper era were not lofty. To assist stability it is essential that the hull should be as light as possible and in *Marie Sophie* the plank on frame hull, using 5-ply frames about 2″ apart and planked with ⅛″ western red cedar, came out very light and strong. This of course meant more lead external ballast and to my surprise the model was so stiff, that she could carry full sail in a really strong breeze.

KEELS

This brings me to keels. If you want to do any serious sailing you must fit an external detachable keel with lead well down. Some purists insist on internal ballast only, but without an external keel you cannot beat efficiently to windward, and the ballast is not low

enough to keep the model sailing at a realistic angle of heel.

Before proceeding from design to construction two vital rules must be stated. All adhesives used in the hull and spar construction must be waterproof and no metals other than copper, stainless steel, brass and phosphor bronze may be used for fastenings and fittings. The only exception is lead in bulk on keels. Lead in anchors or fittings is disastrous as it corrodes. On sails it is possible to use 'Unibond' adhesive but more about that later. To return to external keels. In bread and butter hulls I suggest the keel box method.

This is akin to full size dinghy practice. Using a band or power fret saw to ensure a truly vertical cut, make a hole in the bottom plank about amidships say 9″ long and wide enough to take the box, made of resin bonded ply ⅛″ thick. This box, sealed on top, is wide enough to take a tongue of ⅛″ ply. The tongue (main grain vertical) is part of the centre section of the detachable keel. This is made up of three layers of ⅛″ ply, the two outside layers having the grain running fore and aft. The box is finished flush with the bottom of the hull and the external strip keel is left off in this section. The detachable keel has pieces of wood glued on, so that when it is in position, the line of the ship's keel is preserved. The box must obviously be dead vertical, and I also fit a strut across the top of the box inside the hull as a reinforcement.

A close up of the detail on the author's ½″ = 1′ 0″ (1/24) scale sailing model of the Brixham trawler *Ibex*. The hull is plank on frame construction, the decks are planked, and even the workboat is planked.

The keel is held in place vertically by brass plates and bolts fore and aft. The tongue and box must be well varnished, otherwise swelling will occur and you will not be able to remove the keel after a sail. The lead is cast in two strips and bolted each side. I cut slots in the ply fore and aft and amidships, 2″ long. This enables the lead to be moved fore or aft, following the sailing trials, to get the exact trim required. This obviates any internal ballast. The whole of the keel and box must be very robust as the lead may weigh 15lbs or more.

To calculate the amount needed I finish the body of the hull and mark the load waterline fore and aft. Then with wood keel attached, float the vessel in the bath. Bearing in mind that one pint of water weighs 20 ounces, pour pints of water into the open hull until she is brought down almost to the load waterline. I say 'almost' because you must allow for the weight of all the top hamper to come. It is impossible to lay down the law on this as hull shapes vary, as do the fittings, rig and sails. It is best to experiment and allow

at least 3lbs for the top gear. You can always add lead if necessary but this system works well. I cast lead in wooden trays say 1″ x 1½″ x 20″. Careful lining with cooking foil helps to give a good cast. The tray will burn and can obviously be used for two strips only but the finish is satisfactory. Any holes can be filled in with plastic padding and bumps removed with a Surform or plane. Do make a good job of this because so many models are spoiled by crude keels. When the lead is finally fixed in position it can be faired-in, using wood quadrant on top and shaped pieces at the ends, and I suggest it is painted, matt finish, a quiet colour such as grey to show that it is not part of the ship as such. Make a dummy tongue and keel strip for exhibition purposes and, apart from the two small bolt holes, the model will be of scale appearance.

The other method, where it is possible to have a hatch large enough to admit a hand, is to make a keel as above but instead of the tongue and box, a stout brass bolt is fitted into the keel (external) and a hole drilled in the ship's keel and keelson. It is best to line

this with a copper or brass tube a good drive fit. The external keel is then held up with a wing nut and a rubber washer. To locate the ends, fore and aft, brass $\frac{1}{8}''$ studs are set in the external keel and these fit into blind brass tubes let into the ship's keel. This type worked very well on my brig and the trim slots were invaluable. Another advantage is that for exhibition purposes no holes show in the model's keel. I always make keels long to keep the ship from pitching unnaturally and also to help directional stability.

You will gather from all this that conversion of a static to a working model would be difficult and I do strongly recommend that a working model is chosen and built with sailing in mind and special observance of the rules about adhesives and metals.

The mention of hatches raises the need for complete waterproofing of the hull. Mast holes are a weakness and a narrow box should be built up from the keel to the deck surrounding the mast step to keep water out of the hull. Alternatively, embed the mast coat in sealing compound. For removable hatches,

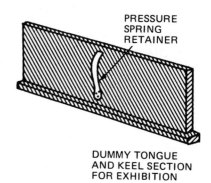

PRESSURE
SPRING
RETAINER

DUMMY TONGUE
AND KEEL SECTION
FOR EXHIBITION

Opposite. *Ibex,* showing more of the fine detail in this model. The line, or 'cut', across the deck planking abaft the stern of the boat was necessary in order to provide a removable section of the deck for handling purposes.
Below. The after end of *Ibex's* deck showing the construction of the transom. The 'reverse tiller' referred to by the author can be seen lying unobtrusively on deck just to starboard of the true tiller.

coamings are built inside the dimensions of the hatch so that they are encased in a lid of $\frac{1}{8}''$ ply surround, capped with $\frac{1}{32}''$ ply. This cover is fitted with a tarpaulin made from tracing linen, washed out and coloured grey, using a very thin solution of matt black paint in turpentine. This is glued round the outer coamings and wedges and battens fitted. The inside and dummy coamings must be well varnished to avoid swelling in water. To keep the whole cover from floating off in a gale, a hook is fitted under the lid and a rubber band goes to a hook in the keelson. Inevitably a small amount of water will seep into the hull somewhere and I fit a drain plug in the deck in the extreme stern. This takes the form of a turned wooden bucket with a plug on the bottom to fit $\frac{1}{2}''$ hole in the deck.

STEERING GEAR

Now for the steering gear which is the very heart of a working model. So often I have seen otherwise excellent models at rallies, where the whole effect was spoiled because they could not be made to sail a course or to run truly before the wind. I use two methods both simple but effective. Firstly for square rig or fore and aft vessels with booms on their mizzens or spankers, the reverse tiller is very effective. The boom is controlled by a sheet where the tackle (a dummy) is hooked onto the reverse tiller and passes through an eye on the boom to a bowsie block running along the spar on a jackstay. This in fact looks like a reef tackle and for exhibition purposes can be drawn tight bringing the dummy tackle right up to the boom. The reverse tiller is fitted with three rings soldered on to allow for adjustment in varying winds. To control the gear a rubber band is slipped over the forward tiller and, after passing through an eye on deck, is adjusted by another bowsie block on a jackstay. This can be camouflaged further by running it up the mast instead of along the deck. It then takes on the appearance of a halliard or topping lift tackle. When fitting rubber bands, preferably brown in colour, into eyes, leave a very small gap in the eye. The band well stretched can be slipped into the eye where it expands again and is trapped. Incidentally do treat all jack lines with beeswax; it saves wear and tear and helps the friction. For beating, the band is tightened up and the rudder is held gently amidships. Also for beating the boom is adjusted so that the end is over the quarter. This works well on a beat as when the wind frees in a puff it bears more on the sail and tends to push her up into the wind. This pressure then pulls the rudder a little to leeward, keeping her on course. The same principle applies on a reach except that both sheet and band are let out more. Most models with masts in designed positions carry weather helm and this has to be corrected in the model.

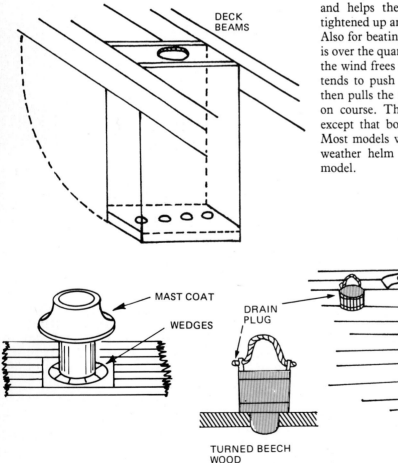

DECK BEAMS

MAST COAT

WEDGES

DRAIN PLUG

TURNED BEECH WOOD

Whereas some working models can sail with few external additions, a period ship such as the *Elizabeth Jonas* usually requires a considerable extension to the rudder as well as a deep false keel.

SAILING

The secret of getting a model to sail well is to adjust the centre of lateral resistance so that the vessel is almost balanced fore and aft with all plain sail set and a slight weather helm. To achieve this in the brig, I made a very shallow wedge attached to the bottom of the keel. It was 1″ deep at the aft end running out to nothing about 20″ forward. This was entirely successful and on the beat if the wind altered, the jibs immediately paid her head off, so avoiding her being caught aback, the bugbear of square rig models. The same principle works equally well on fore and afters and is much easier than altering mast positions. I admit that the adjustment of sheet and band is tricky because the strength of bands varies with temperature

change, and on a very hot day they become quite weak. Also wind velocity varies so that some experiment is needed. It is a good idea to make small marks on the boom or deck or mast to remind you of the position of bowsie blocks when you have achieved successful settings. Remember that as in full-sized vessels, when the wind is strong all sheets need to be hauled tight on a beat whereas in light airs everything except halliards needs to be slack and easy for ready response. In this connection it is essential that rudder pintles and gudgeons be free and easy. I find it best to make only the top and bottom pintles work, the ones between being dummies. This cuts down friction and cannot be seen.

Now for running. I have tried letting the sheet right out as I did in my full-sized boat and slacking the rudder control. This resulted in a series of yaws to leeward, followed by wild gybes and the model proceeded downwind like a snake, in a most

111

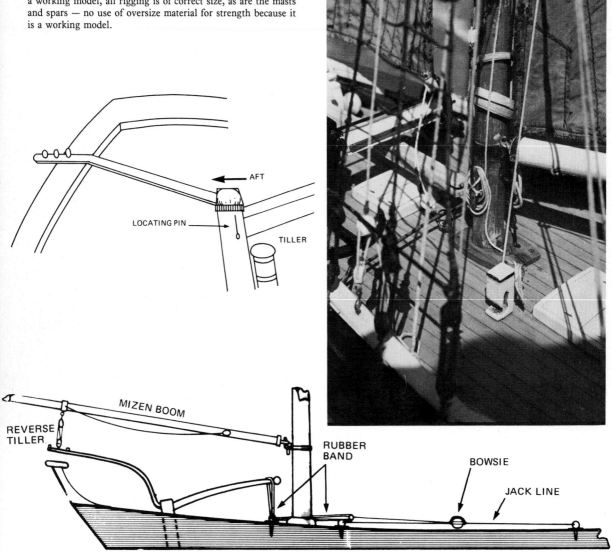

AFT

LOCATING PIN

TILLER

REVERSE TILLER

MIZEN BOOM

RUBBER BAND

BOWSIE

JACK LINE

unrealistic manner. However by leaving the rudder slack but tightening the sheet right up so that the boom is amidships, the sail then has immediate effect on the rudder. This results in a series of quick flip gybes of the sail which waggle the rudder to and fro and the model sails truly before the wind. With the long directional keel mentioned above my brig behaved extremely well with the yards squared in and the spanker sheet really up tight. The most difficult angle is to get the model to sail straight with the wind on the quarter, as this always tends to develop into either a reach or a run. The only thing to do is to slack the sail well out and give a little slackness to the

rudder to pull the ship off the wind. This is very much a matter of pleasant experiment. Try her out in fair weather but with enough wind to make the steering gear work. First, with rudder tight and sheets let out halfway, launch her for a reach at 90 degrees to the wind. If she runs off haul in the mizzen sheet a little and try again. If she runs up to the wind slack off the mizzen a little. If still not balanced slack off rudder control slightly. Notice the word 'little': make all adjustments gradually.

Schooners are very sensitive to the main sheet, and if this is too tight will invariably fly up into the wind. For beating, haul in the jibs gently, brace any yards

well up and set the mizzen over the quarter. Launch her at 45° to the wind and follow the above routine. If she persists in getting in irons go home and make a wedge as suggested, and deepen this as necessary until perfect balance is achieved. Model yachtsmen reading this will wonder why I have not suggested the Braine gear. This is fine in a schooner with a large mainsail providing plenty of power to work the sheets and blocks, but it must be hidden under a deck house or under the deck. The neatest gear I have made was on the brig, where the rudder head is covered with a square wheelgear house. This is close to the taffrail and I made a small reverse tiller coming out through a slot cut in the after side of the house to the point where the spanker sheet was led in the real ship. The control rod and line was covered by the helmsman's grating. This also covered the wide slot in the base of the house to allow movement of the control rod. It was tensioned with a small band carried out at 45 degrees to the starboard rail where it was adjusted by a bowsie block.

VESSELS WITH LOOSE FOOTED SAILS

We will now tackle the difficult task of sailing a craft such as a lugger with loose footed sails. To make it worse there is no jib or bowsprit to balance and the centre of the sail area is well aft. To correct the centre of lateral resistance in my $\frac{1}{2}''$ scale model of *Ebenezer* of St Ives I had to deepen the keel aft with deadwood going down in a wedge 5″ deep. On a 24″ model this looked appalling out of the water but it was all detachable and it worked. It followed that with all that keel below water the scale rudder had to be enlarged. I made a bolt on, dagger-like, deep addition so that for exhibition purposes only a $^1/_{16}''$ hole showed in the scale rudder. I also found it necessary to insert a piece of lead into the addition to keep the whole rudder from floating off the pintles. The usual reverse tiller was fitted to the rudder head using a brass band with a locating pin for easy removal, but the problem was the loose-footed sail.

After some thought I hit on the idea of making the outrigger boom swivel from its inboard cleat, putting

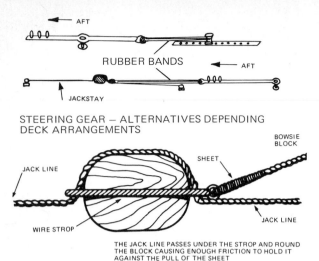

AFT

RUBBER BANDS

AFT

JACKSTAY

STEERING GEAR – ALTERNATIVES DEPENDING
DECK ARRANGEMENTS

BOWSIE
BLOCK

JACK LINE

SHEET

JACK LINE

WIRE STROP

THE JACK LINE PASSES UNDER THE STROP AND ROUND
THE BLOCK CAUSING ENOUGH FRICTION TO HOLD IT
AGAINST THE PULL OF THE SHEET

Opposite top. This radio controlled model of the Manx
Nobbie *Gladys* by A J Brown is a good example of a working
model having loose footed sails.

Opposite bottom. At ¼″ = 1′ 0″ (1/16) scale every detail is
possible, and a nice touch, as well as the figure at the helm, is
the inclusion of some fish boxes on deck. This model is fully
described in *Model Shipwright* Number 14.

Below. The mackerel drifter *Ebenezer*, another working model
built to a large scale, is described in the text.
(Photo: Max Davey)

a brass pin down through the metal band and through
the deck. Where the spar is normally lashed down to
the rail on the quarter I substituted a rope link from
an eye in the deck giving the boom freedom to move
sideways an inch each way. The outer end was
supported by the sheet and sail so that the spar swung
clear of the rail. After a good deal of experiment I
connected the outrigger to the reverse tiller using a
length of stiff stainless steel wire engaging in a slot
cut in the tiller, as shown in the figure. The whole
gear was centralised as before by looping a band over
the tiller proper, through an eye on the deck and up
the mast. Also as before, for running, the difficult
operation, the sheet which runs in the spar to a cleat
was made up tight. The rudder control was slacked
right off. Provided the rudder is big enough this
works perfectly. The sheet on the fore lug can of
course be let right out, the same applying to ketches,
schooners and the fore and aft sails on square riggers.

The lugger behaves well on the reach and beat but
the mizzen must not be over tightened as the leverage
over the stern will force her up into the wind.
Luggers beat at a high angle of attack and are prone to
be taken aback. When this happens, the foresail
belayed at the rail acts as a brake and the vessel drifts
slowly sideways to leeward. For a long time I could
not overcome this but we have found a solution.
Make a horse of stiff brass wire painted black to fit
across the model amidships. This horse is pinned into
the rails using brass clips and pins soldered on. The
pin holes are arranged so that the horse is set at an
angle, the lee side being about 1″ farther aft than the
windward. The fore sheet has two double blocks and
the friction of the sheet in these is quite sufficient to
hold the sail once it has been adjusted. Now the
model is launched with the sheet pressing on the lee
side. If she is caught aback the ring on the horse flies
across with the sail as the angle forward releases the
pressure. Now all the foresail except the small piece
before the mast is pulling and the model will sail to
windward on the other tack, although at not such a
sharp angle. It is most unlikely that she will go aback
again. On the reverse tack, the pins are extracted and
the horse set at the opposite angle. Now I agree that
this looks 'odd' on the bank but 'at sea' it cannot be
seen and the horse can be removed ashore and the
sheet hooked on to the scale bumpkin. I found that
the clips and pins were necessary because there is a
strong upward pull on the horse on the beat and any
other fitting pulls out.

Now to turn to other sheets and braces. In fore and
aft vessels the topsails will have to be taken in during
a blow and I have evolved almost invisible means of
doing this. When fitting sails and running rig make
the halliards and sheets as for full size but when you
get to the point where the lines are shackled to the sail

cringles, introduce a neat hook for rapid removal of the sail. The shackle will keep the halliard or sheet from unreeving and falling back to the deck. The tack is shackled on to the foot of the sail and a bowsie block 'tackle' made up so that the fall can be hooked over a cleat or belaying pin and tightened, as topsails need to be bowsed down. Also on fore and aft types the fore staysails on barges, ketches and merchant schooners all sheet down to iron horses running across the foredeck and can take care of themselves on going about. Where there are several headsails the solution is, fit the sheets through the appropriate bullseyes on the fo'csle or main rail but instead of belaying them, gather all together each side and lead one line to a bowsie block running on a jackstay along the straight side of the ship. It is easier to deal with if the line runs inside the pin rails and is adjusted amidships between the fore and main shrouds. For these jack lines I use dark grey 'rope' as it looks more like wire and is inconspicuous. To change tacks it is only necessary to let out one side and take in the other. This system also allows good settings for all the jibs on reaches and runs. Remember to slack the weather side right off so that they do not interfere with the set of the sails on the lee side. When the weather is light keep the sheets slack but harden them right in for a blow.

Opposite. Very few models — let alone working models — of junks are to be seen, which is a pity for they make interesting and out of the ordinary subjects. Moreover, to judge by the performance put up, even under boisterous conditions, by this model by Roy Johnston the remarkable sailing abilities of the prototypes are reproduced in their miniature counterparts. This model is only about a couple of feet long. With the simple rig and sail plan this type of craft should prove attractive to beginners as well as the 'older' hands.

Below. Another simple model, and again one rarely seen as a working model, is this Norfolk Wherry. This model is slightly larger than the junk, and is even more simple in its design and construction.

SAILING SQUARE RIGGERS

With square rig we have braces to contend with. One of the problems is that in the lower yards fitted with trusses, the length of the braces varies as the yards are

braced up. On my topsail schooner *Little Mystery* I solved this by making the fore and topsail yard braces continuous but led through blocks at the foot of the mainmast. These blocks, about 2″ above the deck and hidden by the winch, were held down by rubber bands to take up any slack. Fortunately in *Little Mystery* the lead blocks came under the crosstrees so that it was easy to work the braces up and down the mast. This would have been impossible had the lead blocks been lashed to the main shrouds as in so many schooners. However you can always use builder's licence in cases like this because every skipper had his own ideas about leads and ships rarely remained the same throughout their careers. The standing topgallant braces were continuous and merely led through a friction block on the mainmast cap.

With the brig, the multiple lower braces with tackles came down to the rails. I got over the varying length by making the yard brace pendants of black silk-covered heavy shirring elastic. Further, when building the hull and before decking, I fitted a length of ³⁄₈″ diameter plastic tubing in the form of a 'U' across the inside of the hull, coming up to and glued to the covering board each side under the pin rail

where the brace lead blocks were situated. Thus I could brace up merely by pulling them through the tubing. Some water resistant silicone grease greatly helped to reduce friction. The royal and topgallant braces were continuous because there were only parrals on the yards. The main braces led to bumpkins right on the quarter. Here I drilled holes in the poop side planking and set a plastic tube athwartships under the deck. Being immediately below the bumpkins, the braces could be led through the lead blocks, through the tube and through the lead blocks on the other side. To make the illusion more complete I fitted dummy falls from the lead blocks to the taffrail where they were made up on belaying pins. In case anyone gets the wrong idea, all these 'gadgets' on the schooner and the brig were removed and proper rigging fitted throughout, before they entered the National Maritime Museum.

With earlier ships of the Tudor period where spankers had not come into existence, the problems of steering are more difficult. Two modern sailers of reproductions of these ships, Captain Villiers of *Mayflower II* and Captain Marsh of the *Nonsuch* explained that use of the sails helped a good deal with

Opposite top. A large ship-rigged vessel under full sail, even as a model, is an impressive sight. False keels are usually required to make successful sailing, and some simplification of the running rigging has to be carried out to ease the problems of trimming, and furling, the sails. This particular model is about 4′ 0″ long overall.

Opposite bottom. Going back in period, but still square rigged, this model of the frigate *Inconstant* always sails well. The model, by A J Lench, is built to a scale of 1″ = 5′ 0″ (1/60). Ships of this type as models have several advantages over the previous model — fewer sails to deal with, and the slightly loftier hull above water makes for a better and more visible model when under way. Once again a false keel has been fitted for stability.

Below. John Mayger's beautiful model of the brig *Waterwitch* is excellently detailed, and looks well upon the water. Under way it puts up a good performance. This type of rig really brings out the art of sailing square rigged vessels. Notice how, though the water is calm and the breeze gentle, the topgallants have been furled.

the steering. The spritsail was a great help in keeping the head off the wind and this was helped by, if need be, brailing up the lateen on the poop. The worst feature was the high poop which tended to push the head up to the wind. This could be overcome on a model by deepening an external keel aft. Also as the hull lines were always full, plenty of lead externally could keep a model sailing fairly upright; Tudor ships did not sail on the ears. For steering, the best gear I have seen was a vane on the poop made to look like the large ensign usually flown. This was connected to the rudder (enlarged) by a pair of equal sized gear wheels under the poop. A telescopic tube arrangement on the ensign gave a friction twist, so that the vane could be set at any angle in relation to the rudder. Incidentally I have also seen the same idea

Opposite. These two views of the galleon *Elizabeth Jonas* under way show that if big enough these picturesque vessels can be made to work. Their operation calls for a degree of experimentation, not only to acquire the knack of dealing with this particular sail plan, but also to overcome the problem of the high poop catching the wind, and so acting almost as an additional mizzen.

Top right and bottom right. The author's Brixham trawler *Ibex* and (below) his ½″ = 1′ 0″ (1/24) scale sailing model of the Thames barge *Kathleen*. Both these fine working models show, among other things, some excellent and realistic sails. They illustrate well the advantage of the fore and aft rig, with its clean simple layout and minimal amount of rigging, as a useful prototype for working models.

applied to a model clipper ship where the vane was made of clear plastic and was practically invisible at any distance. The gear was most effective and when set the model sailed as straight as a vane yacht.

Although only one tack could be sailed at a time without bringing the model ashore for sail adjustment, the fitting of proportional radio control for the rudder would be a very good thing for Tudor ships. All the gear could be concealed below decks and it would obviate the real difficulty of keeping such models from being caught aback and they could be made to run truly before the wind. I will have more to say about radio later.

Below and opposite. Another fine performer under sail is John Mayger's brigantine *Dolphin*. The model is to the builder's customary showcase standard, and apart from some minor modifications to the rigging for sailing purposes, the only departure from the scale plans is the addition of an external false keel. This is a plank on frame model, with planked decks. Notice how this builder, too, adheres to the principle that masts and rigging do not have to be overscale for sailing models. The sails are in keeping with the rest of the model, well made and setting well — note the reef points.

SAILS

Sailmaking and setting need consideration. For material I have found a British-made cotton called 'Tarantulle'. The fine white is coded 72.2/2 and being all cotton dyes well. It is best to dye all the material for brown sails first to shrink it, before ironing and cutting out. At the same time bolt ropes must either be spun from Terylene (non-shrinking) or pre-shrunk by boiling in water. This is to avoid the sail being puckered up when it gets wet. Cut out paper patterns for all sails to ensure that they will fit. Rig the spars in position temporarily with cotton to get the angles of booms, gaffs, etc correct. Remember once the mainsail on a ketch has been made you cannot alter the angle of the gaff and the topsail must be seen to fit beforehand, so hoist your topmast. Next ensure that all sails except the topsails (fore and aft) are cut with the selvedge in line with the leech. Topsail cloths were in line with the head of the sail. Now consider the figure showing the roach of the sails. You will have to calculate the amounts required but they are essential as when the bolt ropes pull taut the sails belly out and look realistic. Lay out your patterns on paper and draw in the curved edges before cutting out. Allow $\frac{1}{4}''$ all round for turning in twice.

'Unibond' glue on cloth resists water so glue and turn in two $\frac{1}{8}''$ hems. You can run a machine stitch over this if you wish but use terylene thread. My wife's Swiss machine has a very fine stitch and I have discovered that lines of stitches on the sails to represent seams can be very inconspicuous. If you cannot use Terylene sew the sail through a sheet of brown paper and tear it off afterwards. On my $\frac{1}{2}''$ scale barge the single stitched lines are just visible and are the nearest approach to realism which I have achieved so far. With my brig I started with white sails but tinted these, using a very watery solution of artists' acrylic colours, which are mixed with water but dry waterproof. I use a mixture of burnt umber with a little black to obtain that dirty grey look of flax sails. Experiment first on odd pieces bearing in mind that the solution dries much lighter in colour. Reef points are glued down in position on the finished sails using 'Unibond'. This looks much more realistic than allowing them to curl up and stand away from the sail. Sew the bolt ropes on with the lay of the cord. I attach the rope to the back of a chair and pull gently as I sew the sail on gripping the sail between two fingers. With practice you will find that the finished sail will set well in a breeze. I should add that 'Unibond' dries clear and should be invisible if used sparingly. It was thoroughly tested on the fore staysail of my schooner which dipped in and out of sea water for six years with no ill effect.

As lofty square riggers cannot be expected to carry full sail in the scale gales which we experience, we must be able to take in kites and upper sails: if royals and upper topgallants and flying jibs are removable it should be sufficient. Strictly speaking the yards should be lowered but as this involves shortening braces and either letting go halliards, or undoing tiny hooks at the bands on the yards, I do not recommend it. However I have seen a very successful brig where the royal halliards are let go and the sails merely belly out. This takes the steam out of them and looks realistic. Alternatively leave the yards in position and remove the sails altogether.

It is impossible to furl neatly a model sail on a yard, so I fit my upper sails with small loops of shirring elastic, dyed light brown, at the ends of the head rope. These are slipped over the yardarms. I make small wire hooks sewn into the head of the sail and they engage with the jackstay on the yard and are invisible. On the yard below I shackle the chain sheet to the clewline block and merely hook the clew of the sail to the shackle. Again you have to look closely to see this. Work on these small hooks at the pond side can be very trying and I strongly recommend you to carry a pair of tweezers or jewellers' pliers. If you wish to be a purist you could of course make up dummy furled sails with elastic loops and slip these on in lieu, but I can assure you that in heavy weather, the onlooker from the bank does not really observe the lack of a sail on the yard. What is much more important is that the model will sail along at a reasonable angle of heel, and the bare rigging aloft looks good. I think the

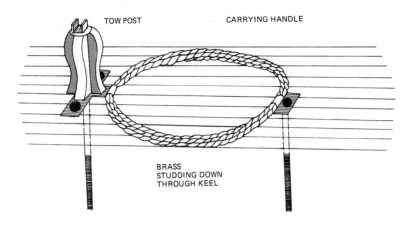

TOW POST   CARRYING HANDLE

BRASS
STUDDING DOWN
THROUGH KEEL

background to this is that our forefathers who lived with sailing vessels, saw them more often than not under reduced canvas.

With jibs and staysails I rig the sail with the downhaul attached to the halliard at the head of the sail. The sail is hooked to the shackle and at the foot to the downhaul block. The spectacle runners on the stay have to be made up as hooks. I have tried sliding the sail down the stay and furling it, on say the jibboom, but it is impossible to do this neatly because of the stiffness of the bolt rope and canvas. Again if you wish, you could make up dummy furled sails to clip on the jibboom. The inner headsails of course have hanks sewn on.

RADIO CONTROL

Over a period of many years I have fairly well exhausted the possibilities of sailing working models. However times change and we must follow and owing to the frequent presence of pleasure motor boats on my local water, I have been forced to enter the world of radio control. I do not regret this because having overcome the initial expense, it has opened up a new dimension in model sailing. Using only proportional rudder control on my trawler *Ibex*, I can feel that I am again at the helm of a real vessel. Further by fitting all the receiving gear in one small box, I can switch this in about two minutes to my new barge model so that I have a choice. There is also the spur of being able to compete with other radio control modellers. Basically you need only rudder control but this involves setting the sails for a fairly broad beat, so that you can reach and run without altering anything. I find this is quite good except that the run is necessarily slow.

The next step is the use of a second channel as they do in model yachts to bring in sail control. From the point of view of the scale ship modeller there are

limitations, because square riggers present great mechanical problems and luggers will not sail aback satisfactorily. The gear is therefore restricted to cutters, ketches, yawls, barges, fore and aft schooners and models of odd craft such as Norfolk wherries. (These traders with their single loose footed sails, have to my knowledge, so far defied working enthusiasts. However with radio control of rudder and sail these quaint craft become a real working possibility.) There is an excellent book on the whole subject by C R Jeffries called *Radio control for Model Yachts*. I would like to add that there is now no need to have any real knowledge of radio working as everything is already assembled.

TRANSPORTATION

Transportation of working models can be difficult. A model of 36″ or over needs to be carried in one hand when negotiating doors, stairs and low openings such as car doors. The time to think of this is early on before the deck is fixed. The ideal is a handle securely screwed into the bottom of the hull at the point of balance as in 'M' or 10-Rater yachts. The arrangement does however assume that there is a removable hatch large enough to admit a hand. Barges, ketches and smacks are all right but my trawler had no hatches of any size. I got over the difficulty by having a coil of rope (dummy warp) amidships fastened to strong brass eyes so that the model could be lifted safely. With square riggers with small hatches it may be possible to make the roof of the main deck house abaft the foremast removable, so as to admit a hand and to bolt on the keel. Another idea would be a tool like a corkscrew with a wooden handle and a wide hook on the end. The small clipper ship hatch could be removable and the hook engaged in a large ring standing up from the bottom of the hull. The hook and ring would need to be fairly big because the model will jump about in a seaway and the 'catch' must be positive. It would be essential that the ring be at the precise point of balance.

If the model has to be rigged down, some of the running rig such as buntlines would have to be dispensed with in square riggers. Shrouds which are joined by a sheerpole can all be unhooked at once. Make up the deadeyes with their lanyards but instead of the lower deadeyes having strops with pins, they are stropped with wire ending in hooks facing inboard. In many vessels the chain plates come up inside the topgallant rail and with holes drilled in the ends, the deadeye hooks are out of sight. The bowsprit is held down in nearly every case by a heavy chain or wire rope, fastened to a chain plate bolted to the stem. In my schooner, where it would have been shackled to the chain plate, I substituted a heavy brass pin bent into the shape of an eye.

The pin's head is pulled down hard and engages in a keyhole slot in the chainplate. The tension keeps the head from jumping out. By fitting a beheaded

screw into the butt of the bowsprit, or a hinge at that point, the whole of the jibboom and bowsprit assembly can be unshipped and slid inboard. This of course slacks off all the headstays and if the shrouds have been unhooked, allows the masts to be withdrawn and laid on the deck. Alternatively the masts can be stepped on deck, but you will then be faced with making all stays and shrouds adjustable, as I have found that the masts will never set up twice at the same angle, owing to stretching cord. If possible it is best to make the lower masts a fixture, with shrouds and stays all set up and then slide or hinge up the headgear. Similarly the topmasts can be made to slide down as in the real ship. My trawler and barge are both fitted like this and are manageable and can be quickly set up again at the waterside.

There is growing interest in working models and with summer rallies becoming more numerous there is encouragement to join the fraternity of builders. You will always get a warm welcome at rallies with plenty of advice and help. There is a general feeling of enthusiasm and many lasting friendships ensue.

Hove Regatta. Just some of the many entrants at this annual get-together for builders of sailing models of sailing ships. Almost all the models illustrating this chapter have been seen at this and other rallies, demonstrating the value and interest afforded by such meetings both to modellers and spectators.

Miniature scenic models

by DEREK HUNNISETT

The construction of miniature ships offers advantages that are not to be found in the making of larger models. Most of the work can be carried out on the kitchen table and in the living room, no really elaborate tools need be used, and apart from the initial sawing and carving out of the hull, there is not a lot of mess to be cleared up each evening. With the average family house, models constructed to a large scale can present storage problems when finished,

whereas a considerable collection of miniatures can be kept in a comparatively small space.

The amount of detail that is put into a miniature ship model rests with the individual modeller and his requirements, whether he wants to build a super exhibition model, or a good replica omitting a lot of the smaller details, like coils of rope on the pinrails, ratlines, reefpoints and so on. However, it is my opinion everything that can be put on should be included and the end product is well worth the extra effort.

There is one thing that must be adhered to and that is scale; if building to $1'' = 50'\ 0''$ (1/600) always keep that in mind, no matter what item is being made. A lot was said in the past about selection and rejection of detail; almost everything can be put on that is on the real ship, and if it looks overcrowded then the scaling must be wrong somewhere. Always try, if it is a waterline model, to give the impression of a miniature ship in preference to a model ship — believe me there is quite a big difference. Take a look at the models in a shipping office window, everything about them is so highly polished and clean. Give *your* model atmosphere. Do not have all the rigging taut but leave some hanging slack in a slight curve. Coils of rope on the deck should not be too neatly coiled; a sail perhaps partially furled, and partially blowing out in the wind, and men working on the deck. In fact there are lots of ways to make it look lifelike.

TOOLS AND MATERIALS
Although most people have the tools necessary for fashioning the hull, there are some others which are essential: a pin vice for holding small drills (these can be bought from a good watchmaker); a steel rule marked in the scale selected, in my case $1'' = 50'\ 0''$, the very best tweezers that you can buy; the smallest table vice you can get; a pair of dividers; a fine toothed X-Acto saw, and some needle files. The best

Opposite and below. Two models, both at 1″ = 50′ 0″ (1/600) scale, of the French 74 *Le Superbe* (1785) by Derek Hunnisett. These are two separate models, not the same one put into a different setting! The stand model conveys some idea of the detail included on the decks, whilst the scenic model does the same for the exterior detail. In a scenic model it is the smaller details which add life to the setting. Here the ship is riding to anchor in an oily calm sea — note the tension in the bow cable and the slackness in the stern cable. The boat is at the boom and the bowman is facing forward to grasp the rope ladder suspended from the end of the boom. Figures make all the difference to a model, bringing it to life. The sails are shown clewed up to the yards, not furled as are those in the static model, and the hammocks are in the hammock nettings — which on the static model are empty.

wood to use is one which is very hard with the finest of texture. I use mostly holly and boxwood, and find these excellent to work with, especially the holly which is really hard and has very little marked grain. I do not advise using soft woods as they are very difficult to finish to a clean cut edge. I also use the holly and the boxwood when taking plane shavings, which I use for quite a lot of the detail work. To obtain the shavings, I take a short piece of wood about $\frac{1}{2}$″ to 1″ wide, clamp it in a vice, and with a bit of practice shavings can be taken off with a sharp plane. They will come out in tight rolls, so soak them in water then iron them flat with a hot iron, and finally glue the rough side down onto a piece of tissue; this helps to stop them splitting when being cut for small items.

For the rigging I use mostly copper wire. I have found that it is easier to put on than thread or hair,

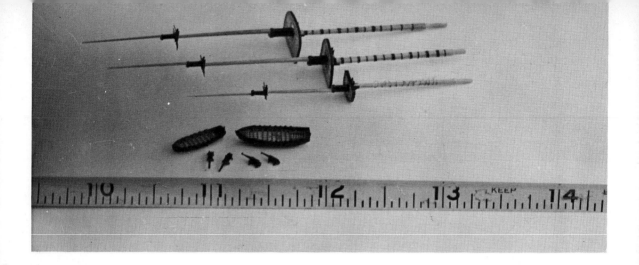

and it hangs better in shape. The trouble is getting it fine enough for the purpose, but it can be done by hunting round for old electric components. I have collected various diameters down to 48 SWG and the thinnest I have been able to buy is 0.020 mm, which can hardly be seen, but was very expensive. 45 or 48 SWG is quite suitable for most of the rigging. If thinner material is needed, as for the reef points, the best currently available is Gutermann M303 Spun Polyester, made in West Germany. As long as it is unravelled in small lengths of about $1\frac{1}{2}''$ or $2''$ it is suitable, but is very difficult to unravel. If using it for, say, reef points unravel it to three or four filaments and draw each through your finger and thumb dipped in diluted glue, to hold them all together.

The glue that I find best for bonding together the layers of wood for the hull, or any solids, is Cascamite Resin glue, but for the lighter work and the rigging something easier to work with is needed and I find Lepage's Seccotine is best. In some cases a very slight watering down stops it stringing out into whiskers, but this must be done only sparingly and only where essential. At all points of contact put a touch of paint and matt varnish, which helps to strengthen it and keeps the atmosphere away, which otherwise in time may weaken the glue. At all times keep the glue to a minimum, for nothing looks worse than blobs of glue on a model; always wash off any excess glue straight away with a moistened paint brush.

PREPARATION

Before starting on a model I always prepare most of the materials I shall require; this not only gives ample time for the application and drying of the several coats of paint, but enables the work on the ship to proceed without having to stop and prepare something. So paint some strips of plane shavings in the different colours that will be needed, also some pieces of card and tissue. Cut lengths of wire about 3" long, straighten them by rolling on a piece of glass with a steel rule, and paint them for the rigging. The quickest way to do this is to grip the left hand end with a pair of tweezers, hold it on a piece of card run a full loaded brush of paint along it, draw the wire away to the left. Drop it onto a clean piece of card and pick it up straight away, then leave it on a further piece of card to dry. Doing it that way stops any little blobs of paint forming on the wire.

Prepare the deck material. Either use lined paper (the lines being 0.01" apart), and paint the paper deck colour — paint by using the finger rather than a paint brush, it does not cover the lines that way — or alternatively plank the decks to scale. This is quite easy to do; take a strip of prepared shaving a little longer and wider than the hull, cut off strips 1/100" wide using a razor blade and steel rule. Glue the corners of a piece of tissue onto a piece of glass, and onto that glue a piece of shaving about $\frac{1}{8}''$ wide, pressing it flat with the rule, and checking that it is absolutely straight. Pick up one plank with a sharp pair of tweezers, run it along a brush loaded with glue, and lay it alongside the first wide piece, making sure that it is flat and hard up against the edge, using a steel rule. Repeat this process until there are enough planks to cover the width of the hull, and wash off any surplus glue.

Three ply strips made out of shavings are always useful — glue three pieces together, the centre piece with the grain running at right angles to the outside pieces. If the ship has rails, begin by making a frame about 7" long by 4" wide of $\frac{3}{4}''$ by $\frac{1}{2}''$ strips. On the short sides mark the spacing of the rails by making little nicks in the edge of the wood, put in a small pin at one end where the centre rail comes, and wind very fine wire round this pin and round the frame through each nick in turn, keeping the tension even. Repeat this process on the longer side for the stanchions, but

Left. The masts, two boats and some of the guns for *Le Superbe.* If the size of the model was not apparent in the two previous photographs, this should help. The mainmast (top of picture) is only just over 3″ long. The boats are less than $\frac{1}{2}$″ in length and are fitted with thwarts and bottom boards. The guns, complete with trucks on the carriages, are less than $\frac{1}{4}$″ overall. The masts are well tapered and woolded, and the tops are complete with trestle- and crosstrees.

using a slightly thicker wire. Having done that spread glue along the outside of the frame so that all the wires are fastened to it. When it is absolutely dry cut away all the wires on the underside of the frame, and paint the rails still on the frame, on both sides, with enamel paint. When this in turn is dry, cut each wire carefully from the frame top, trim one end of each stanchion flush with the top rail, and cut the other end to leave a short length to reach the deck, at the same time leaving every fourth or fifth stanchion just a little longer to go into holes drilled in the deck.

PLANS

As most of the plans which can be bought are invariably to scales like $\frac{1}{8}$″ = 1′ 0″ (1/96), it is necessary to reduce them to our working scale; nothing very elaborate is needed just the bare outlines to be able to arrive at the correct shape, but they must be done very accurately. I find the best way is to draw on a sheet of card a vertical line about 5″ long on the

right hand side, marking this number 1. Next measure the distance between the first and second station lines on the original plan (always think in feet), if the scale on the plan is $\frac{1}{8}$″ = 1′ 0″ and the distance is 2″ then it will be 16′, so set the dividers to 16/50″ on the rule and mark off this distance on the card to the left of line 1. Do this for each station line in turn, always working from line 1 as the datum point, to the last station line. A series of vertical lines will result. Then draw a horizontal line across the card to represent the centre line of the deck of the model, and set off at each station line in turn, the distance from the centre line to the edge of the deck, and also the distance of the bow from line 1, and the stern from the last station line. By drawing a fair line through all these points the outline of the deck is obtained. The same process is used to obtain the sheer plan, by drawing another horizontal line across the card well clear of the first drawing, to represent the load waterline of the ship, and measure off on the plan the distances from the waterline to the deck. Plot them on the appropriate station line, and draw a fair line through them. Finally mark in the shape of the stem and stern on this sheer drawing. Allow some extra on the hull below the load waterline, to compensate for the thickness of the material used to represent the sea. Once this amount has been decided, draw out the shape of the bottom of the hull in the same way as before, by selecting on the plan a waterplane below the load waterline which corresponds to this thickness.

To get the correct form of the hull during carving, use templates which show the shape at the various stations. To make these templates it is necessary first to draw out the body plan to the scale size, using the same procedure to that adopted for the sheer and deck plans. Now cut out in thin plastic sheet a template for

WOOD FRAME
FOR WIRE RAILS

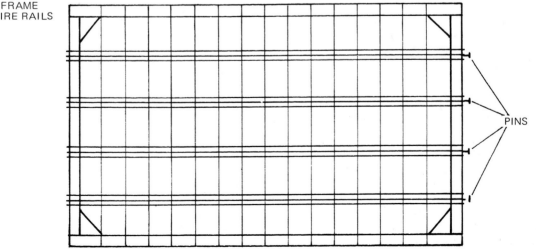

PINS

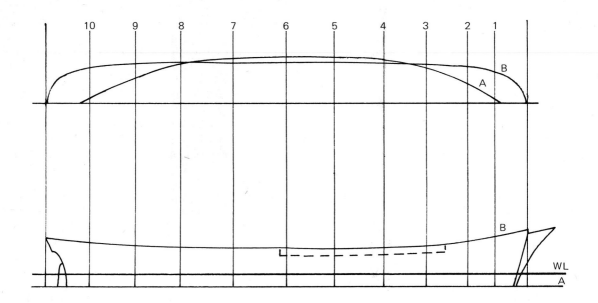

HULL LINES

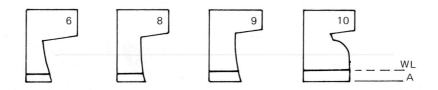

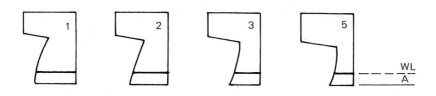

HULL TEMPLATES

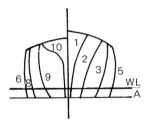

BODY PLAN

each section, and that completes all that is necessary to be done to scale down the lines; all the other details can be scaled down as work progresses.

HULL CONSTRUCTION

Using the templates continuously the model can be shaped out of one solid block of holly. That is satisfactory for a vessel such as a clipper ship, but if the model is of a man-of-war, then shaping it requires a different technique because of the gun ports. In the accompanying sketches, I have shown a 64 gun ship, but the principle is the same whatever the number of guns or size of ship. Scale down the plans in the same way as before, but build up the hull in layers instead of one solid block. Shape the first piece, which is about $\frac{1}{8}''$ thick, roughly to the shape and the sheer up to the bottom of the lower gun ports. Then prepare a strip of holly equal in thickness to the height of the lower gun ports, and cut to shape; carefully mark the positions of these ports and cut them out with a piercing saw. Next measure the distance between the top of the lower ports and the bottom of the second row of gun ports, and cut and shape a strip to that thickness. Prepare another strip of holly, equal in thickness to the depth of the second row of ports, shape it and mark out the positions of the ports, and cut these out. Afterwards cut away the section representing the waist so that there is one piece to go on the bow and one on the stern. Glue and pin all these pieces together and put the assembly in clamps. When this is dry, glue the deck material into the recess on the gun deck. Next cut and shape a piece of thin veneer with a hole cut in the centre to represent the forecastle-gangways-quarterdeck and glue this into position. Finally cut to shape the poop and poop cabin pieces and glue and pin into place, the smaller piece going on top of the larger one.

Carry on shaping the hull, checking frequently with the templates, but not rubbing down too much at this stage. Fill in the gap in each side with a three-ply shaving, rebating them into the hull and underneath the top deck. Mark out the positions of the gun ports, drill a hole in the centre of each and make these holes into the square ports with a square needle file. All this part of the work must be very carefully done, and constantly checked, for it is so easy to get the deck heights a fraction too high or low if the thickness of the strips is wrong. The gun ports must be very accurately marked off and cut, otherwise later on when rigging the model, a gun may appear where a shroud should be.

The bulwarks at the stern, are cut from three-ply shavings and let into a rebate in the deck edge, cutting the gun ports as before with drill and file. Following this, finish shaping the hull and smooth off with sandpaper. Make a thin saw cut vertically in the bow and stern, and fit the shaped stem and rudder; I prefer to fashion these from thin plastic, as this is less likely to split.

THE MOUNTING AND CASE

On all my models when I have reached this stage, I have found it is better to make a working block to hold the model. Also I make the sea and the case. The working block need not be elaborate. Cut a piece of hardboard about $3''$ longer and $2''$ wider than the model (including the bowsprit), screw this to a block of wood about $1''$ thick and wide enough to allow the model to be tilted without overbalancing. Drill two holes $\frac{1}{8}''$ in diameter in the bottom of the hull, glue a piece of dowel about $1\frac{1}{2}''$ long into each hole, drill two corresponding holes in the top of the working block; the model can then be held in place there until it is finished without touching it. As an extra precaution to prevent the block from suddenly coming back on an even keel after being tilted, a strip of stiff plastic can be screwed to each side of the block, so that when

Another of the author's 1/600 scale scenic miniatures, the French 64 *Le Protecteur* (1760), showing the extension to the hull below water for setting into the sea. This model is some $4''$ long.

131

TOP OF LOWER GUNPORTS

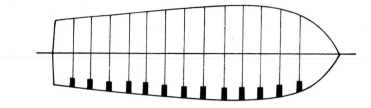

HOLLY STRIP BETWEEN GUNPORT ROWS

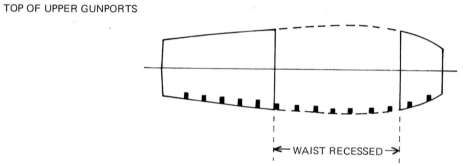

TOP OF UPPER GUNPORTS

◄— WAIST RECESSED —►

QUARTERDECK — GANGWAYS — FORECASTLE LEVEL

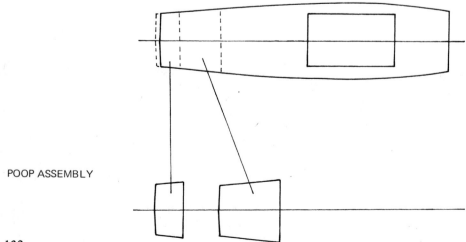

POOP ASSEMBLY

THE HULL AFTER SHAPING

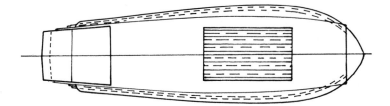

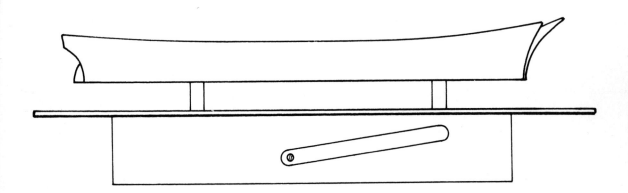

THE HULL BEFORE ADDING BULWARKS

BUILDING BLOCK

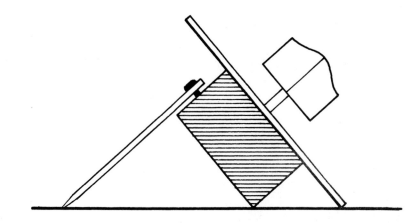

Right. *Le Superbe* under construction. Externally the hull has been completed, but it is still on the working supports.

Below. Photographs such as this are invaluable for giving an indication of the wave patterns and 'seas' created by a vessel under way. Though it must be remembered that both the shape of the hull and its speed have a bearing on the resultant wash and wake created as the vessel moves through the waves. The state of the sea, on the other hand, depends upon the weather, tidal and other factors.
(Photo: Conway Picture Library)

Opposite top. *France II* with all sail set in a choppy sea. This gives a good idea of the amount of sail set by these huge cargo carriers of the earlier part of this century.

Opposite centre. *Le Protecteur* with a 'topgallant breeze' just off the stern, a setting which is full of atmosphere.

Opposite bottom. In contrast the tiny *Mayflower* is lost in the immensity of the Atlantic rollers. The vastness of this ocean has been caught by setting the little ship in a large area of sea — not readily conveyed by this photograph.

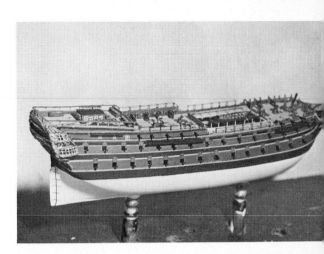

it is tilted on its side, the strip can be swivelled down and the free end, just touching the table, stops it coming back into the upright position.

The style and quality of the case is a matter of personal taste. Before starting on the sea, the base and the wood edge moulding must be finished. Personally I find decorating filler is an ideal medium in which to fashion the sea. First I drill two holes in the base to correspond with the two pieces of dowel in the model, in the position in which the model is to be set. To make a key for the filler when it is applied, I insert a lot of small tacks all over the base, leaving the heads just clear of the surface. Then I cut four strips of glass to put round the edge of the base temporarily whilst applying the filler; they need only be a fraction higher than the level of the sea. After putting the model in position and securing it firmly in place with a single screw inserted from below, I fix a narrow strip of tissue round the hull, with a tiny spot of glue to hold it into place. Then I mix some filler into a fairly stiff consistency, spread it over the base and round the hull and out to the strips of glass, and mould it into the necessary wave formations with a $\frac{1}{2}''$ brush, bearing in mind all the time the force and direction of the wind in relation to the model. I let it stand for several hours and then lift the model out; the tissue will be left behind and a good recess formed to take the model when completed.

Painting the sea is, to me, one of the most difficult jobs of all, and I must confess that I have never been really satisfied with my results. All I can suggest is to study paintings and photographs of seas, and try to create what it should look like, to the best of your ability. I think I spend more time painting and re-painting a sea than anything else! Once it is finished to your satisfaction give it several coats of picture varnish to give it a transparent look.

PAINTING

Very often an otherwise good model is ruined by bad painting. Always apply several thin coats of paint rather than one thick coat, rubbing each one down when it is dry, until a perfectly smooth finish is obtained. The final coat is the most demanding, for on it depends much of the success of the model. If there are a number of coloured bands, or areas of colour, on the hull — as there were on the models of *Le Superbe* and the *Mayflower* — painting these straight on to the hull can present considerable problems if true and clear-cut lines are to be preserved. I overcame this problem on these two models by cutting strips from pre-painted tissue and glueing these on to the hull. The result was clean, sharp bands of colour. On models of this type, I prefer to use matt paints, except for the sea.

On most of the old time sailing ships there was a lot of gilded carving and fancy 'gingerbread' work on the

Top left. *Royal Katherine,* a Second Rate of 1664 in a calm sea, with even the sprit topsail set. The fact that she is under way in a gentle breeze is ably conveyed by the treatment of the flags and pennants — not board stiff but just fluttering; note the realistic way in which the long pennant at the main is drooping more than its shorter counterparts. Because the ship is moving slowly there is just a little froth of broken water at the stem, and almost no following wake aft clear of the rudder.

Bottom left. This aerial view of *Le Superbe* under construction shows the incredible amount of detail on the decks, which incidentally are planked. The guns are complete with tackles, the pump handles are fitted, the gratings are in place, and a number of coils of rope have been placed ready to be 'joined' to the appropriate leads of the rigging — an example of the forethought and planning which has to go into working out the constructional sequence.

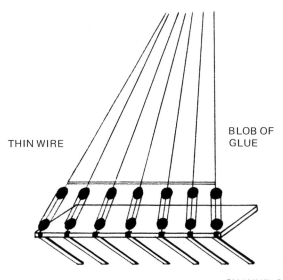

THIN WIRE

BLOB OF GLUE

CHANNELS

bows and stern. After fashioning the stern galleries from shavings and so on, I build up the carving with glue, dabbed on with the smallest brush, and if it is to be gilded, I mix a little gold powder with the glue. If done with due care and not hurried, very good results can be achieved; I use the same method for the figurehead and scroll work on the bows.

DECK FITTINGS

After trying several different ways of making the ship's boats, I found that the best results were obtained by the first method that I tried, namely by carving them out of a strip of holly. Mark the inside first, on a strip a little larger than the beam and the depth of the boat; place it in a vice and carve out the inside using a sharp-pointed modelling knife and a small chisel made from a suitable size needle, ground down and sharpened. Shape the sheer next, and when satisfied with the inside, form the external shape with file and sandpaper, making it as thin on the gunwales as possible. Finally remove it from the strip and mount it on a pin for painting. Once the paint is dry the bottom boards, thwarts, and so on, made from paper and shavings can be fitted.

If the model has channels for the lower shrouds, it is best to cut them to shape in three ply shavings, and carefully cut a slight rebate in the side of the hull with a sharp pointed knife, and glue them in place.

The pin rails are narrow strips of shaving glued to the inside of the bulwarks, with a triangle piece glued underneath for extra strength. The fife rails round the mast vary in shape, some being just straight each side, and some U-shaped. If I am making the latter I cut the shape out of three-ply shaving, drill a hole in the two ends and two corners and drill corresponding holes in the deck, then I glue short pieces of wire in the holes in the fife rail, and into the deck. If there are no coils of rope to go on any of the rails, then I simply drill holes and glue short pieces of wire in each to represent the belaying pins.

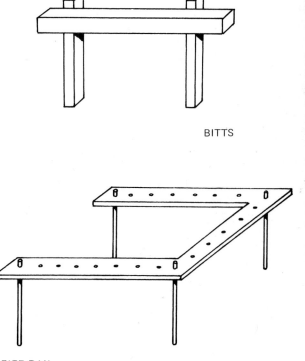

BITTS

FIFE RAIL

Coils of rope on the pinrails enhance the look of a model, and they are not hard to fit. Take a length of the thinnest wire and wind it round a needle of the right size, then slip off the spring-like length, cut off three coils at a time, flatten these with a rule and squeeze them together with tweezers, and bend up one end and glue this to the pinrail. When all are fixed in place, paint them to the colour of the rigging.

I think one of the most intricate jobs is making the steering wheel. First make a wire ring using a needle of the right diameter. Press this ring flat, and glue a length of very fine wire across it, then build up the other spokes from the centre. When dry press flat with a rule and trim off the ends of the spokes to the right length, and paint it. Keep the amount of glue used to the very minimum.

Ladders are another of those awkward jobs, but if made in the right sequence they turn out quite well. First cut enough strips of shavings to complete all the ladders to be fitted. These strips should be 1/50″ wide and long enough to fit between the two decks, with the top and bottom ends cut on a slant. Lightly glue half the number on edge, on a piece of tissue. Now cut another strip, with the grain running across it and as wide as the treads are long, and cut off pieces across the strip equal to the width of the ladder side pieces. With a pair of fine tweezers pick these up one at a time, put a touch of glue on one end and lay them in place against the side pieces, spacing them about the equivalent of 10″ apart. When all these treads are in place on all ladders, glue the other side pieces in place against the other ends of the treads. When dry give them a coat of matt varnish; the varnish makes the tissue transparent and thus almost invisible when the ladders are glued into place.

There are dozens of ring and eye-bolts on a ship, which I fashion by twisting very fine wire round a small needle to obtain the ring, leaving a short length attached to it which is glued into a hole drilled in the deck.

The gratings present a bit of a problem at this scale. By drawing fine horizontal and vertical lines as close together as possible on a piece of paper, cutting out a 'grating' of the correct size, and adding a coaming of painted paper or shaving round the edge, obtains good results. I have used a coarse screen from a printed photograph, found by hunting through a magazine or paper, which looks good also, if one can find the right sort of picture!

The deckhouses are built up from a solid piece of holly, cut to the right shape, mounted on a pin and painted in the correct colour. When the paint has dried I add the doors and windows, all cut from pre-painted paper. The windows are drawn with a draughting pen with the finest nib, cut out and glued on; if it has port holes, they are small wire rings glued

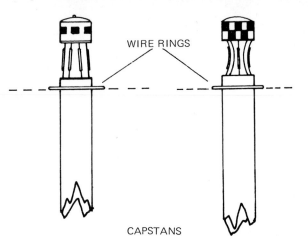

WIRE RINGS

CAPSTANS

on. If there is any beading round the edge or on the roof, I find it best to build this up with different widths of very narrow strips of paper or shavings, or both; it depends upon the type of beading. When I am satisfied that it is as near to the original as it is possible to get I remove it from the pin and glue it into position on deck. Most have a weather board round the base, and I find it is better to add this when the house is fixed in position, making it from a strip of painted paper.

Capstans are very easily made from short lengths of holly filed and sandpapered round, then shaped with a round needle file and painted. I find it neater to paint a very narrow strip of paper to represent the holes for the capstan bars and glue that round the top, but using two strips for those which have two rows of holes. Once I have completed all the work on the capstan, then I cut it from the strip with a razor blade and glue into position. Whenever I have to glue items to a deck which has been painted, I scrape all the paint off first, and if possible put a small pin or dowel underneath the item to be glued, and into the deck.

From time to time, and when all the deck fittings are in place, I hold the hull or rather the baseboard and give it several sharp taps on the table; if anything comes off I re-glue it firmly. It is better to find out at this stage if anything is likely to come adrift rather than when all the rigging is on, when it is very nearly impossible to get at it.

If the model is to be a man-of-war, there will naturally be quite a few guns to make. It is worth taking some care with these, as well made guns enhance the appearance of the deck layout. Do not just make them from a piece of wire stuck on a roughly shaped carriage. In fact, guns can be made quite easily, but if there are, say, 18 to go on the deck make all 18 at once. First take a piece of wire just a little thicker than the finished barrel, put a short piece in a pin vice and file it to a taper, with a slight flair at the muzzle, using needle files, then cut it off with a

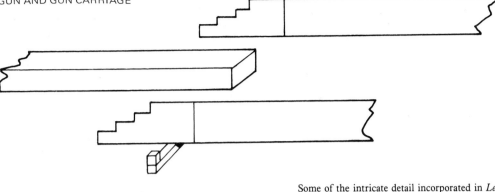

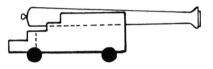

Some of the intricate detail incorporated in *Le Protecteur*. Note the hammocks stowed in the nettings, the triced up gun port lids, the neatness of the rigging. Not many miniatures can 'survive' close-up photography of this nature.

sharp knife to the correct length, and round off the end. Finish the number required, and store them away for the time being. Next are the carriages. First cut a strip of shaving or wood to nearly the correct width and height to the underside of the barrel to form the bottom of the carriage; put that to one side, and cut from another strip of shaving or paper shaped pieces to form the two sides of the carriage, bearing in mind the right length. After producing the required number, take the first strip, glue two of the side pieces to it at the free end, and glue another two strips of very thin wood or wire underneath, a fraction wider than the carriage, to represent the trunnions, and glue the barrel in between the two sides. Finally fix a small wire ring round the muzzle of the barrel, and a small flower seed on to the other end. Lobelia seeds are quite good but a hunt through your seed packets if you are a gardener will produce some to the right scale. Once the glue has dried I paint the whole assembly in the correct colours, cut if off the strip, and glue it into position. When all the guns are in place, I add the gun tackles, which are short pieces of painted wire. Of course the guns which are shown projecting through the lower gun ports are a lot easier to do, as only the barrels have to be made and glued in. The gun port lids are cut from shavings or paper, and the hinges of very thin strips of pre-painted paper.

To include hammock netting to scale is very near impossible. The nearest suitable material which I have found so far is a piece of a silk stocking dyed black; it is not easy to fix in place, for once cut to the correct height and length it tends to come apart. However, I find that if I glue thin strips of wire along the top and some for the upright pieces before I cut it to size and glue into position it is quite strong. I represent the hammocks with a thin strip of white card with small nicks along the top; glued in between the netting makes this even stronger, and it looks quite good. The netting round the bows of course is only single and is a little bigger which makes it easier to fix.

FIGURES

On some models the inclusion of figures adds to the realism and gives that little extra atmosphere to the setting. Their presence also gives a good indication of the size of the ship. Such figures are not very hard to make, but scale must be adhered to. Having built them by several different ways, I found my last method to be the easiest. Place a short length of 40 SWG wire in a pin vice, measure the length from the nose to the top of the thigh on a human body, bend

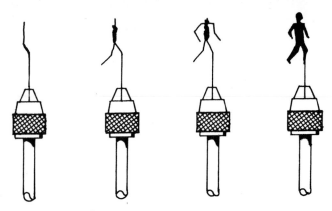

MAKING FIGURES

the wire at that point, then bend the leg to whatever angle is wanted. Cut another short length, bend it for the other leg and glue that half way up the body. Bend a further length for the arms, this time in 43 SWG wire, and glue into place. Build up the head with a blob of glue, then similarly build up the rest of the body, and the arms and legs. Paint the figure in appropriate colours and cut off, leaving one leg longer than the other — this is glued into a hole in the deck. It is best to make about six at a time, glueing each item in turn on each figure, so that by the time the sixth has been reached the first is dry. With a bit of practice, and varying the shape of the arms and legs, very lifelike figures can be made.

MASTING AND RIGGING

I find rigging a model is one of the most enjoyable aspects of ship modelling, for at last it is really taking shape and beginning to look like the real thing. Starting with the mast and spars, I find it is best to shape them all first, and start by carefully measuring all the lengths and copying them down on to a piece

Opposite. A much enlarged view of *Le Protecteur's* main and mizzen masts and associated rigging; note the reef points on the topsail.

Right. *France II* under construction. It is essential on models of this type to work out beforehand a sequence of rigging if damage and frustration are to be avoided. Here basically the method is from forward to aft and from inboard outwards. Note how much of the standing has to be completed before the yards and sails are fitted.

Below. *Le Protecteur's* bowsprit and foremast. Among the many outstanding features of the author's miniature models is the careful selection of the appropriate sizes of rope for his rigging. Even at 1/600 scale this is important, and is yet a further instance of the necessity of paying attention to such matters in order to obtain an authentic appearance in the completed model.

of card to the correct scale. To my mind the best material to use is holly strips, held in a pin vice. If several grooves of different depths are made in a flat piece of wood, the strip can be laid in these, starting from the deepest and filing while twisting the pin vice, then finishing off with sandpaper. Thin doweling or even cocktail sticks can be used, but these have a tendency to split when very finely tapered.

When all the masts and spars are fully shaped, I glue the lower masts to the topmasts and add the topgallants, then fit all the tops, made from shavings, and resting on the cheeks, trestle and crosstrees, also made from thin strips of shaving glued on. The wooldings, if any, on the lower masts I make out of narrow strips of pre-painted paper glued round and trimmed off. I twist a short length of fine wire round the mast in the position where each yard is to be fitted, and cut off the ends, leaving about 1/16" to which I attach the yard later.

Complete each mast as much as possible before stepping into the model, that is, put all the shrouds on the topmast and topgallant while holding the mast in a pin vice, then the halyards etc. The easiest and neatest way of making the shrouds and ratlines is to glue the shrouds, cut from wire of correct diameter, in position then cut ratlines from the finest wire, and glue them across the shrouds, giving the completed assembly a coat of black matt polish. Step the masts and complete the lower shrouds, the same as the topmast shrouds, put a blob of glue to represent the deadeyes in the correct positions and when dry add short pieces of wire glued on each side for the lanyards. Then fit all the halyards, of painted wire, from the mast top to pinrails, and complete the standing rigging with the backstays, and so on.

I put most of the fittings on the yards, such as footropes, before fixing them to the masts. First I hold the yard in a pin vice by twisting a loop of wire in the centre, with a touch of glue to hold it in place, then fix the thinnest wire for the footropes from the

centre. I glue the stirrups on and, working alternately from each side, glue the footropes to the stirrups bending it carefully to shape so that it looks as if it is hanging loose in between, and finally cut and glue to the ends of the yard arm.

A great deal of thought should go into the sequence of rigging all the running gear, especially between the main and mizzen; it is best to complete the foremast first, leaving off the fore course braces until last, then, working alternately between the main and mizzen: work upwards, otherwise you will find it very awkward to get some braces on, as others will be in the way. Once again it is essential to keep all glue to a minimum with a spot of paint and matt varnish on the point of contact.

SAILS

I find tissue paper is the best material for the sails. First draw a series of very thin lines just over 1/50" apart, using a hard pencil sharpened to a chisel point, to represent the cloths, on a sheet large enough to

Below. HMS *Victory* under full sail. This was an early model, and at that time the author had not developed the techniques which now enable him to produce more realistic sails. These, he points out, are too stiff and lack the correct shape.

Bottom. The Dutch, formerly British, 18 gun brig of war *Irene*. Seen here heeling over in a stiff breeze, these sails are an improvement and have a somewhat more realistic appearance.

Opposite top. A totally different kind of setting for a scenic model — the *Herzogin Cecilie* as she was after running aground in Salcombe Bay in 1936. A sad, yet interesting scene, but one which is rarely tackled by modelmakers. A nice little touch is the inclusion of a couple of small yachts 'having a look'.

Opposite bottom. *Royal Katherine,* a Second Rate of 1664. A truly superb example of the miniaturist's art, which richly deserved the award of the Championship Cup for Miniatures at the 1976 Model Engineer Exhibition in London.

(Photo: John Bowen. All uncredited photos by Derek Hunnisett)

complete all the sails. Soak it in a solution of very weak, brown coloured water to remove the whiteness. It is well nigh impossible to get the right shape into the sails, but the most successful method I have managed so far is to cut out the sail slightly deeper than is wanted, dip it in water then put it on a wooden former, (experiment with different curved shapes first) put a handkerchief over it, twist this tight and dry over heat. When dry, and while it is still on the former, spray it with hair lacquer. It will come away with a slight belly to it, which improves the look immensely. Trim the sail straight along the top and glue to the yard.

When the sail is fixed to the yard, hold it in a pin vice by the piece of wire in the centre, take three or four filaments of cotton, run them through the fingers and thumb which have been dipped in watered down glue, to hold them together; when dry, cut off pieces and glue to the top and bottom of the sail to represent the leach lines and clew lines. Then cut smaller pieces for the reef points: if cut on a piece of white card they can be seen easily. With the sail laid down in front of you, pick up a reef point with tweezers, touch one end to a brush loaded with glue, and place it in position on the sail; complete all one side of the sail, then the other. It sounds a bit tedious but it is surprising how quickly it can be done with a bit of practice. Complete the rest of the details on the yard — blocks represented by flower seeds, grommets of wire rings, and jackstay a thin length of painted wire glued to the mast. Then finish the rest of the rigging, lifts, clew lines and so on.

CONCLUSIONS

Summing up, in general there is no golden rule or essential quality needed for the successful creation of these miniature ships, in contrast to the larger models; some people have said to me 'what a lot of patience you must have', but that is not true at all. If you want to make something and you are really interested in the subject, patience does not come into it. Having said that, the only other advice is check everything and double check, especially at the start, when scaling down the lines, and shaping the hull. Every now and then during the construction have a long look at it, and if there is any doubt in your mind about any item, or one which you think you could improve, scrap it and make it again; it pays in the end.

Presentation of a model is all important, and much must depend upon, or relate to, the type of vessel being modelled. This 1/75 scale model of the French galley *La Reale,* by the author, is shown complete in every detail. The oars were an essential part of these craft so they are shown in position; thus it follows that the furled sails must be included, and so too must that other prominent feature of these early vessels, the flags and pennants. They put to sea with all these flying, and it is unthinkable that they should be omitted from the model. Painting, painted decorative work and some carving were part and parcel of their finish, and so these must be effected with care and with consideration of their appearance. Gloss paints as we know them today were unknown in those days, so such finishes must be avoided — except possibly on the gilded work. Flags and banners are tricky items to produce realistically, and much care and attention must be given to the way they are made — and finished — if they are not to spoil a model.
(Photo: Science Museum, by courtesy of the author)

144

Painting and finishing

by P HERIZ-SMITH

The chapter devoted to 'finish' does not bring the book to a conclusion: but it does complete a circle, for the end is implicit in the beginning. In the world of model ships, it does not mean slapping a coat of varnish or paint on a structurally complete job. It is the logical development of the original intention, and this intention must not be lost sight of at any stage during construction of the model.

ATMOSPHERE

I suppose that every modeller seeks a balance between (to adopt the terminology of ice skating competitions) artistic impression and technical merit. At one end of the scale is the dockyard type of model, with its cool perfection of exact craftsmanship; at the other is the scenic or waterline model which seeks to portray the ship as she might actually have appeared in prototype.

Thus it is possible for two models of the same ship, each absolutely accurate, to appear to be quite different because of a difference in intention and aim. Let us imagine a model of a small schooner, correctly framed and with a number of hull strakes omitted to show the construction. It is built of boxwood and pear to the highest standards of accuracy and impeccable craftsmanship, is left 'in the white' and is formally mounted on turned pillars. Then imagine another version, also built correctly on frames, also with a number of strakes omitted. This time, however, the model is mounted scenically on the stocks amid the confusion, the scaffolding and the litter of the builder's yard. The work and skill involved will be very similar in both models, but they will not be interchangeable. The difference in intention will have affected the end products in some subtle way which defies definition. Yet, if an otherwise excellent model has the wrong 'feel' about it, it may well be that the builder started out without any very clear picture in his mind of what he was aiming to achieve, or else he changed his mind during the course of construction.

I do not take sides: either type of model is equally enchanting to the eye and equally fascinating to build.

However, I often feel that craftsmen who produce excellent models are more concerned with producing a ship model rather than a miniature ship — a distinction usefully made by Donald McNarry.

In the Science Museum there is an excellent model of a Lamu Dhow. It was built by an Arab craftsman living at Lamu, and examples of his craftsmanship are in the possession of a number of old East African hands. They cannot be faulted for accuracy of detail and construction, and they are a valuable record of a type of vessel which may well disappear from the Indian Ocean. They are, like the prototypes, graceful and ornamental; but they are idealized and are entirely lacking in atmosphere.

The craftsmanship in the Lamu Dhow is comparatively crude. Frames are rough hewn, so are the beams. Masts are generally crudely finished and the long lateen yards seldom pretend to disguise their mangrove pole origins. Sails are patched and irregular, paintwork is crude. The half decks are cluttered and dirty, and the stench from the bilges unattractive, to say the least. None of this is hinted at in the model, which makes it a failure to anyone who has experience of the prototype. Yet it is a fine model within its own convention, and I envy a friend of mine who possesses a good example.

When it comes to modelling historical vessels, there is obviously no opportunity of making a comparison of this nature, so imagination has to replace personal experience. The danger of idealization or of simply making models of other models is obvious.

None of this should be read as a justification for botched, careless or second-rate work. It is merely a plea to the modelmaker to remember that he is building a miniature of a real ship. It is this continual awareness of the prototype which helps to impart to a model that elusive whiff of the sea.

If this sounds unhelpfully vague, I can only apologise. Atmosphere is easy to recognise but impossible to define, so let us turn to some more practical considerations.

G

HULLS AND PLANKING

I am a great believer in planking hulls and decks, whether or not the hull is solid or built on frames, and even if the hull is subsequently to be painted. The labour of filling and rubbing down bare timber until all shadow of grain is lost is excessive and, to my mind, dangerous in the long term, for paint is apt to become more transparent with age, and wood may prove to be unstable under different atmospheric conditions. On the other hand, a veneer of planking is bound to look right whatever happens. Similarly with decks. Lining with Indian Ink or even scribing just will not do. The device is screamingly obvious. Decks must be laid properly — three or four step butt — trennelled and joggled into the margin planks where necessary.

Opposite. A totally different method of presentation — the scenic model — and one which has considerable scope for interesting interpretations by the modelmaker. Here the author of this chapter has chosen to depict a typical sixteenth century shipyard, set on the banks of a river or estuary. The ship on the stocks is nearing the launching stage and this model, only a few inches long at its $\frac{1}{16}''$ scale, is planked. Note how the atmosphere of the scene is caught by the figures of the shipwrights at work, the rough baulks forming the keel blocks, the shores supporting the hull, the supports for the staging along the side, the rough and ready access gangway, and the short ladder from the staging amidships.

Below. Another way to show a model, on a simple stand mounted on a block to raise the model from the base which takes the glass of the case. The $\frac{1}{16}''$ scale model of the author's mediaeval English ship is only a few inches long, but the hull has been planked.

Left. Three views of a miniature schooner, again to $\frac{1}{16}''$ scale. To show off the hull lines the builder has set the model well clear of the baseboard by using two slender pillars to support the hull, so that the keel and rise of floor can be seen. This hull is planked, but on deck it has been constructed on the Navy Board principle referred to previously, thus allowing the deck beams and so on to be seen.

Opposite. Yet another presentation — the diorama. This is part of Harold Hahn's superb $\frac{1}{8}''$ scale diorama of a colonial shipyard of about 1765. The backdrop is painted, but the three similar vessels in the foreground are all full hull models set into the 'sea'. These three ships have all been launched from the fully detailed shipyard which adjoins the right hand side of this photograph, and they are shown here in various stages of completion. Note the great impact created by the activity going on along the shore and on the jetty.
(Photo: Mariners Museum, Newport News)

A brief word about trennelling. In model work it is tempting to show these fastenings as much darker than the timber they secure. Examination of a real ship will show this to be wrong. Trennels should be just discernable, but not obtrusive. If you stand back from the *Victory* how many can you actually see? How visible are they when you look down one deck from another?

You might conclude that they could be omitted. If you do so, you will save yourself a deal of boring (in both senses) work. But if you decide to include them, it is essential to make sure that they correspond to the frames and beams underneath them — even in a solid unframed model. At a recent exhibition I noticed a model which was trenelled only at the plan station lines — about six scale feet apart. This sort of gaffe must be avoided at all costs, and so must the temptation to make a model more 'decorative' by substituting brass pins for the wooden trennels.

The actual boring does not take an excessive amount of time, especially if you have a miniature electric drill. Insertion of genuine trennels does, and so does the cleaning up of the surface afterwards; but the end result makes it all worthwhile.

If you feel you cannot face this tedious job, I offer a 'cheating' alternative. This is to fill the drilled holes with a suitably coloured Brummer stopper. This means, of course, that you lose the benefit of the trennel as a fastening and will have to rely on glue alone to hold the planks. If you are prepared to risk this — and the use of a good glue will minimize the risk — the difference between a genuine and a false trennel will be imperceptible. You might consider using the genuine article on exposed decks and the false one on lower decks which will not be available for close inspection.

One does not normally have occasion to use plywood in a serious model. Indeed, most authorities reject this material outright, particularly in view of the fact that (unless particular care is given to painting) the edges only too obviously betray their origin.

On the other hand there are rare occasions when no other material will do a job quite as well. The solution in this case is to select a piece of hardwood the colour of which approximately matches that of the ply face, and to take off shavings with a fine-set plane. The curled shavings can be straightened by damping, and then glued, smooth side out, to the edge that needs to be concealed. White glue should be used. When it is quite dry, the whole thing can be sanded flush. The ruse, if the work is carefully done, will be undetectable.

Whatever the finish is to be, the hull and deck must be meticulously cleaned up. This is particularly important where planking is to be stained. There is nothing so infuriating as to run a coat of stain over a hull only to find that some unnoticed glue creates leprous patches. It is safer, of course, to find a wood which does not need staining, but this is not always possible. If planking has to be stained, it is not a bad idea to stain it before fixing it in place. This will prevent unsightly white lines at the glue line between planks.

Coarse sandpaper should not be used on a planked hull for obvious reasons. One should start with a medium fine grade and work down to flour grade. Silicon carbide paper is better than ordinary sandpaper.

Scraping is another useful finishing technique, though the cabinet maker's scraper will be of little use. Fortunately it is easy to improvise one. The first way is to use the edge of freshly broken glass (you are sure to have a few pieces knocking around the workshop, especially if you make your own glass cases.) Cover the glass with newspaper and give it one sharp tap in the middle. It will break into segments, one edge of each being sharp. The cutting edge will blunt fairly quickly and then the segment can be thrown away. A blunt scraper will tear the wood, not plane it.

The second method is to take a blade of the Stanley kind and, using an ordinary domestic knife-sharpening steel, sharpen one edge only. This turns the cutting edge slightly and converts the blade into a useful scaper. If something narrower is required, it is not difficult to snap the blade using a vice and a hammer.

PAINTS AND STAINS

There are a number of reliable wood stains on the market which imitate natural timber colour. Some of them are, however, apt to be a little too 'postive' in colour for small scale work, and they should always be tested on a spare scrap of the same timber that you intend to stain. I have on occasion had recourse to permanganate of potash. This can be diluted to various shades of a pleasant neutral brown which does not obtrude on the eye.

It should be remembered that any stain with a water base will raise the grain of the wood, however carefully smoothed by the methods already referred to. The remedy is slightly to damp the surface of the wood first and rub it down again before the stain is applied.

On unpainted wood, a matt finish is best, or one having a very slight sheen at the most. The 'grand piano' mirror surface should be reserved for the case; it has no place on a model. Varnish should therefore be avoided. Shellac (the basic ingredient of French Polish) well diluted with methylated spirit gives a satisfactory and easily controlled result. It needs two or three applications, each very lightly rubbed down. Again, practice on odd scraps of wood until satisfied that your technique is right. This will protect and mellow the wood, and bring out its natural colour and character. Experiments can also be made with wax polish or Teak Oil.

Burnishing to a final sheen can be done with the handle of an old toothbrush, the back of an old bit of sandpaper or a finger nail — which gives great control in awkward corners.

Wood fillers are not really necessary if a close-grained wood has been used, but the following are suitable:

'Sanding Filler' which is intended primarily for balsa, but which is perfectly suitable for other timbers; Brummer Filler which can be bought to match the wood and which, although a bit messy to use and clean up, gives a perfect finish.

If a painted surface is required, there must be no relaxation in the preparation of the surface. Contrary to what some people think, paint never disguises blemishes — it accentuates them.

In the case of period ship models, there is not normally much painting of large areas to be done; but this does not mean that care need not be exercised, for one still sees models of excellent craftsmanship which are spoilt by indifferent paintwork.

The obvious choice of paint is the Humbrol range which is specially designed for modellers. It is put up in small tins and does not cost much. The paints can be bought in gloss or matt finish. The latter are preferable, for it is easier to burnish a matt surface to a slight sheen than to reduce a gloss one using, say, pumice powder on a damp cloth. I have found these colours to be quite reliable and easy to use.

Artists' Oil Colours can be used. Admittedly, they do not flow on easily, they take a long time to dry really hard, and take patience to rub down to a fine finish. There is no doubt, however, about their permanence, and they have the advantage of being easily mixed to an exact shade. If you are using oil-based paint, white is a tricky colour, for it has comparatively little covering power, and there is a danger of building up an out-of-scale and crude looking layer in an attempt to achieve opacity. It is best first to apply a couple of coats of white undercoat — ordinary decorator's quality — thinned and rubbed down. The final thin coat of matt white will then behave well. Rubbing down should be done with wet-or-dry paper, used wet, the model being meticulously dusted off before each new coat is applied.

When slow-drying paint is being used, dust is your major enemy. It is surprising to anybody but a

housewife how much dust there is in suspension in the cleanest house. I suppose that ideally painting should be done in a sterile operating theatre, but ideals are not easy to realise. The best we can do is to choose a room which is unlikely to be used for a few hours, and to threaten any member of the family who comes near it with sudden death or worse. If you have an unoccupied glass case, this could possibly be used.

A comparative newcomer to the artistic scene is the Acrylic Polymer paint. This, being designed for artists, is made from the finest ingredients, and the colours are permanent. It is, until it dries, water-soluble, but it dries waterproof. It can be thinned with a Matt Medium and dries quickly so several coats can be applied in quite a short time. As with any other paint, several thin coats are better than one thick one, and the final coat can be burnished to a pleasant sheen. It is not particularly cheap, but a 40 cc tube will last a very long time.

Poster Colour (or in its more refined form, Designers' Gouache) has good covering power, but it

is not waterproof. It is valuable for the painting of flags and heraldic shields: so is Artists' Water Colour. However, I feel that the Acrylic range will do everything that these colours can achieve, with the added virtue of being waterproof. It is worth experimenting with this material.

Just as important as the paint — indeed, more important — is the quality of the brushes used to apply it. A cheap brush is hopeless. It probably has no shape to start with, and even if it has it soon loses it and ends up looking like a miniature lavatory brush. Furthermore, it will probably moult.

What you need are artists' best water colour brushes, sables if you can afford them. You will need one or two flat 'one stroke' brushes for covering large areas and painting accurately up to a line, and ordinary pointed ones for detail work and getting into awkward corners. You will need at least one really small one, 00 size, and miniaturists will also need an 000 size, if one can be found.

Below and opposite. Contrasts in the presentation of full hull models. The Dutch yacht, a $\frac{1}{16}''$ scale model, is part of a scenic model. By depicting a scene where the tide is out, the builder has been able to include a full hull model by showing it sitting quietly on a mud berth. Taking advantage of the fact that the vessel would naturally list over on to one bilge in such a situation, the full underwater body is revealed. The anchor is realistically embedded in the mud, with the cable lying in a slack bight. In this case the inclusion of sails is essential to the scene, as the ship is obviously in commission. The Roman Ship, on the other hand, is mounted on a simple conventional cradle on a block on a baseboard, and the hull and deck details are visible. There is little decorative work on this ship, and much of what there is is in fact part of the structure. Sails have been included in this static model, but they might equally well have been omitted.

Even Students' quality brushes are not cheap, so brushes are worth looking after. They must be meticulously cleaned before whatever paint is being used even *starts* to dry, and particular attention must be paid to the roots of the hairs where they are held by the ferrule. If an oil-based paint is being used, the brush should be squeezed out with a rag to rid it of as much paint as possible, and then be washed out several times in paraffin until every visible trace of paint has disappeared. Finally, the brush should be washed out in soap and water, the soap being worked well into the brush with the palm of the hand. You will be surprised to find even more paint emerging. The hairs should be moulded back into their proper shape — tongue and lips are the most effective instruments here.

There is one other way of applying paint, and that is by Airbrush. These instruments are capable not

only of depositing a very fine mist of colour — useful for covering large areas, but also can be adjusted to give an incredibly fine line.

When it comes to selecting a paint, it is a safe rule to choose a shade which is slightly less positive than that which would appear on the full-scale prototype. There is a scale to colour effect which must be observed. There is a fine model of the *Victory* at Portsmouth which to my mind is marred by excessively bright and raw yellow on the upperworks. For all I know, this may be historically more correct than the yellow ochre that is used on the *Victory* herself. But even so, something more muted would have been better *to scale*.

Painting should be carefully thought out and planned in advance. Indeed, every component should, if practicable, be finished before it goes into the model. Much of a model becomes inaccessible as work progresses. To take an obvious example, if you are working to a large scale and wish the decoration of the stern cabins to be visible through the after windows, the painting must be executed at a relatively early stage. In fact, it should be accepted as a general principle that you should not be in too great a hurry to instal any item permanently.

In this connection, I have had the privilege of being allowed from time to time to watch the progress of the definitive model of the *Wasa* being built for the Science Museum by Mr C J H King. At quite a late stage in the construction, the hull, fully framed and planked, appeared to be an empty shell; but a 10 foot glass fronted case contained every single beam, carling, grating, stanchion, and so on, each cut to an exact fit, carefullly identified and perfectly finished. Everything can be slipped into place and removed again as required at the time.

To illustrate what I mean by advance planning, let us take a practical problem. Some bulwarks are open with stanchions exposed, and the stanchions are painted a different colour from that of the hull planking. This entails some very precise painting work where the two colours meet. If, however, the plank from which the stanchions are to be cut is painted on both sides, the problem is at least partially solved. The sides of the timbers will be cleanly finished — and it is these faces which are most difficult to paint accurately when the timbers are in place. Painting the planking up to the stanchions is comparatively easy.

Black wales often feature prominently on period ships. Their edges obviously cannot be painted after fitting, so they need to be stained before fixing. Black Indian ink does the job well, and so does black leather stain, obtainable from leather specialists. One word of caution. Some glues act as solvents to some paints or stains and a horrid mess can ensue. The answer is, as usual, to test beforehand on scrap wood.

WATERLINES

Cutting in a waterline is a task which drives many modellers, myself included, mad. The theory is fine. You rest your hull the right way up or, more effectively, upside down in such a position that the designed waterline is parallel to the table. You then fasten a sharp, hard pencil to a block of wood thick enough to raise the pencil point to waterline level. Making sure that the hull is steady and upright, the pencil is run round the hull and an accurate waterline is the result. Easy. The only snag is the line crosses so many subtle planes that when you come to examine it, it is apt to look wrong and although you know for a fact that there is no error you begin to doubt the evidence before your eyes.

All that remains now is to paint up to, but not over this line. The experts will tell you to use adhesive tape or masking tape and then to paint away light heartedly up to and even over the tape; peel it away and a faultless waterline is the result if you can persuade a tape which is flexible in two dimensions to lie flat on a surface which curves hither and thither in three; if the paint does not creep under the tape; if the paint does not form a ridge a couple of scale inches thick where the edge of the tape has been.

It is *not* as easy as the experts make it sound. To mask a waterline you need a very narrow strip of masking tape, which can be persuaded to take a straight line across multiple curves. But just you try to cut a thin strip off a roll of Sellotape and see where it gets you. Better to cut off a strip from the paper backed type of adhesive plastic, colour it with a felt-tip if it is transparent so that you can see what you are doing, strip the backing and then apply it. A sound

alternative is to cut a thin strip of ordinary gum-strip, which will take the curves even more easily and can be washed off when the paint is dry.

Of course, if you can rely on a steady hand, you can simply paint freehand up to the line. In the event of any irregularity, all is not lost. A scalpel used carefully will remove unwanted paint, an artist's fine brush will touch up gaps. I have read of modellers who change from a dark to a light coloured wood at the waterline, a very precise and difficult operation that would offer plenty of scope for disaster to the unskilled.

GINGERBREAD WORK

Gingerbread work is the generic name given to the elaborate gilded carvings which appear, often in great profusion, in seventeenth century ships. This can be very daunting, and can well persuade a modeller to avoid this period altogether.

Of course, if you are a skilled woodcarver already, you have nothing to worry about, although you will probably have to make your own miniature carving tools from old hacksaw blades, or needles, for the normal woodcarving chisels and gouges are too clumsy for the job. Much can be done with a scalpel, and with the wide range of blades to be had for modelling knives. Some people like to use dental burrs in a miniature drill, though their use demands a rather different form of skill.

It is essential that only a close-grained hardwood be used in this work. Small pieces of pear and cherry are easily come by, especially if you live in the country, and so is holly. One should never lose an opportunity to collect bits of these timbers. They can be kept to season until needed. Even if you have never tried carving before, it is worth experimenting. You might surprise yourself. Certainly in a pure dockyard type of model, there is something greatly satisfying in a skilled miniature carving, left ungilded. If, however,

French Xebec
'Le Singe'

Above and right. Three views of the French xebec *Le Singe* of 1714. There can be no doubt that these Mediterranean vessels make interesting and attractive models. In this model the wood used for the planking of the hull and decks has been left in its natural colour, painting and staining being confined largely to the decorated areas of the hull, the fittings, and the masts and spars.

as is more common, the carving is to be gilded, you can be much freer in your approach and use of materials. In fact, it can be said that, provided the end product looks right, anything goes. Wood, paper, wire, modelling paste or any other material that ingenuity suggests for the job in hand, can be blended together with a unifying coat of red or orange paint before gilding.

For larger figures, carving is still the best method, but a figure can be jointed and built up puppetwise, which incidentally makes for a stronger job, and details can then be modelled on to the basic figure. I have even used cloth to indicate free flying drapery, which would have been difficult to carve and rather fragile. I used tracing linen, which I dampened, teased into the required folds and allowed to set dry again. I then painted it with several layers of glue, which both stiffened and thickened it. I was left, not with wood trying to imitate drapery, but with cloth trying to imitate wood!

Smaller figures can be built up with a modelling paste over a wire skeleton, the paste being made from powder colour and glue or plaster filler and glue, and applied with a brush. If you wish to experiment with this technique, which is basically a miniaturist's one, try various glues and powders until you find one that suits you. Small relief figures can be cut in silhouette from thin Bristol Board to establish their main shape, and then contoured with successive layers of the paste mix. Formal decorations such as the typical 'war trophy' plaque of spears, shields and banners can be be built up from scraps of wire, paper and card on a thin paper base, and then unified with a coat of clear dope before painting and cutting out. Small seeds can be used to form garlands. Miniature mouldings can be suggested by glueing oversize strips of Bristol Board together with a stepped edge, which is then parted off with a sharp knife or razor blade.

These are merely a few hints to indicate what can be done, and done very effectively, by the use of a little imagination and ingenuity. It may offend the purist; it may, indeed, offend you when you achieve more skill — but it works.

The ideal way of gilding a carving is by the use of gold leaf applied over gold size using a soft brush. Most modellers will, however, from considerations of expense if nothing else, opt for gold paint. In this

156

French Xebec
le Singe
1764

Another view of the xebec which demonstrates the effect on detail achieved by this treatment of the model.

case, only the best should be bought, and there is little doubt that Liquid Leaf is the most reliable. Cheaper makes are coarse in effect and tarnish quickly.

A NOTE OF FLAGS

The general subject of flags has been dealt with in Chapter 8, but since I am here preoccupied with atmosphere, I must record my personal dislike of flags and banners which stick out flat as though made of tin. It is, I know, tempting to leave a beautifully detailed and emblazoned flag flat so that its full beauty can be seen; and it takes a masochistic sort of courage to crumple it up and tease it into natural hanging folds. However, if you wish the flags in your static glass case model to defy every law of gravity, that is your privilege and you will find plenty of examples in museums to quote as precedents.

One thing cannot be justified in any circumstances, and that is the two-dimensional cut-out painting of a fluttering flag. Ugh!

FIRST AID

Perhaps I should end this chapter with a few hints on how to deal with minor errors which inevitably creep into your work. When you look at a model built by an expert, the mind is apt to boggle, and the standard of superlative craftsmanship fills you with despair. Thoughts of taking up knitting instead of ship modelling run through your head. It should never be forgotten, however, that these experts were once beginners themselves, and that they probably have a few early skeletons hidden away in the cupboards of their memories. Even in their best work, it is safe to assume that everything did not go smoothly all the time. *Ars est celare artem.*

You should be guided by the principle that not a single item should be admitted to the model, however insignificant, until you are satisfied that you cannot improve on it. This counsel of perfection sounds tough, for it may demand that a single component may have to be remade half a dozen times. However, the building of a ship model entails many thousands of small individual operations, and each one should be treated as an important and worthwhile end in itself. This will lead to better craftsmanship.

However ruthless you may be in discarding the imperfect, self-discipline can relax and some small part will be accepted on the 'to hell with it, it will have to do' basis. Maybe the error will be minor and near to invisible: nobody may ever spot it — but you know it is there, and it will for ever after make you feel uncomfortable, like the Princess with a pea under her mattresses. So work which falls below the standard of which you are capable must be rejected. And that means that you must be prepared to scrap an entire partly completed model and to start again. Set your sights high and good work will follow.

However, we are all human. Major mistakes are easily spotted and can be corrected in time; but what of the hairline cracks where mating surfaces have become divorced, the slight gaps where no gaps should be between adjacent planks, the deck house or deck machinery which just fails to meet flush with the deck at some minor point? Should you turn a blind eye to it, or is cosmetic surgery in order? This must be a matter of judgement. It can happen, especially with unpainted wood surfaces, that a hairline gap will be much less noticeable than a clumsily filled one. Perhaps the fault is in such a position that a coil of rope could naturally conceal it.

With a painted surface, however, any imperfection must be filled for, as stated earlier, paint does not hide faults — it accentuates them. In fact it can happen that you yourself do not realise the fault is there until a coat of paint shows it up. If some form of filling is necessary, do not rush out and buy a tin of plastic wood. It is fine for large jobs, but is intractable stuff to use on a small scale, for it shrinks on drying. The traditional cabinet maker's solution is a mixture of glue and sawdust from the wood being treated. Better still, and easier to use and finish, is Brummer Stopping. This can be smoothed in with a palette knife, and does not shrink. This stopping can be obtained in various wood shades, and it is important always to select one that is slightly darker than the timber being treated. If it is lighter, it will shine out like a searchlight.

To suggest that Plasticene can be used may sound like heresy. However, it has its uses and a few coloured sticks from a child's modelling set can come in very handy. It can be mixed by kneading to whatever shade is required, and will take paint well. It has good adhesive qualities, is clean to handle, does not shrink or crack, and appears to have indefinite life. It is, of course, softened by heat, but shows no sign of movement under any normal variation of temperature; besides which, one is using it to fill cracks, not for any structural purposes. It is particularly useful to stop a gap between a painted and unpainted surface, because it can be smoothed into place perfectly with a palette knife, and will not stain the unpainted wood. If a matched colour has been used, it will not even need to be painted.

Finally, I will counsel the modeller to guard against haste. There are thousands of things that can go wrong even in the simplest model, but if you are always aware of the possibility, accept it as a fact of life and continually guard against it, you are unlikely to go seriously astray. Every operation should be regarded as an end in itself, and there should be genuine satisfaction in the production of even an insignificant ring bolt or block.

Monotony inevitably attaches to repetitious tasks, and boredom can engender carelessness. The tedium can beneficially be broken by turning your hand to a totally different type of job. Some people like counting up the number of hours spent in the construction of a model — possibly because it is one of the irrelevent queries made by admiring non-modellers. This seems to me to be a completely futile, if harmless, statistical exercise. A model ship takes as long to build as is necessary to the task — no more and no less. If it is to be worthwhile, it will take a long time, perhaps a couple of years of spare time work. But it is the result that counts, not the time taken to achieve it. Similarly, it is dangerous to set oneself a deadline. A determination to exhibit a model in a certain year can very easily lead to skimped work.

Friends will express envy or admiration of your patience; but modelmaking, treated as a hobby, is essentially a timeless business. It is an art, a craft, an intellectual exercise, a refuge from the world: it can be repetitious and boring and can lead to moments of breath-stopping anxiety: exhilaration can be followed by exasperation and depression. Always it is an adventure and a challenge, an exploration of new techniques to deal with new problems which you have deliberately set yourself. Always aim for perfection; invariably you will be disappointed. But there is unrivalled pleasure simply in the act of sincere creation.

If the completed ship is praised by knowledgeable friends or favourably noticed at an exhibition, that is a pleasant bonus. Basically, however, it is you yourself who are the final critic.

Getting the flags correct 8

by ALEC A PURVES

There is no doubt that a few carefully selected flags, well made and correctly hoisted, make an attractive and colourful addition to most ship models. Equally there is no doubt that a distressing proportion of ship modellers, who go to considerable trouble to get their hull, deck details, and rigging correct, spoil their models by hopelessly incorrect or badly made flags.

To those who know something about flags, it is always pleasing to see them correct, both in design and usage, and perhaps this chapter will assist the not-so-experienced ship modeller in the right direction.

EARLY FLAGS

For all practical purposes we can consider the late middle ages as the earliest period in which flags of consistent and meaningful design were in use. True, there were some earlier ones, but most of these were either ephemeral or of indeterminate design. The equivalent of the modern ensign, to denote nationality, was limited to a masthead flag of the personal arms of the king (or other head of state), flown by warships or by merchant ships sailing under royal patronage. The remaining flags were almost entirely decorative streamers and pendants, sometimes bearing heraldic devices, or banners frequently of a religious nature, depicting saints or christian emblems. We are mainly dependent on artists' representations for these, but care must be taken in copying them, to be sure that the artist is regarded as accurate in his work on hulls, rigging, etc, since many of the flags shown are often merely fanciful creations, while others are only approximately correct in such matters as heraldic detail. A noticeable example of this is seen in the many pictures, both by ancient and modern artists, where the first quarter of the Tudor arms is shown as blue with three *white* fleurs-de-lis instead of yellow, while others show the English lions in the first and fourth quarters, whereas the French fleurs-de-lis should occupy these positions.

FLAG TERMINOLOGY

Perhaps at this stage we ought to note the various terms used in describing flags. The part of the flag nearest the mast is known as the 'hoist', and this term is also used to describe the width of the flag, ie the length alongside the mast. The far end, away from the mast, is called the 'fly', and similarly the word can be used to describe the length. Thus we could say that a flag, 6′ x 3′ is 6′ in the fly, with a 3′ hoist. When a flag is divided into quarters, they are numbered; 1st, upper hoist; 2nd, upper fly; 3rd, lower hoist; 4th, lower fly. The first quarter is usually referred to as the *canton*, although strictly speaking, in heraldry, a canton is a small rectangle in the same position, but appreciably smaller than a quarter. The sleeve of canvas along the hoist, into which the bunting of the flag is sewn, and which, in modern flags, holds the tack-rope, is called the heading. The rope usually has either a toggle at the top (which slips into an eye-splice at the end of the upper halliard), or an Inglefield clip — a specially fashioned piece made of bronze, which clips into a similar piece at the end of the halliard instead of the eye-splice. The tack line extends below the flag, usually equal approximately to the hoist and, again, ends in an eye-splice (which is bent to the lower halliard, which ends in a back-splice or a whipping, by a sheet-bend), or both tack line and halliard have Inglefield clips. There are variations on these fittings; many foreign flags have just an eyelet or a ring at each end of the heading, and the halliards are merely 'tied on'. Also some flags have a very short length of rope below the flag.

FLAGS FOR SOME FAMOUS SHIPS

Many ship modellers, particularly in their early days, favour such famous ships as Columbus' *Santa Maria*, Drake's *Golden Hind*, Henry Hudson's *Half Moon*, and, of course, the Pilgrim Fathers' *Mayflower*. So let us have a look at the flags for these.

The *Santa Maria* was essentially a small merchant ship, and when Columbus took her westward in

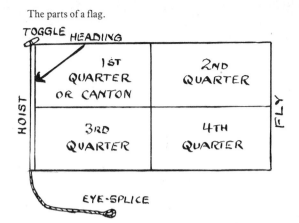

1492, he was sailing under the patronage of Ferdinand and Isabella of Spain. There is no doubt that he flew a much more elaborate set of flags and streamers than was normally used by such a small vessel. The designs as accepted by both historical and maritime experts, are fairly certain. The masthead flags were not hoisted, as today, by halliards, as these had not then been invented. They were fixed by rings or ties to flagstaves, which were lashed to the mast, or by rings slipped over the mast with the top ring made fast at the truck or finial.

At the foremast was a white flag, probably cut in the fly, with a green cross flanked by the crowned initials, F and Y (Ferdinand and Isabella) — the monarchs' personal flag, presented to Columbus by Queen Isabella herself. At the main was the flag of Spain — the quartered arms of Castille and Leon, red with a gold castle, and white with a red rampant lion, crowned gold.

There is some doubt about the flag at the mizzen mast, but it was probably a white flag with a black eagle bearing a shield of another version of the arms of Spain, half showing the quartered Castille and Leon (as above), and half Arragon, in vertical stripes, five yellow and four red. In addition there were streamers and pendants, with a short staff at the head, depicting again the arms of Spain, and slung from a mast or mizzen yard, in the same way as they are today when decorating coronation routes. There was no stern ensign, but a large crimson banner with a representation of the Virgin Mary ('Santa Maria') was set up at the break of the poop.

For the *Golden Hind*, it would seem probable that the correct flag at the mainmast was the flag of St George — white with a red cross — indicating English nationality, but it is possible that Drake could have flown the Tudor royal standard at the main if he had royal patronage, and St George's flag at the fore. She almost certainly flew other decorative flags and pendants, but no direct evidence exists. Many Elizabethan ships had a stern ensign, but frankly we

are not quite sure what purpose they served. They were certainly not national ensigns, as nationality was indicated by the masthead flag; they all seem to have been striped horizontally (blue and white or green and white were the usual colours) with a red St George's cross either in the canton (top left corner) or superimposed over the stripes. They may have been personal flags of individual owners or masters, varying according to personal preferences, in the Tudor livery colours plus the English cross of St George, or they may have been squadronal flags of the navy — some of this type were certainly used as admirals' masthead flags by the fleet which went to Cales in Andalusia in 1596, indicating both the rank of the admiral and his squadron. But it is most unlikely that the *Golden Hind* flew one of these striped flags at the foremast, as proposed for the 1973 replica, since the only indication of its use as a masthead flag was by naval ships as stated above; however, she may have flown one at the stern, but we have no evidence for or against.

The larger royal ships, particularly in earlier Tudor days, carried deck banners of royal badges and religious emblems, but Henry VIII abolished the latter except for those of St George and (possibly) St Edmund, King and Martyr.

A ship with an interesting story, and one always popular with modellers, is Henry Hudson's Dutch ship, *D'Halve Maen* (1609), which we call the *Half Moon*. Like the *Santa Maria* and the *Mayflower*, she was purely a merchant ship, of only 80 tons burden, sailing under the auspices of the Amsterdam Chamber of the Dutch East India Company, in an attempt to discover the North-West Passage to the Indies.

There has always been some controversy regarding her flags (as with so many of these old ships, and while one can often say that certain flags are wrong, it is not always possible to say which are correct), but it is generally accepted by Dutch ship modellers and research workers that the flags described by F Baay,

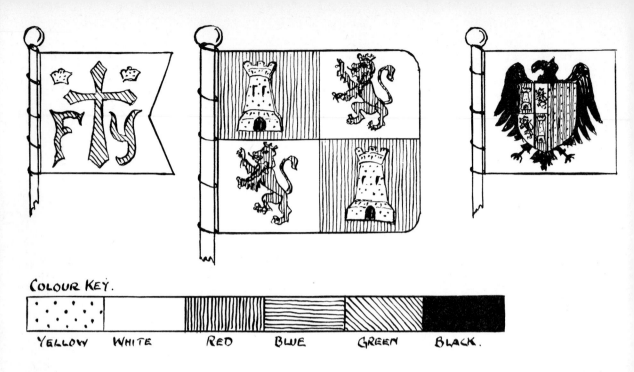

COLOUR KEY.

| YELLOW | WHITE | RED | BLUE | GREEN | BLACK. |

The *Santa Maria's* flags. Left — foremast; centre — mainmast; right — mizzen.

in his booklet (1941) on his model based on the ship built at Amsterdam in 1909, and on the famous model by that great Dutch authority, the late G C E Crone, are the most likely to be correct. He shows at the main, the red, white, and blue horizontal tricolour with the entwined cypher of the Dutch East India Company in black — VOC, with an A above, for Amsterdam. At the foremast is a smaller flag of the arms of Amsterdam, red, black, red, horizontal, with three white saltires on the black (the arms themselves have vertical stripes). At the mizzen is a small flag in the popular colours of the 'Prinzenvlag', orange, white, and blue, while at the stern is another large red, white, and blue tricolour, with the full arms of Amsterdam in the centre, the shield having golden lions as supporters. One writer quotes this last flag as having stripes of red, white, and *black,* the colours of Amsterdam; while this might be possible, the views of Mr Crone are preferred by most modellers.

The *Mayflower,* which made her epic voyage to America in 1620, was a very similar type of ship, although she was virtually a late sixteenth century vessel, being very much in her old age when the Pilgrim Fathers entrusted themselves to her creaking timbers. If depicted as at 1620 (which she invariably is) she would carry the 1606 Union Flag at the main, as this was some fourteen years before the first proclamation (1634) requiring that none but naval ships and others in the king's service, were to wear the Union Flag. She would have flown a St George's

flag at the fore, to indicate that she was English (as opposed to Scottish) which also had the Union at the main, but a St Andrew's cross — diagonal white cross on blue — at the fore).

It is unlikely that the *Mayflower* flew any flag at the mizzen, and we have no information that she carried a stern ensign — the first red ensign, with a small white canton containing a cross of St George, did not come in until 1621, and was mainly used at first only by naval ships.

For eighteenth and early nineteenth century naval vessels, do not make the common mistake of always hoisting a white ensign (with either the 1606 or the 1801 Union flag in the canton). It was not until 1864 that the White Ensign became the distinctive ensign of the Royal Navy. Before that date the *normal* indication of a naval ship was a red ensign at the peak of the gaff or at the stern, and a Common Pendant at the main, ie horizontally striped red, white, and blue, with a St George's cross in the hoist; if at anchor or in harbour, the Union Jack (1606 or 1801 type) was hoisted at the jackstaff in the bows; the jack was also flown at sea in the days of the spritsail topmast.

If a ship was attached to a squadron, she wore the appropriate ensign and pendant. Thus a ship of the Rear, or Blue Squadron wore a blue ensign and a blue masthead pendant with a St George's cross in the hoist; the Centre, or Red Squadron wore red ensigns and pendants, and the Van, or White Squadron had, of course, white ensigns and pendants. Flagships also

162

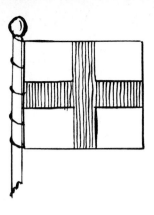

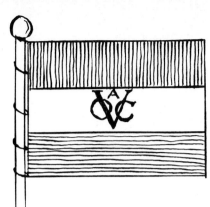

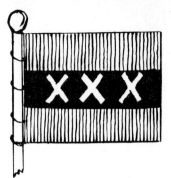

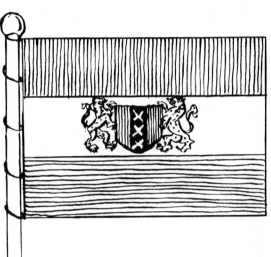

Top left. St. George's Flag for mainmast of the *Golden Hind,* and foremast of the *Mayflower.*

The three on the right. Flags for the *Half Moon.*
Above left — mainmast; above right — foremast. Below — Stern ensign.

wore the appropriate ensigns, but no pendant. Instead they flew the flags of their respective admirals, full admiral's flag at the main, vice-admiral's at the fore, and rear-admiral's flag at the mizzen. It should be noted, however, that prior to 1805 there was no rank of Admiral of the Red. Before that date either the Lord High Admiral or the Admiral of the Fleet had commanded the Red Squadron. The former flew the royal standard up to 1702, and subsequently the red flag with the yellow foul anchor (but he rarely went to sea, anyway), while the latter flew the Union Flag at the main. But from 1805 to 1864, when squadronal colours were abolished, and Admiral of the Red flew a plain red flag at the main.

Since 1864 all flag officers (ie admirals) have used a St George's flag, proportions 3 by 2. In three masted ships, the old order was retained: Admiral — St George's flag at the main; Vice-Admiral, at the fore; Rear-Admiral, at the mizzen. In ships with less than three masts and in boats, a vice-admiral was distinguished by having one red ball in the upper canton, and a rear-admiral by two red balls. In 1898 the rear-admiral's flag was amended, with one red ball in the upper and one in the lower canton.

It would take a whole book to deal with the flags of all the types of ships which attract the attention of ship modellers, and in our restricted space we can only cover a few of the most popular items. So let us leave the earlier centuries, and have a look at the flags carried by clipper ships and windjammers.

1606 Union Flag, for *Mayflower's* mainmast.

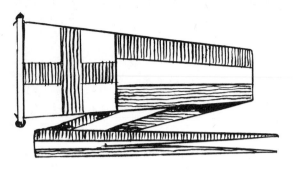

Common or Union Pendant.

THE NINETEENTH CENTURY

For those of British nationality the red ensign is almost always the appropriate national flag, usually shown at the peak of the gaff, but sometimes worn at the ensign staff at the stern when in harbour. This should be twice as long as the width, with the union occupying exactly one quarter of the flag (and please, please do not let the diagonal red cross run through the St George's cross, as so many ship modellers do!). During the first half of the nineteenth century, ensigns tended to be shorter in relation to the width, roughly 5 by 4 or 6 by 4, with the union often less than a quarter, but from the middle of the century onwards, modern proportions seem to have become standard.

It must be noted that the figures of 2 by 1 do not apply to the majority of foreign ensigns, and if you are making a model of a foreign ship, it is essential to find the correct proportions of the flag of the country concerned. We can briefly note that, in modern times, the merchant ensigns of the following countries are in the proportions of 3 by 2: the Netherlands, Belgium, France, Italy, Portugal, but the Scandinavian countries all have unusual proportions: Norway, 22 by 16; Sweden, 16 by 10; Denmark, 37 by 28; and Finland, 18 by 11.

The house flag of the owners is usually flown at the main (except for T & J Brocklebank, whose house flag was flown at the foremast). These are usually in the proportions of 3 by 2, and details must be sought in books of house flags or in histories of the clippers and windjammers.

The foremast was often adorned with a national flag of another country, although this was not fixed by regulation but rather by practice. When leaving a British port, a British ship often hoisted the flag of the next port of call, while when entering, tied up in, or leaving a foreign port it was (and is) customary to hoist the flag of that country, known as a trading or complimentary ensign.

Signal flags, hoisted at the mizzen, or where best seen, can also be incorporated to advantage, according to the setting in which the model is represented. It has not been unknown for modellers to show a hoist of perfectly correct flags, but selected at random from one or other of the recognized signal codes of the period; alas, when looked up in the signal book, the hoist has proved to be quite unsuitable for the setting. For instance, if a ship is shown in a harbour setting, or just entering or leaving harbour, it would be quite wrong to show her with MQS of the 1857 Commercial or International Code — *Just lost sight of land* (this has been known, because the flags hoisted were the initials of the modeller); Blue Peter — flag P of the International Code — can be hoisted at the foremast of a ship shown in a harbour setting, as indicating that she is about to sail, but would be quite wrong if the ship is shown out at sea. A clipper ship requiring a pilot can hoist flags PT of the International Code (but today vessels hoist flag G), or the white bordered union jack at the foremast. Under Marryat's Code, up to, say, 1880 when it fell out of use, the latter was the signal usually employed.

When hoisting signal flags on a ship model, it is very important to consider not only the suitability of the signal, but also the date at which the ship is represented. The first signal code for merchant ships as such, was Marryat's Code, referred to above. This was designed by Captain Frederick Marryat, RN (well known as the author of *Mr Midshipman Easy*, and other books for boys), in 1817, using fifteen (later seventeen) well designed flags (plus the Pilot Jack), similar to but different from the naval signal flags of the period. These have stood the test of time, and ten of them are still in use today in the current International Code, while three are also still used with only slight alterations. From 1817 to 1840 signals can be taken from the first seven editions of the code, but with the eighth edition in 1841 the whole numbering was revised and remained thus up to the last edition in 1879, although during this period several additional signals were added.

In 1855, with the coming of steam power and the wide development of shipping, a need was felt for a more comprehensive code. One using lettered flags instead of numeral flags provided very many more signals, and thus the Commercial Code of Signals, of 1857, was instituted by the British Board of Trade. In about 1871 its name was changed to the International Code of Signals. This code, which omitted all vowels so as not to include any rude or objectionable words, also X, Y, and Z, lasted until 1 January 1902. From 1 January 1901 to 1 January 1902 it ran concurrently with the revised (1901) International Code, and during that year signals made from the new code were distinguished by hoisting the code pendant with the fly tied to the halyards and with a black ball above (I have never seen this on a ship model — who will be the first to show this correctly? Remember, the signal must be from the 1901 code book, and the ship must be shown as she was during the year 1901). We should mention, of course, that the 1901 code was replaced by the 1931 code, which came into force in 1934.

Overleaf we show some suitable signals from the various codes, suitable for nineteenth and twentieth century ships, including clipper ships and windjammers.

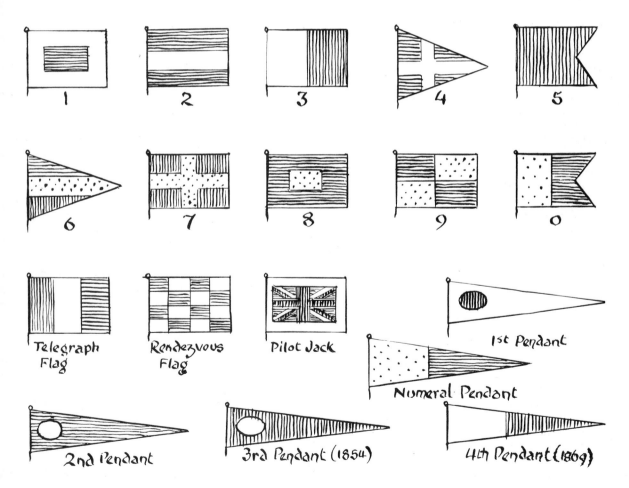

Marryat's code flags.

		Marryat		International Codes		
	1817-40	1841-80	1857	1901	1931(34)
Cargo is damaged	365	1328	NJT	HZS	CVQ
I am going into port	751	3897	DNJQ	OCB	RHM
Shall I take you in tow?	918	6018	KRG	XY	XZ
Am coming to your assistance	23	683	HF	DC	DN
The coast is dangerous	397	1475	MRD	IXW	—
Have you any letters for me?	634	2860	BRL	EPA	RD
Wish you a pleasant voyage	—	6389	FCSW	TDL	WAY
Signal not understood	873	5072	CWF	WCX	VB
Where are you bound?	321	1084	BPF	SH	RV
London	R520	R4072	BDPQ	AEHV	AJLZ
Liverpool	R536	R4036	BFGN	AEUV	AJJO
Glasgow	R387	R3251	BFKG	AEYZ	AGJV
Southampton	R834	R5912	BDRQ	AELW	APFY
Bristol	R143	R2078	BDVT	AEQC	ACEG

Note: R before Marryat's Code numbers indicates Rendezvous flag over the number.

The flags of the three International Codes are fairly well known and are shown in most flag books. Sufficient to say that those of 1857 are almost identical with the modern ones, with the following exceptions: C — white pendant with red ball; D — blue pendant with white ball; F — red pendant with white ball; G — pendant, yellow in hoist, blue in fly; L was quartered, *blue* and yellow (blue in the first quarter).

The 1901 code flags were as the present 1931 flags, except for the following: C, D, E, F, G, as the modern pendants 1, 2, 3, 4, 5. There were no substitute flags in the 1857 or 1901 codes, consequently there were no hoists with any repeated letters in either of these codes.

BIBLIOGRAPHY

For those who want to pursue the study of flags further, there are many books available. Some are, of course, out of print but are often to be found in secondhand book shops. The most authoritative work on our own flags is W G Perrin's *British Flags* (Cambridge University Press, 1922); although over fifty years old, it is not difficult to obtain secondhand, but is rather a difficult book for the beginner to use, owing to copious footnotes, bad arranging, and bad indexing — but I would not be without it for anything. The present writer's little book, *Flags for Ship Modellers and Marine Artists*, was published by Percival Marshall & Co Ltd in 1950, but has since been taken over by Model & Allied Publications Ltd,

Hemel Hempstead, Herts, and a few copies are still available. Covering a wider field is *Flags of the World*, which started as a small book by F E Hulme, in about 1890, and has since appeared much enlarged and revised by several editors, including W J Gordon (from 1915), V Wheeler-Holohan (from 1933) with the title, *A Manual of Flags*, but reverting to the original title in 1939, H Gresham-Carr (from 1953), and now, from 1969, under the able editorship of Captain E M C Barraclough, CBE, RN. These have all been published by Frederick Warne, Ltd, and all are useful, as although much of the information runs through them all, each has some topical items which, by becoming obsolete, are not included in later editions.

Other recommended books include the following:
The International Flag Book in Colour, by C F Pedersen (London; Blandford Press, 1971).
A Handbook of Flags, by P Kannik (London; Methuen, 1958). (Both the above were originally Danish publications, but have been translated into English and revised for the British market).
Sea Flags, by Commander Hilary P Mead, RN (Glasgow; Brown, Son & Ferguson, Ltd, 1938).
Traflagar Signals, by Commander Hilary P Mead, RN (London; Percival Marshall & Co Ltd, 1936).
The Observer's Book of Flags, by I O Evans (Observer's Books, No 29. London; Frederic Warne & Co Ltd).
Flags, by I O Evans (Hamlyn All-Colour Paperbacks, No 43. London; Hamlyn, 1970).

The official Admiralty book, *Flags of All Nations,* started as a large folio format volume, published by Hounsell Bros, in about 1876, under the patronage of the Admiralty, but from 1889 it has been published, in various formats, by HM Stationery Office. From time to time supplements have been issued for each edition, and new revised editions have appeared, including those of 1907, 1915, 1930, and 1955 (which was a loose-leaf edition, and can thus be kept up-to-date by additions and substitutions).

Books on house flags are not too common, but you might be able to find, in a public library or in a secondhand book shop, the following: *Flags, National & Mercantile, House Flags & Funnels,* by James Griffin (3rd edition, Portsmouth, 1895); *Lloyd's Book of House Flags and Funnels* (London, 1904; enlarged edition, 1912); *Brown's Flags and Funnels,* by F J N Wedge (Glasgow, 1926). Several other similar books exist.

Naval signal books are, of course, very difficult to obtain, since during their currency, many of them are confidential documents, but information can be obtained regarding early naval signals. Particularly useful are two books, by Julian S Corbett, in the *Navy Records Society publications* — *Fighting Instructions, 1530-1816* (London, 1905), and *Signals and Instructions, 1776-1794* (1908) both of which have been reprinted by Conway Maritime Press Ltd. The latter corrects and expands the former, as Corbett discovered a lot of previously unknown MSS just as the earlier volume was in the press, and thus the two volumes should be used together for that particular period. Two other useful books in the same series, which give considerable information on signals, are *Logs of the Great Sea Fights, 1794-1805* (2 vols, 1899, 1900).

Occasionally naval signal books containing the general signals can be found. These, of course, were not secret, but were published at frequent intervals and possibly numerous alterations were made, so that it may be dangerous to use signals taken from them unless the ship is shown at just the year in which the signal book was published (or very shortly afterwards). For example, editions were published in 1827, 1839, 1853, 1859, 1868, and so on; examples are in the Admiralty Library and can be referred to by special permission, but the extent to which they differ can only be known by inspection.

Signal books for merchant ships are not too difficult to find, and it is worth while buying any of the nineteen editions of Marryat's Code which, incidentally, also includes the ships' numbers (you will know the phrase, 'Making her number'). These were allotted on application, so not every British ship has a Marryat's number. Copies of the Commercial or International Code of 1857 onwards can often be found. To be complete, these should have a blue paper covered supplement, giving the signal letters of British ships (later editions included some foreign ships), entitled *The Commercial Code List* or *The British Code List;* these are often missing from the code book, but can be found separately. Right up to 1900, these are, unfortunately, only 'one-way' lists, enabling one to identify a ship from her code letters, but to find the signal flags relating to a particular ship, one has to search right through — Marryat, fortunately, worked on an alphabetical basis and thus ships' numbers can be traced both ways. Later International Code books, and *Signal Letters of British Ships* are fairly common, and current editions can be bought from HM Stationery Office.

Some other useful signal books which, if found, can be used to advantage include *The Liverpool & Holyhead Telegraphic Vocabulary* (Lt W Lord's Code, 1845), which used Marryat's flags; *Watson's Code of Signals,* 1841, compiled by Barnard L Watson, who operated a chain of telegraph (ie semaphore) signalling stations around and near the coast, and who also exchanged signals with shipping, using his special flags.

Another useful code, which I have never seen used on a ship model, is *Reynold's Code,* published by the French naval officer, Captain Charles de Reynold-Chauvancy and accepted by the British Admiralty and by many other nations, for international communications. It was instituted in 1855, and editions exist in English, French, Danish, Russian, German, and several other languages. It appears to use the current naval signal flags of each country plus a special Reynold's code flag, while Marryat's flags, with special pendants, were used for merchant ships; in addition, the signals could also be made by combinations of three objects — a square flag of any colour, a ball or similar shape, and a pendant. Although it had its good points, Reynold's Code was not in use for long, as the introduction of the 1857 Commercial Code displaced it.

The British Signal Manual was published by HMSO, and was authorised for use between HM ships and British merchant ships. The earliest edition I have been able to trace is that of 1905, and I have the 1912 edition, also a 1918 edition, enlarged and revised, under the title of *Allied Signal Manual.* This is sometimes called the 'Union Jack Code', as many of its signals make use of the Pilot Jack. The signals relate largely to convoy matters and other messages likely to be exchanged which are outside the scope of the International Code. Another interesting but very rare item is the *Lighthouse Signal Code,* published by Trinity House in 1908, using International Code flags, and hoists from it could be shown on models of Trinity House vessels, including Lightships; such signals would always include a cone with point either down (2) or up (3), with just one or two flags. Thus we have QB2 — *Your light was not showing well last night,* or B3L — *Whitby Lighthouse.*

The present writer has covered some of these topics in a series in *Model Shipwright,* the issues concerned being Nos 1-5 (Volume I, 1 — II, 1), No 8 (Volume II, No 4), No 10 and No 13. J L Loughran has also written in this journal about house flags and funnel markings. The issues are No 9, No 10 and No 11.

The foregoing notes have really only touched on the fringe of the interesting world of maritime flags and signals, but it is hoped that they will encourage the keen ship modeller to devote the same enthusiasm and research to his flags as he gives to the rest of the ship — the resuls will certainly repay the effort.

SHIP

A FIRST RATE SHIP of WAR with Rigging &c at Anchor

Bibliography

Compiled by John Bowen

A. GENERAL INTRODUCTION TO SHIP MODELLING
(All these works are in print or readily obtainable)

The Neophyte Shipmodeller's Jackstay by George F Campbell (published by Model Shipways, Bogota, NJ, USA). Although basically a guide to techniques of modelling from a wood kit, it contains a great deal of detail about seventeenth to nineteenth century vessels, well illustrated by numerous clear line drawings and sketches.

Ship Modelling Hints and Tips by Lt Cdr J H Craine, RNR (Retired) (first published 1948 by Percival Marshall Ltd, London, second revised edition 1973 by Conway Maritime Press Ltd, London). Contains short but useful chapters on such matters as woods and other materials, the story of anchors, rope making, how to make gratings, early guns, sea settings, and making glass cases.

The Ship Model Builder's Assistant by Charles G Davis (a 1970 reprint by Edward W Sweetman, New York of the original 1926 work). The value of this excellent book lies in the chapters on masting, with its description of how mast sizes are deduced and the tables of mast scantlings, standing and running rigging, deck fittings, ironwork, boats and davits, and appendices showing block and rigging sizes for several vessels circa 1750-1815 (roughly the period covered in the book). Of particular interest are the details of the Swedish, Danish, English and French methods of sparring ships; that is determining their lengths and diameters.

The Built-Up Ship Model by Charles G Davis (a 1966 reprint by Edward W Sweetman Company, New York of the original 1933 work). A very detailed description of the construction of a model of the United States brig *Lexington*, 16 guns. The chapters on the constructional methods used in building vessels of this type are most detailed and informative, as too are those on deck fittings, guns, boats, masts and rigging.

American Ship Models and How to Build Them by V R Grimwood (published W W Norton & Co, New York in 1942). Contains plans of a dozen American sailing ships, with emphasis on local and small craft types such as skipjack, bugeye, sloop, brig, schooners, and privateer. The accompanying text covers briefly the principal aspects of model construction, though not in great detail. The value of the book lies in its plans.

Lusci's Ship Model Builder's Handbook by Vincenzo Lusci (published 1970 by Vincenzo Lusci, Florence, Italy; English language edition also published). Outlines all phases of the construction of models of, mainly, sixteenth to nineteenth century vessels. Hull construction based on the egg-box principle. Copiously illustrated with line drawings, photographs and plans. The remarks in Chapter 1 should be borne in mind when considering the plans in this book.

Plank on Frame Models (2 volumes) by Harold A Underhill (published by Brown Son & Ferguson, Glasgow 1958, reprinted 1974). The text has been written round the construction by the author of a model of the brigantine *Leon*, built in Norway in 1880. This is a very comprehensive work covering the whole subject of plank-on-frame construction for vessels of this era in great detail, the whole illustrated by clear sketches and plans. Long considered as *the* book on the subject. The second volume covers the masting and rigging, concluding with chapters on clinker built models, sailing models and sawn-frame construction. Apart from the plans of the *Leon*, there are those for some Scottish fishing vessels — ring net boat and zulu — a motor fishing vessel, and clinker-built boats.

The Techniques of Ship Modelling by Gerald A Wingrove (1974, Model and Allied Publications Ltd, Hemel Hempstead). There are chapters on all the recognised principal phases of constructing ship models of various types and periods, but much of the work described has been carried out with the aid of an exceptionally well-equipped workshop.

B.   DETAILED MONOGRAPHS ON PARTICULAR SHIPS OR TYPES
(Most of these works are in print)

HMS 'Victory': Building, Restoration and Repair by A Bugler, 2 vols (Her Majesty's Stationery Office, 1967). The most highly detailed account of the *Victory's* construction available. The second 'Volume' in effect is a boxed set of plans.

A Handbook of Sailing Barges by F S Cooper (Adlard Coles Ltd, London 1955 and 1967). A useful guide to details of the hull and gear of the Thames sailing barges, illustrated with black and white sketches and line drawings.

The Construction of Model Open Boats by Ewart C Freeston (Conway Maritime Press Ltd, London 1975). Although describing a method for constructing models of open boats of all types to a largish scale, the information contained in this book is of considerable value when it comes to making the boats for a model.

Modelling Thames Sailing Barges by Ewart C Freeston and Bernard Kent. (Conway Maritime Press Ltd, London 1975). Describes the building of a small scale model of a sailing barge, with a section on building and sailing larger working models of these craft.

How to Build Clipper Ship Models by Edward W Hobbs (Brown, Son & Ferguson, Glasgow 197). A reprint of the original work, like its companion volume below it describes the construction of a typical clipper ship, so the same remarks apply.

How to Make Old Time Ship Models by Edward W Hobbs (Brown, Son & Ferguson, Glasgow, 1972). This is the third edition of the original 1929 book. The major portion of the book is devoted to a detailed description for a model of a typical 100 gun ship of the period 1690-1710. The constructional methods used may provide some answers to the 'how do you do this . . ." type of question.

HMS Victory as in 1805 (Neptune Models Ltd, Guildford). Described as a portfolio of plans by Basil Lavis, this booklet contains plans and photos of the *Victory*, and includes some plans of her guns. It is intended as an introduction to the 11 sheet set of plans of the ship as in 1805 prepared by Basil Lavis, and obtainable from David MacGregor Plans.

The Anatomy of Nelson's Ships by C Nepean Longridge (Model and Allied Publications Ltd, Hemel Hempstead 1955, reprinted 1972). A detailed step by step account of the construction of a model of HMS *Victory*. Apart from being a book which contains a great deal of practical modelling know-how, amply illustrated by sketches, drawings and photographs, it is an authentic guide on the art of ship construction and rigging of the period.

The 'Cutty Sark' by C Nepean Longridge (first published by Percival Marshall Ltd, London, reprinted as one volume by Edward Sweetman, New York in 1959, and again by Model and Allied Publications Ltd, Hemel Hempstead in 1975). Generally considered to be the most authoritative work on the construction of a scale model of this vessel, the methods used, and much of the information, can be applied to other types of ship models. Some differences in the model in this book and the vessel at Greenwich may be apparent as the result of all the information acquired for the restoration of the vessel in recent years. The plans for the book, by Harold Underhill, should be compared with those prepared by George Campbell for the restoration work.

The Galley and the Galleon by E Armitage McCann (reprinted 1967 by E W Sweetman, New York). Describes the construction of models of a Barbary pirate felucca and of a Spanish galleon, the models being described as lying between a purely decorative ship and an exact scale model; they were achieved by using a simplified method of building.

'Sovereign of the Seas' by E Armitage McCann (reprinted 1967 by E W Sweetman, New York). Describes in detail the construction of a 1/144 scale model of the American clipper ship of that name built in 1852. Contains many sketches of the vessel's fittings.

How to Make a Model of the US Frigate 'Constitution' by E Armitage McCann. (Originally published in 1928, reprinted by E W Sweetman). Monograph – but lacking in detail – on this famous ship. Plans banded inside back cover also lack detail.

Clenched Lap or Clinker by Eric McKee (National Maritime Museum, Greenwich, 1972). A booklet on the clinker technique of boatbuilding, with card templates for building a model of a 10' 0" workboat. Beautifully illustrated.

Modelling the Brig-of-War 'Irene' by E W Petrejus (published in Holland in 1970, text in English). Described as a handbook for the building of historical ship models, it covers in great detail the construction of a model of the Dutch 18 gun brig-of-war *Irene*, originally the British *Grasshopper* of 1806. Apart from being lavishly illustrated with numerous plans and sketches, the author also discourses widely both on other ships of the period and on variations of a fitting to be found on, or be suitable for, other types of contemporary vessels. An invaluable guide for the shipmodeller not only for its wide ranging and detailed content, but for the clarity of the numerous detailed sketches, which indicate so lucidly the art of ship and model construction and rigging practices.

'Speedy' by Bill Shoulder (Conway Maritime Press Ltd, London, 1975). Describes and illustrates the construction of a model of a naval cutter of 1828, based on contemporary drawings. Full size plans for a $\frac{1}{4}'' = 1' 0''$ (1/48) scale model are included.

Modelling the Golden Hinde by Arthur L Tucker (Conway Maritime Press Ltd, London 1973). Step by step account of building a static model of this well-known vessel, illustrated with photographs and detail sketches. Full size plans for a model 24" long (hull length) supplied with the book.

C. BOOKS AND ARTICLES OF PARTICULAR RELEVANCE TO THE CHAPTERS OF THIS BOOK

Chapter 1.   Beginnings
There are sections in Chapelle's *Search for Speed under Sail* and Abell's *The Shipwright's Trade* on reading plans and understanding draughtsmanship.
Model Shipwright articles:
I/3 (No 3) 'Converting Scales' by John Bowen.
I/4 (No 4) 'Tools for the Ship Modeller' by Arthur L Tucker.
II/1 (No 5) and No 9 'Breaking the Barrier' by J V Armstrong. How to get started on serious ship modelling.
No 12 'The Draughts Collection in the National Maritime Museum' by D J Lyon.
No 13 and No 14 'Researching Wooden Warships' by Robert Gardiner.
No 17 'Laying off the Head' by K M Hobbs.
No 18 'Laying off the Stern' by K M Hobbs.

Chapter 2.   Hulls and Decks
Further information can be found in Volume 1 of *Plank on Frame Models, The Anatomy of Nelson's Ships, Modelling the Brig Irene,* and *The Built-Up Ship Model,* which are probably the best sources for this aspect of modelling.
Model Shipwright articles:
I/1 to II/3 (Nos 1-7) 'Building a Seventeenth Century Dockyard Model' by Ewart C Freeston.
II/2 to II/4 (Nos 6-8) 'The Schooner Halifax' by Harold M Hahn.
II/4 (No 8) 'Framing — A New Approach' by Clyde M Leavitt. Framed hull model.
No 15 'Olivebank' by Harry Boyd. Bread and butter construction of a large barque.
Nos 16 to 19 'The bomb ketch Granado' by Bob Lightley. Framed hull.

Chapter 3.   Deck Fittings
The Model Shipbuilder's Manual of Fittings and Guns by Captain A P Isard (Faber & Faber, London, 1939) contained some useful information on fittings and armament but was necessarily limited. For specific vessels' fittings usually it is necessary to consult

photographs in books of 'background information'. The classic work on early armament is *Armada Guns* by M A Lewis (London, 1961) although it does not include the latest evidence from underwater archaeology, which can be found in past issues of the *International Journal of Nautical Archaeology*. Peter Padfield's *Guns at Sea* is readily available but it is a book curiously devoid of technical details on the dimensions and appearance of early guns. F L Robertson's *Evolution of Naval Armament* (London, 1921, reprinted 1968) is a good general account of the background, but again lacks detail.

Model Shipwright articles:

I/1 to I/4 (Nos 1 to 4) 'Photo Album'. Contained photos of sailing vessels *Olivebank, Mozart, Pommern* and *Killoran*.

I/2 (No 2) 'Labour Saving Devices in Sail' by A A Hurst.

I/3 (No 3) 'Braces and Brace Winches' by A A Hurst.

No 16 'Brigantine Raven of Rye' by Roger Glen.

No 16 'Olivebank' by Harry Boyd. Deck fittings for a four-masted barque.

Nos 17, 19 and 20. 'Fittings for Wooden Warships' by Robert Gardiner.

No 19 'Building a Model Whaleboat' by Jack Kitzerow.

Chapter 4. Masting and Rigging

Seventeenth Century Rigging by R C Anderson (Model and Allied Publications, Hemel Hempstead 1955, reprinted 1972). This is almost entirely a repetition, with the sections on foreign ships omitted, of *The Rigging of Ships in the Days of the Spritsail Topmast, 1600-1720* published in 1929 by the Marine Research Society of Salem, Mass. It is the most authoritative work on the subject, and shows, by means of diagrams and photographs, the details of every separate item of rigging, its composition and lead, for vessels of that type and period. Essential to modellers interested in such ships.

The Art of Rigging by Captain George Biddlecombe, RN (a 1969 reprint by Edward W Sweetman, New York of the original 1848 work). This book deals with the practicalities of rigging a vessel, describing the way the rigging is prepared, illustrating the various blocks, knots and bends employed, and how it is set up in place, or, in the case of running rigging, reeved. There is a section on bending sails, and one on the rigging of brigs, yachts and smaller vessels. Finally there is a series of tables giving the dimensions of the standing and running rigging of merchant ships of various types and tonnages, including fore and aft schooners. The nucleus of this book was originally Steel's work on rigging published in 1794, which

with the major revision made by the author in 1848 is indicative of the period covered.

Steel's Elements of Mastmaking, Sailmaking and Rigging. (A reprint by Edward W Sweetman Ltd, New York of the 1932 book, which itself was from the 1794 edition of Steel's work). This is the most comprehensive and authoritative work on the operations described in its title. Apart from the section giving the proportions for the lengths of the standing and running rigging of all ships calculated from the lengths of their masts and yards as given in tables, it has further detailed tables of the dimensions of rigging, with block sizes and numbers for all manner of vessels, ranging from 110 gun ships to 14 gun ships, from 1257 ton merchant ships to 60 ton sloops. Finally, in addition to the numerous diagrams in the text there are five folding plates showing in detail the way masts and bowsprits were made for 100 gun ships, 74 gun ships and 36 gun ships — with yard details as well for the latter two vessels.

The Art of Rigging by David Steel (1818 reprinted, 1974 by Fisher Nautical). The earlier work of 1794 was republished in 1818 in a set of revised and updated volumes. This is the rigging volume and represents the practice of the Royal Navy towards the end of the Napoleonic Wars.

Sailing Ships and Rigging by Harold A Underhill (Brown, Son and Ferguson Ltd, Glasgow 1938, reprinted 1975). Authentic sail plans of 32 different rigs, with descriptive notes of each vessel, ranging from the five-masted ship *Preussen*, to barques, brigs, schooners and a Humber Keel.

Masting and Rigging by Harold A Underhill (Brown, Son and Ferguson, Glasgow 1946, reprinted 1976). Sub-titled *The Clipper Ship and Ocean Carrier* this book covers in depth the masting and rigging of nineteenth and twentieth century sailing ships. After discussing the principles of rig and rigging, the succeeding chapters are devoted mainly to the masts, spars and rigging of iron and steel ships. The final chapter, entitled 'Use of tables and formulae', gives calculations for arriving at mast and spar sizes for various sizes and types of vessels and includes many tables of proportions for masts and spars, and rigging sizes in wire and hemp. A definite and authoritative work on the period, it takes up at the point where earlier works leave off.

Apart from the above there are also the less easily obtainable *Treatise on Masting Ships and Mastmaking* by John Fincham (London, 1829), *Sails and Sailmaking* (1858) and *The Elements of Sailmaking* (1851) by R Kipping, *Mast and Sail in Europe and Asia* by H Warrington Smyth (London 1906) and *Fore and Aft — The Story of the Rig* by E Keble Chatterton (London 1912).

Chapter 5.   Working Model Sailing Ships

Radio Control for Model Yachts by C R Jeffries (published by MAP Ltd) is a useful guide to R/C for working models, and *The Voyage of Mayflower II* by Warwick Charlton sheds some light on the problems of sailing early square riggers.

Chapter 6.   Miniature Scenic Models

Shipbuilding in Miniature by Donald C McNarry (1955, Percival Marshall Ltd, London). Covers in detail not only the author's constructional techniques in building a variety of miniature scale models, but in displaying them and building suitable cases. The data about each of the models mentioned includes valuable material on paint colours on the ship.

Ship Models in Miniature by Donald McNarry (1975, David and Charles Ltd, Newton Abbot). Contains illustrations, accompanied by brief details, of 65 superb examples of the miniaturist's art, ranging from a Phoenician Galley to the training schooner *Sir Winston Churchill*. The seventeenth century (17 models) and nineteenth century (30 models) are extremely interesting, but the eighteenth century has only 6 models. Although the descriptive matter for each is confined largely to details of the vessel, it is most valuable for the information they include regarding the sources from which the necessary plans and/or other information required to build the model was obtained.

D.   BACKGROUND SOURCES

(Some of these works are difficult to obtain.)

The Shipwright's Trade by Sir Westcott Abell (published in 1948 by the University Press, Cambridge). Covers the development of the art and craft of the shipwright from the days of the dug-out canoe to World War II, with some useful material on the design and laying off of ships of the late sixteenth and early seventeenth centuries.

The Sailing Ship by Romola and R C Anderson (published in 1963 by W W Norton and Co, New

York; many other editions). Originally published in 1926, this work is a compact account of the development of the sailing ship over the past 6000 years, illustrated by pen sketches. Useful as a survey of ship types through the ages.

Restoration of the Smack 'Emma C Berry' by Willits D Ansell (1973 by The Marine Historical Association, Inc, Mystic, Conn, USA). A fully detailed description, accompanied by numerous line drawings of constructional details, of the restoration of this sloop rigged well-smack built in 1866. The book has folding plate plans — lines, rig, deck layout — of the vessel.

The Kedge Anchor by William N Brady (Reprinted by Library Edition 1970 from 1876 edition). In essence an American version of D'Arcy Lever (see below).

Le Vaisseau de 74 Canons by Jean Boudriot, 4 volumes (published by Editions des 4 Seigneurs, Grenoble 1973-76). Although in French, this magnificently detailed anatomy of a 74 gun ship is worth consulting for the illustrations and plans alone. It is safe to say that no other vessel has ever been treated in such depth in a single work.

China Tea Clippers by George Campbell (Adlard Coles Ltd, London 1974). A definitive work dealing with the development of the tea clipper, with numerous highly detailed two and three dimensional sketches showing every aspect of the construction of the hull and deck erections for wood, composite and iron hulls, together with detailed sketches of deck and mast fittings. Plans for the *Foochow* are included. This book will be most valuable when used in conjunction with the plans of the vessel being modelled. Much of the information about deck fittings will be of use for other contemporary vessels. The chapter (No 14) on deck planking is particularly recommended, whilst the details in chapter 5 of the ornamentation of deckhouses cover an area on which little is written.

Sailing Barges by Frank G G Carr (published 1931, revised 1951, reprinted by Conway Maritime Press Ltd, 1971). The definitive work on sailing barges.

The Baltimore Clipper by Howard Chapelle (1930, reprinted by Sweetman, New York, 1969). The origin and development of this peculiarly American type. The late Howard Chapelle's first important work, and one in which he developed the approach later applied to *American Sailing Ships* and *American Sailing Navy*.

The History of American Sailing Ships by Howard I Chapelle (Bonanza Books, New York, first published by W W Norton & Co, New York in 1935). A survey of the development of sailing vessels in America from colonial times to the present day. The seven chapters cover the Colonial Period, Naval Craft, Privateers and Slavers, Revenue Cutters, The American Schooner, Merchant Craft, and Sailing Yachts. Each is copiously illustrated with lines, arrangement or sail plans, and many pen drawings of the different types of vessel.

The History of the American Sailing Navy by Howard I Chapelle (Bonanza Books, first published by W W Norton & Co, New York in 1949). The history of the sailing men-of-war of the United States Navy from the Colonial period to 1855. Each section is amply illustrated with plans, and there are reproductions of many ship models. As with the other books by Chapelle, there are plans of many interesting and intriguing ship designs, which in this case includes those for several humble service craft. There are tables of spar dimensions for various brigs, frigates, corvettes, schooners, sloops and ships of the line, and a short section on boat establishments with plans for several different types of ships' boats. Finally there are several building specifications, containing useful information about scantlings and materials.

The Search for Speed under Sail by Howard I Chapelle (Allen & Unwin, London 1968). Covering the history of the development of sailing vessel design in the United States between 1700 and 1855, the book contains numerous lines, arrangement and sail plans of a wide variety of sailing ships. Although covering the same period as MacGregor's book, from the variety of craft presented, and the generally larger size of the plans, this book has, perhaps, the edge over the other so far as this aspect of a modelmaker's interest is concerned.

American Sailing Craft by Howard I Chapelle (published 1936, reprinted by International Marine, 1975). Contains much information, and many scale plans on small local craft, yachts and dinghies.

The American Fishing Schooners by Howard I Chapelle (published 1973). Chapelle's last work, in his usual style of combined history and naval architecture.

The National Watercraft Collection by Howard I Chapelle (published by the Smithsonian Institution and International Marine, Washington, 1976). A beautifully produced volume cataloguing — with copious photos and plans — the ship models of the Smithsonian Institution.

Architectura Navalis Mercatoria by F H Chapman (originally published 1768 but reprinted many times recently in editions of reduced size). The most famous of all eighteenth century works on naval architecture, it is a folio of plans ranging from Chapman's own designs for privateers and merchantmen, to draughts taken off the fast sailing vessels of the principal European navies and mercantile marines. However, there is rarely much detail either of deck fittings or masts and spars.

A New Universal Dictionary of the Marine by William Falconer (1815 revised by William Burney, reprinted 1970 by Library Editions, New York). A most useful compendium of information on the construction, fitting and operation of ships — particularly warships — in the eighteenth century. It is very comprehensive in matters of armament, masting, rigging, and nautical terminology. Illustrated with some valuable engravings.

Sailing Craft of the British Isles by Roger Finch (William Collins Sons & Co Ltd, London, 1976). After an introduction well illustrated by photographs, the author describes 52 types of traditional sailing craft once found round the coasts of the British Isles, illustrating each with an elevation of the hull and rigging. A useful guide to these craft.

Prisoner-of-War Ship Models by Ewart C Freeston (published by Nautical Publishing, 1973). A history of the bone and wooden models produced by French prisoners during the Napoleonic wars. These are very much collectors' items nowadays.

The Merchant Schooners, 2 volumes by Basil Greenhill (first published 1951 by Percival Marshall & Co Ltd, London: new and revised edition by David & Charles Ltd, Newton Abbot in 1968). The definitive work on the fore and aft rigged merchant sailing vessels of England and Wales from 1870 to 1940. It describes and illustrates the building, rigging and operation of these vessels in detail, and contains lines, sail and arrangement plans for a number of vessels of different types, such as the steel three-masted schooner *Result*, wood three-masted topsail schooner *Rhoda Mary*, West Country sailing barge *Mary*, and ketch *Clara May*.

Sailing Ships by Bjorn Landström (Allen & Unwin, London 1969). A very useful and accurate exposition in words and pictures from papyrus boats to full riggers, it provides the modelmaker with a clear, concise and amply illustrated guide to ship types, and is particularly of benefit in clarifying the vessels of the sixteenth and seventeenth centuries. It is a concise edition of Landström's classic work *The Ship*.

Old Ships' Figure Heads and Sterns by L G Carr Laughton (1925, reprinted 1967). A highly regarded work on ships' decoration, but unreliable in some details. However, no other comparable survey exists, and the book is very difficult to obtain.

Gaff Rig by John Leather (Adlard Coles Ltd, London 1970). Traces the history of the gaff, and fore and aft, rig. The text contains much information about the details of this rig and its rigging, with many explanatory sketches, line drawings of vessels of many types, supplemented by numerous photographs. Although it concentrates principally upon vessels found round the coasts of the British Isles, it does include material on American schooners and fishing vessels. A useful book for the modeller of vessels with the fore and aft rig.

The Young Sea Officers Sheet Anchor by D'Arcy Lever (1808, many revisions during nineteenth century, reprinted by Sweetmans, New York, 1968). *The* work on rigging and seamanship. Not only a detailed text but fine illustrations of ship-board operations from getting in masts and spars to moving anchors, setting up the rigging to manoeuvres under sail.

Vintage Boats by John Lewis (1975, David and Charles Ltd, Newton Abbot). Although primarily directed towards the many problems involved in the preservation of old ships, the book contains a great deal of information about many of these vessels which have been saved for posterity. There are plans of several vessels, mainly fishing craft and inshore vessels, and a wide range of photographs. The information about the construction of wooden vessels is of value to modelmakers.

The Log of the Cutty Sark by Basil Lubbock. The best known of a large number of works on sailing ships by this prolific author. Others include *Last of the Windjammers* (2 volumes), *The Tea Clippers, The Opium Clippers, The Colonial Clippers, The Blackwall Frigates, The Down Easters* and *The Western Ocean Packets* all of which are kept in print by Brown, Son and Ferguson. They are often useful as general background but are by no means exhaustive, and offer little by way of detail information on the ships.

Fast Sailing Ships 1775-1875 by David R MacGregor (Nautical Publishing Company,

Lymington 1973). A definitive work dealing with the design and construction of fast sailing ships, amply illustrated by original plans, detail drawings, photographs of all types of vessels. Its value to the modeller lies not only in the wide variety of craft covered, from privateers, merchant ships, packet ships, yachts and revenue cutters, to schooners, brigs, smacks and the fast ships for the eastern trades with accompanying plans, but also for the bibliography and source references it contains. The notes on tonnage measurement are most valuable in elucidating a side of ship design which puzzles many modellers, but which is encountered quite frequently when researching a vessel's history and endeavouring to establish its dimensions.

The Tea Clippers by David R MacGregor (first published 1952 by Percival Marshall Ltd, London, new revised impression by Conway Maritime Press Ltd, London 1972). This is not only an account of the China Tea trade and some of the British ships engaged therein, but also a work incorporating information about the design developments of the vessels in the period 1849 to 1869. Lines, deck or sail plans are included of several well known vessels, all prepared by the author from original source material.

The Practical Shipbuilder by Lauchlan McKay (1839, reprinted 1970 by Library Editions, New York). A treatise on shipbuilding by the brother of Donald McKay who designed many of the best-known American clippers. Some plans, constructional detail and proportions for masts and spars.

Spritsail Barges of the Thames and Medway by Edgar J March (first published by Percival Marshall Ltd, London 1948; new edition by David and Charles Ltd, Newton Abbot 1970, 1976). A history of the various types of Thames sailing barge, with details of their construction and rig, amply illustrated, and with detailed plans of the typical trading barge *Kathleen* — but note that the lines plan is incorrect.

Sailing Trawlers by Edgar J March (David and Charles Ltd, Newton Abbot). A very detailed account of the building and operation of the British sailing trawler. Numerous sketches, photographs and trawler plans.

Sailing Drifters by Edgar J March (David and Charles Ltd, Newton Abbot, 1976). The companion book to *Sailing Trawlers* but dealing with the sailing drifters.

The Last Days of Mast and Sail by Sir Alan Moore (1925, reprinted by David and Charles, 1970). Described as 'an essay in nautical comparative anatomy' it is really an outline history of the development of masting and rigging.

The Seaman's Vade-Mecum by William Mountaigne (1756, reprinted by Conway Maritime Press Ltd, 1971). Information on masting, rigging, armament and the internal administration of merchant vessels in the eighteenth century. Very useful.

Seamanship by G S Nares (many editions in middle and late nineteenth century). A first rate work for anyone interested in scenic models; it gives detailed descriptions of manoeuvres under sail, and aspects of rigging and sail drill, with very fine engravings in the best editions.

Souvenirs de Marine by Admiral Paris (6 volumes, 1882 on, reprinted in 3 volumes by Editions des 4 Seigneurs, Grenoble 1975). A magnificent series of plans of ship types which had disappeared or were becoming extinct, collected by a historically minded French naval officer in the 1870s. It covers almost every type of sailing vessel from ships of the line to local craft from about the seventeenth century on. There is some text — in French — but its real value lies in the plans, some of which are very detailed.

Rees's Naval Architecture (sections from 'Cyclopaedia', 1819-1820, republished by David and Charles Ltd, Newton Abbot, 1970). This is an essential book for those whose interests lie in the vessels of the early eighteenth and nineteenth century. A comprehensive guide to naval architecture of the period, not only does it cover matters of design and the methods of laying off different parts of the ship, but it deals with ship construction, rigging, masts, yards, blocks, sails and sail-making, ropes and rope making. Each section is backed up with large diagrams and many fold out plans: Much of the text is based on Steel's *Naval Architecture*, 1806.

West Country Coasting Ketches by W J Slade and Basil Greenhill (published by Conway Maritime Press Ltd, London 1974). An illustrated study of this type of vessel and its operations, the book contains sail plans of four vessels, plus one arrangement plan and sundry constructional cross sections (midship sections), and many detailed photos.

Ship Models by C Fox Smith (1951, Country Life: new impression 1972 by Conway Maritime Press Ltd, London). Dealing with the history of the ship model from earliest times to the days of the tea clippers, and including votive models, bottle models and sailors' models, the book is useful for the 78 photographs of models of sailing ships and pulling boats.

Workaday Schooners by Edward W Smith, Jr, (published in 1975 by the International Marine Publishing Co, Camden, Maine). Illustrated by a very fine collection of photographs taken in Narraganset Bay between 1895 and 1905 of American fishing schooners and coastal schooners, chiefly under way, this book also contains a number of small scale

lines and sail plans of various examples of these vessels.

Deep Water Sail by H A Underhill (published 1952, frequently reprinted by Brown, Son and Ferguson, Glasgow). A useful account of the types, and technicalities, of rigs during the last era of commercial sail.

The World of Model Ships and Boats by Guy R Williams (André Deutsch, London 1971). A lavishly illustrated survey of ship models throughout the ages.

E. PERIODICALS

The Mariners' Mirror. The quarterly journal of the Society for Nautical Research. The most prestigious of all journals in this field, containing academic but very useful articles on all aspects of naval and maritime history. Further information from The Secretary, The Society for Nautical Research, The National Maritime Museum, Greenwich, London, SE10.

The American Neptune. In many ways the American equivalent of *The Mariners' Mirror,* dealing with topics of interest specifically to the Americas. Information from The Peabody Museum of Salem, Massachusetts 01970, USA.

Le Petit Perroquet. A French research journal published five times a year. Unlike the above two, this periodical is profusely — and beautifully — illustrated, so that the French language text need be no drawback. Published by Editions des 4 Seigneurs, 39 Rue Marceau, 3800 Grenoble, France.

The International Journal of Nautical Archaeology. Perhaps only of marginal interest to modelmakers, nevertheless this journal publishes some articles (on guns for example) which form the only sources of information on the actual dimensions and appearance of early ships and their fittings. Published by Seminar Press Ltd, 24-28 Oval Road, London, NW1.

The Nautical Research Journal. An American quarterly, produced by the Nautical Research Guild and aimed mainly at modelmakers. As its name suggests it emphasizes background and research rather than modelling technique. Further information from Harry S Bowman, 1743 Dana Street, Crofton, Maryland 21114, USA.

Model Shipwright. The only journal devoted entirely to scale model ships of all types and periods. Published quarterly by Conway Maritime Press Ltd, 2 Nelson Road, Greenwich, London SE10.

F. PLANS

David MacGregor Plans, 99 Lonsdale Road, London, SW13 9DA.
Plans for several tea clippers, sailing warships, fore and aft craft and fishing boats. Large scale prints

available of plans appearing in *Fast Sailing Ships 1775-1875.* Agents for the Vincento Lusci range of plans, which include a number of fifteenth to eighteenth century vessels. Catalogue available.

Bassett-Lowke Limited, Kingswell Street, Northampton, NN1 1PS, England.
Distributors of the Harold A Underhill range of sailing ship plans prepared specially for modelmakers. The collection comprises mainly plans for late nineteenth and twentieth century square riggers, but includes many smaller fore and aft craft, sail training ships, and fishing vessels. Catalogue available.

Model and Allied Publications Limited, PO Box 35, Hemel Hempstead, Herts, HP1 1EE, England.
Publish plans for a wide range of vessels of all types; these plans have been specially prepared for the modelmaker, and vary quite extensively in the amount of detail shown. Catalogue available.

Model Shipwright, 2 Nelson Road, London, SE10.
Plans service contains a small number of sailing ship plans.

A & A Plans (London), 102 Mattison Road, London, N4.
Publishers of plans of modern naval vessels only. Catalogue available.

Clyde Leavitt, 707 Beach Boulevard, Pascagoula, Mississippi 39567, USA.
Plans for eighteenth century plank-on-frame Admiralty type models.

Model Shipways Co, Bogota, New Jersey, 07603, USA.
Agent for plans for ship modellers published by several leading suppliers in this field. Catalogue available.

Maritta Models, Box 1156G, Newport News, Virginia 23601, USA.
Importers of ship model kits and plans. Catalogue available.

The National Maritime Museum, Greenwich, London, SE10, has the largest collection of ship's plans in the world, although by no means all are copied and hence many are unavailable to the public. Select lists are available, but requests must be specific as to vessel, period or at least the type required. These plans can be supplied at full, half or quarter size of the original which usually means 1/48, 1/96 or 1/192 scale.

The Science Museum, South Kensington, London, SW7, can provide photographs of many plans not held in the Museum, including the Hilhouse Collection.

The Smithsonian Institution, Washington, holds a large collection of plans of American vessels. Further information in Howard Chapelle's books.

Musée de la Marine, Palais de Chaillot, 75116 Paris, publishes a number of 'monographs' specifically for modellers. These contain plans, photographs and some text.

Glossary of terms

ABAFT. Near the stern; behind, aft of.

AMIDSHIPS. The middle of the vessel, either from stem to stern, or athwartships.

ARM. The part of the lower end of an anchor to which the palm is attached. (see also YARDARM).

ATHWARTSHIPS. Across the ship from one side to the other.

BACKSTAYS. Stays which support a mast from aft, leading from the upper part of a mast to the ship's side abaft the shrouds.

BEAKHEAD. Originally the projecting, pointed beaks of ancient times. Later it referred to a small platform at the fore end of the upper deck in large ships.

BEAM. (i) The breadth of a vessel; the moulded beam is the breadth to the inside of the planking at the widest part of the ship, usually midships.
(ii) Strong timbers placed across the ship to support the decks and to keep the sides the correct distance apart. They are secured to the frames by heavy knees.

BELAYING PIN. A round wooden pin, about 16″ long and $1\frac{1}{2}″$ diameter, the upper end turned as a handle. They are inserted in holes in the pin rails and used for belaying ropes, mainly running rigging. Sometimes made of iron.

BELAY. To make fast a rope.

BELFRY. The shelter under which the ship's bell was hung.

BEND. (i) To fasten one rope to another, or to an object.
(ii) To fasten a sail to a yard or stay.

(iii) In conjunction with another word, such as a 'fisherman's bend', denotes a particular type of knot.

BENDS. See WALES. Strong thick planks in the ship's side.

BETWEEN DECKS. Sometimes 'tween decks, the space between two decks of a ship.

BIGHT. The double part of a rope when it is folded.

BILGE. Originally that part of the floor on either side of the keel which was more or less horizontal; it also refers to the (flat) part of the bottom on which a ship would rest when on the ground.

BIB. A piece of timber bolted to the hounds of a mast to support the trestletrees.

BILL. The sharp point at the extremity of the palm of an anchor.

BILLET HEAD. An ornamental carving or scroll at the top of the stem in place of a figurehead. Also called a FIDDLE HEAD.

BINNACLE. A wooden casing, column, or box which contains the compass, incorporating a window through which to view it, and two lamps to illuminate the card by night. On either side is a bracket to carry the iron balls used to compensate for the metal of a vessel's hull.

BITTS. Very strong timbers fixed vertically in the fore end of a ship, usually passing through one or more decks and projecting about 4 feet above the top deck, to which the anchor cables are secured. Each timber is supported on its foreside by a heavy knee secured to the deck and the bitt. On the after side of the bitts, and well fastened thereto, is a strong horizontal beam, set about one-third of the height of the bitts, below their tops, and extending by about the same amount on either side.

BITTER END. The part of the anchor cable abaft, or inboard of the bitts — hence the extreme end when the cable is paid out.

BLOCK. A wood or metal shell or casing, with one or more grooved pulleys or sheaves set therein, over which a rope is rove. To the shell is fitted a hook, eye, or strap by which it can be attached in place. A block is designated single, double, etc by the number of its sheaves. Other types of blocks are:

Cat block — a double or treble block with an iron hook, used to bring the anchor up to the cathead.

Cheek block — a half shell bolted to the mast, the sheave pin being the main securing bolt to the mast.

Long-tackle block — two sheaves one above the other in the same shell. The lower sheave is two-thirds the size of the other: stropped with an eye at the top.

Sister blocks — similar to two single blocks end to end, but with a single piece shell, which is reduced in size between the sheaves to take a seizing.

Snatch block — a single sheave block with an opening cut in one of its cheeks to allow a rope to be put in or be taken out without reeving the end of the rope through first.

BOBSTAY. Stays fitted between the end of the bowsprit and the stem to hold the former down and to counteract the pull of the forestays.

BOLTROPE. The rope sewn round the edges of a sail to strengthen it.

BONNET. An additional small sail secured to the foot of sails with lashings, and exactly similar to the foot of the sail to which it is attached. Only fitted in calm weather to increase the sail's area, they were about one third of its area in size.

BOOM. (i) Any small spar. Across the waist of a ship, booms or SKIDS carried the boats and spare spars.
(ii) The spar used to extend the foot of fore and aft sails.
(iii) Stunsail, or studding sail, booms are spars used to extend the yards to carry studding sails.

BOTTOM BOARDS. Lengths of board laid over the bottom of a boat as flooring. They are usually fastened together in sections.

BOWLINE. (i) A rope attached to the centre of the leech of square sails to keep it taut when close-hauled.
(ii) A type of knot.

BRACE A rope leading from the yardarm to an adjacent mast or to the vessel's side, and used to haul the yards to the required position.

BRACE PENDANTS. Short lengths of rope, with one end attached to the yardarm and the other end carrying a block through which the brace is rove.

BRAILS. (i) Ropes used to haul up the bottoms and lower corners of (square) sails to the yards ready for furling.
(ii) Ropes led through blocks on the mast, and down either side of a spritsail or spanker, to gather the sail to the mast.

BRAKE. The handle by which a ship's pump is operated.

BREAK. The part in a ship or deck where it terminates and the next deck below commences.

BREASTHOOK. Heavy, thick pieces of timber fitted in the fore end of the ship directly across the stem to unite it with the planking on either side.

BRIDLE. A short two-legged rope.

BULWARK. The side of a ship above the upper deck.

BULLSEYE. A form of wooden thimble, having a hole in the centre, and a groove round the circumference.

BULKHEAD. An upright partition fixed transversely across the ship to divide it into compartments.

BUMKIN. Sometimes BUMPKIN or BOOMKIN. A small spar, of wood or iron, projecting from the ship's side, to extend the clew of a sail.

BUNT. (i) The middle part of square sails.
(ii) The part of a square sail furled to the centre of the yard.

BUNT LINE. Ropes fastened to the foot of square sails and used to haul the sail to the yard for furling.

BURTHEN. Sometimes BURDEN, the weight of cargo a ship will carry, and hence a conventional measure of tonnage.

BURTON. A small tackle, formed by two blocks, and used principally for setting up topmast shrouds. It also refers to any similar tackle used for moving any heavy objects around on deck or in the holds.

BUTT. (i) The end of a plank in a ship's side or deck, uniting with the end of another.
(ii) The lower end of a made mast.

CABLE. The large, thick strong rope to which the anchor is attached by its ring. Cable-laid is the method by which the cable is made up, namely three ordinary laid ropes laid together, with a left-hand twist.

CAMBER. The curve, transversely, in a ship's deck; the amount by which the deck is higher in the middle than at the sides. The curve nowadays is usually of parabolic form.

CANT FRAMES. Those frames at the bow and stern of a ship which are not at right angles to the longitudinal centre line of the ship.

CAP. A heavy block of wood, later metal, used to connect the head of one mast to the lower portion of the mast above. Of the two holes in it for this purpose, the one for the head of the lower mast is usually square. There are definite proportions for the size of caps.

CAP SQUARE. The thick metal plates which fit over the trunnions of a gun to secure it to the carriage.

CARLINGS. Short pieces of timber set fore and aft between two deck beams, and with their ends set into the beams.

CATHEAD. A short heavy beam projecting nearly horizontally over the bow of a ship — one on each side — securely fastened to the deck, and having two or three sheaves set in the outboard end through which a rope is rove to connect with the cat-block; this tackle is used to haul the anchor from the water's edge to the bow.

CAT-HARPING. A small rope used for bracing the shrouds of the lower mast behind their yards to allow the yards more room to swing, and also to tighten the shrouds.

CAULK. To drive oakum or spun yarn into the seams of the planks of a ship's side or decks to prevent the entry of water; afterwards it is covered with hot melted pitch.

CAULKING IRON. The flat bladed tool used in caulking a seam.

CAULKING HAMMER. The specially shaped wooden mallet used for striking the caulking iron.

CAVIL. See KEVEL.

CEILING. The inside planking of a ship, also used at times to refer to the planking across the bottom of the hold.

CHAIN PLATES. Originally 'Chains'. Strong metal plates bolted to the outside of the hull, or ship's side, to which the deadeyes for the lower shrouds and the backstays are attached.

CHANNEL. Broad heavy planks, projecting horizontally from the ship's side, fitted abreast of each mast, to give greater spread to the shrouds and to keep them clear of the bulwarks.

CHEEKS. (i) The two side pieces of the shell of a block.
(ii) The projecting parts on each side of a mast which support the trestletrees, usually comprising flat pieces of wood bolted to the mast.
(iii) Knee pieces of timber fastened to the bow of a ship to support the knee of the head.

CHINE. (i) The part of the waterway projecting above the deck in order to facilitate the caulking of the lower seam of the spirketting.
(ii) The knuckle made where the sides of a boat meet the bottom to form a sharp angle.

CLAMPS. Thick planks of wood running from stem to stern of a ship inside the frames, and fastened thereto, situated immediately below the deck beams in order to support the ends of the beams.

CLEAT. Shaped pieces of wood of various sizes, usually having two arms, upon which ropes can be fastened: fitted to bulwarks, decks, masts and where required.

CLEW. The lower corner on square sails and the after lower corner of fore and aft sails.

CLEW GARNETS. The tackles by which the clews of the courses were hauled up to the yard when furling these sails.

CLEW LINES. The line by which the clews of the other square sails were hauled up to the yard when furling the sails.

CLINKER OR CLINCHER BUILT. The method of boat construction by which the lower edge of one plank overlaps the top outer edge of the other and to which it is fastened.

CLOTHS. The breadths of canvas in a sail.

COAMINGS. The raised edges of a hatch.

COAT. The tarred canvas fastened round a mast or bowsprit where it penetrates the deck.

COMPANION (WAY). A wooden, or metal, covering over the hatchway giving access to accommodation etc. below that deck.

COURSES. The principal sails of a ship, such as fore course, main course, mizzen course.

CRANSE IRON. The iron band supporting a lower yard and fastening it to the lower mast, rather like a universal joint: it replaced the chain slings.

CRINGLE. A ring or loop in the bolt rope of a sail.

CROSSTREES. Pieces of timber fitted across the cheeks and trestletrees to support the top, and take the upper shrouds of the mast.

CROWN. The lowest end of the shank of an anchor; it unites the arms of the anchor.

CROWSFOOT. An arrangement of small lines spreading out from a long block or euphroe.

CRUTCH. The support for the boom of a vessel when the sails are furled.

DAVIT. A wood, or metal, crane used for hoisting the anchor clear of the ship's side, or for lowering and raising the ship's boats.

DEADEYE. A circular wooden block, scored round the circumference to take a rope or iron band, and pierced with three holes to take a lanyard. Earlier deadeyes were heart shaped with a single large hole in the centre and later with three holes.

DEADLIGHT. The solid cover fitted to a scuttle (porthole) to keep out water. Also refers to a solid piece of glass in a ship's side to admit light.

DEADWOOD. The solid blocks of wood fitted upon the keel at the ends of the ship were the space is too narrow to permit the fitting of cant frames.

DOLPHIN STRIKER. Also called MARTINGALE. The short spar projecting down below the bowsprit to spread the stays supporting the jibboom.

DOUBLINGS. The overlap of the top of one mast and the bottom of the other.

DOWNHAUL. The rope leading from the head of a sail down to the deck by which the sail is hauled down for furling.

DRIVER. The gaff sail set on the after mast of a ship, barque, etc. See SPANKER.

EARING. A small rope used to fasten the upper corner of a sail to its yard.

EUPHROE. A long piece of wood, having a number of holes through which the crowsfoot is reeved.

EYE. A loop in a rope, usually at an end.

EYEBOLT. A length of metal having an eye formed at one end, the standing end being driven into the deck or ship's side, and used for fastening tackles.

FALL. The fall of a tackle is the loose end, or the one which is pulled upon.

FASHION PIECES. The aftermost timbers which terminate the breadth and form the shape of the stern, being secured to the ends of the wing transom and to the stern post.

FID. (i) A short piece of wood or metal resting on the crosstrees, and passing through a hole in the mast to keep it in position.
(ii) A tapered circular length of hardwood used in splicing ropes.

FIFE RAILS. Horizontal pieces of timber supported on stanchions and fitted with belaying pins, at the foot of a mast.

FLEMISH HORSE. A short footrope found at the extreme end of a yard.

FLOOR. The bottom of the ship, or the part on each side of the keel which is nearly or wholly horizontal.

FLOOR TIMBERS. The parts of the ship's timbers which pass across the keel and on which the bottom is framed.

FLUKES. See PALMS.

FOOTROPES. (i) Also called HORSES. Ropes suspended below the yards, and attached thereto by stirrups, upon which men stand when furling the sails.
(ii) The boltrope sewn to the lower edge of a sail.

FOOT OF A SAIL. The lower edge of a sail.

FORE AND AFT RIG. A vessel having all its sails set along the centre line, that is in a fore and aft direction.

FRAMES. See TIMBERS.

FURL. To roll a sail close to its yard or boom and secure it thereto with lashings.

FUTTOCKS. The parts of a ship's timbers situated between the floor and the top timbers.

FUTTOCK BAND. An iron band fitted near the top of a lower mast to take the futtock shrouds.

FUTTOCK PLATES. Iron plates with a ring in the upper end to take a deadeye, and holes in the lower end to take the futtock shrouds.

FUTTOCK SHROUDS. Short shrouds leading from the futtock band to the futtock plates.

GAFF. The spar along the top edge of a fore and aft sail, held in position by the throat and peak halliards. The forward end is fitted with two cheek pieces which form a semi-circle to enclose the mast, called gaff jaws, the other half of the circle being completed by a form of parral round the mast, the ends being attached to the ends of the gaff jaws. A standing gaff is one which remains aloft, that is does not lower, and is attached to the mast by a gooseneck fitting. In this case the sail is brailed up to the mast and gaff.

GAFF TOPSAIL. A fore and aft sail set abaft the topmast, with its foot being spread by the gaff.

GAMMON IRON. The iron band holding down the bowsprit to the stem.

GAMMONING. The rope, or sometimes chain, which binds the bowsprit to the stem. The rope passes over the bowsprit and through the 'gammoning hole' in the stem or the knee of the head; usually there are seven or eight complete turns, and these are drawn together by a separate rope bound tightly round them, between bowsprit and stem.

GANGWAY. Until forecastles and quarterdecks became a continuous upper, or spar, deck, they were connected by narrow gangways. At first these were moveable, but by about 1795 in most warships they were fixed, and wider.

GARBOARD STRAKE. The first strake of planking of the ship's bottom, laid next to the keel, on either side, the inner edge being let into the keel in the groove known as the rabbet or garboard rabbet.

GARLAND. A horizontal piece of timber, fitted to the bulwarks or elsewhere adjacent to the guns, having a number of hemispherical openings in it in which round shot are stowed.

GARNET. See CLEW GARNET.

GASKETS. Short pieces of rope used to secure a furled sail to its yard or boom.

GOOSENECK. A form of metal hook fitted to the end of a boom, and fitting into an eye on a metal band on the mast, to allow the boom to move freely: a kind of universal joint.

GORES. The pieces of cloth in a sail which have been cut at an angle in order to increase the width or depth of the sail.

GRIPES. Ropes or canvas straps used to retain a boat on its chocks, or against the davits when stowed in a hoisted position under the davits.

GROMMET. A ring or wreath of rope.

GUDGEON. Metal clamps bolted to the sternpost of a ship and having an eye on the after end into which the pin or pintle fastened to the leading edge of the rudder fits to allow the rudder to turn.

GUN TACKLES. The ropes and blocks fitted to either side of the gun carriage, and used to run out the guns for use, or to secure the guns in place when not in use.

GUNWALE. A heavy piece of timber fitted in the waist of the ship on each side between half deck and forecastle covering the timbers. Later it came to refer to the top edge of a boat.

GUY. The rope or tackle used to steady a boom: a rope or stay leading to a vessel's side.

HALLIARD. Also HALYARD. Ropes or tackles employed to raise or lower spars, sails, flags.

HAMMOCK NETTING. A trough of netting, suitably supported, on the bulwarks, into which the rolled up hammocks were placed when the ship was in action to provide protection to the crew against spinters and small shot.

HANKS. Rings, of wood or metal, on a stay for attaching a sail to allow it to be raised or lowered.

HARPINGS. The ends of the wales round the bow of a ship and fastened to the stem. Usually somewhat thicker than the rest of the wale.

HATCHWAY. Openings in a deck.

HATCHES. The boards used to cover a hatchway. Sometimes used in place of 'hatchways' to refer to the opening in a deck.

HAWSE HOLE. An opening in the bow of a ship through which a cable passes. Often called the 'hawse pipe' in modern vessels by virtue of its construction in the form of a cast cylinder or tube with flanged, shaped ends.

HAWSER-LAID. Another term for a 'cable-laid' rope.

HEAD. The fore end of a ship, the bow and its adjacent parts. The figurehead or other embellishment at the stem or beakhead. Also used to refer to that part of the ship, lying within the head rails, forming the crew's toilet.

HEAD RAILS. The curved rails at the head of a ship.

HEAD SAILS. The fore and aft sails set between the foremast and the bowsprit. Sometimes also used to refer to the square sails on the foremast of a square-rigged vessel.

HEART. A form of deadeye, shaped like a heart, and having a single large hole in the centre.

HEEL. (i) The lower end of a mast, bowsprit, boom. (ii) The after part of a vessel's keel and the lower part of the sternpost to which it is connected. (iii) To incline.

HOGGED. To curve upwards in the middle; a ship is said to be hogged when the ends are lower than the middle. In this condition the hull is strained and probably leaky.

HORNS. The jaws, or the semi-circular inner end of a boom or gaff.

HORSE. An iron bar, or one of timber or rope, fitted across the deck on which the sheet block of a fore and aft sail slides. Also a footrope.

HOUNDS. The parts of the masthead which project beyond the diameter of the mast to form a support for the trestletrees: their upper part is also called the cheeks.

JACK. A type of flag, flown at the jackstaff.

JACKSTAFF. The pole or staff at the bow or on the bowsprit.

JACKSTAY. A metal bar, or rope, fitted along the top of a yard, or up and down the after side of a mast, to which the sail is attached.

JEERS. The heavy tackles by which the lower yards of a ship are hoisted or lowered.

JIB. A fore and aft staysail forward of the foremast, set on a stay between that mast and the bowsprit or jibboom.

JIBBOOM. The spar fitted on the top of a bowsprit, and projecting beyond it, to which the outer headstays are fitted.
A flying jibboom is one extending beyond the preceeding one, although it was the original term for the jibboom itself.

JIGGER. The aftermost mast in a four-masted vessel.

KEEL. The principal timber in a ship, extending from stem to stern and projecting below the underside of the planking. A 'false keel' is a piece of timber lightly fastened to the underside of the keel to preserve its lower face.

KEELSON. The piece of timber laid upon the middle of the floor timbers immediately over the keel, and secured thereto by long fastenings passing through the floor timbers and the keel.

KEVEL. A fitting composed of two pieces of horn-shaped timber whose lower ends rest on a step or foot set into the bulwark, the upper ends branching out like horns. Used for belaying ropes. Kevel heads are the ends of the top timbers which project above the gunwale and are used for belaying ropes.

KNEES. Shaped pieces of timber or metal used to secure the ends of the beams to the ships side or timbers (frames).

KNEE OF THE HEAD. A heavy piece of timber fitted to the foreside of the ship's stem, and supporting the figurehead.

KNIGHTHEADS. The timbers nearest the stem, on each side of the vessel, continued high enough to secure the bowsprit, originally so called because they were carved to resemble heads in armour. Sometimes called 'bollard timbers'.

LACING. The rope or line confining the heads of sails to their yard or gaff.

LANYARD. The light rope rove through deadeyes for setting up, or tautening, a shroud or backstay.

LARBOARD. The old name for the left, or port, side of a ship when looking to the bow from the stern.

LASHING. A length of rope used to fasten or secure a moveable object.

LATEEN SAIL. The large triangular sail, rather like a jib, having a yard along its fore leech or luff. Usually found on Mediterranean and Far Eastern craft.

LATEEN YARD. The long yard to which the lateen sail is attached. It is suspended from the mast at a point about one quarter of its length from the fore end. The fore end of the yard is made fast to the stem or deck nearby, and the after end is raised in the air abaft the mast.

LAY. The direction of the twist in a rope.

LEECH. The vertical after edge of a fore and aft sail (the forward edge is called the luff). The vertical edges of a square sail.

LIFT. (i) The rope leading from the mast to the end, or arm, of the yard below, or of a boom, and used to support and trim the yard, the other end being led down to the deck. A standing lift is one which is secured to the mast and to the yardarm.
(ii) The horizontal section of the hull of a ship model. In a hull built on the 'bread and butter system', or of a number of horizontal boards fastened together, the individual boards are often referred to as lifts.

LIMBERS. Holes cut through the floor timbers in their lower part, near the keel, to form a channel for the water to pass to the pump well.

LIMBER BOARDS. Short lengths of plank, being part of the ceiling, or lining on the inside of the floors, lying immediately above the limbers, which can be removed easily to give access to the limbers in order to clear them when blocked with dirt.

LINCH PIN. The metal pin passing through the end of the axle tree on a gun carriage to prevent the truck (wheel) slipping off.

LINES. (i) Various small ropes on a vessel.
(ii) The shape of the hull of a vessel as indicated by sections taken through the hull transversely, horizontally and longitudinally. The general appearance or shape of the hull as apparent to the eye.

LINING. The inside planking of a ship.

LUBBER'S HOLE. The space or opening in the top on either side of the mast, allowing access to the top without climbing over the futtock shrouds and the lip of the top.

LUFF. The forward, or weather leech, of a sail.

MAINMAST. The principal mast on a vessel.

MAINSAIL. The principal sail in the mainmast, also called the MAIN COURSE.

MARTINGALE. See DOLPHIN STRIKER.

MAST COAT. Coverings of treated (well tarred) canvas fitted round the mast to prevent water going down the mast hole (in the deck).

MIZZEN MAST. The aftermost mast in a three masted vessel, and also in a two masted vessel where that mast is of secondary importance, for example in a ketch or yawl.

MONKEY RAIL. The second, or lighter, rail fitted above the main rail at the after end of a vessel.

MOULDED. The word used to define the breadth of an object, such as moulded beam, or the moulded dimension of a piece of timber as opposed to its sided dimension.

MOUSE. A knob made on a stay with spun-yarn parcelling to prevent a running eye from going past that point.

MOUSING. The lashing put across the opening of a hook to prevent it coming adrift.

NOCK. The foremost upper corner of boom sails, and of staysails cut with a tack.

ORLOP. The lowest deck in a warship.

PAINTER. The rope attached to the stem of a boat for towing it astern of another craft, or for mooring alongside.

PALM. The broad flat plate, triangular in shape, at the end of each arm of an anchor. Also called FLUKES.

PARCELLING. The narrow strips of tarred canvas wound spirally round a rope prior to serving.

PARRAL. The band arrangement of wood balls and boards (ribs and trucks) on a rope, used to hold a hoisting yard or gaff to the mast, yet allowing it to be moved up and down as required.

PARTNERS. Heavy pieces of timber secured to the frames as strengtheners in way of masts, bowsprit, and capstans.

PAWL. The heavy piece of metal on the capstan or windlass which is so fitted to engage in a toothed rack on the barrel and thereby prevent the latter rotating backwards when under load.

PAWL BITTS. Two heavy timbers fitted vertically in front of the windlass to which the pawl was attached.

PEAK. The upper after corner of a gaff sail.

PEAK HALLIARD. The ropes and tackles by which the outer end of a gaff is hoisted.

PENDANT. (i) A short rope, or wire, having a block at one end, the other end being attached to a yard or boom, or elsewhere as required.
(ii) When pronounced 'pennant', a kind of flag, sometimes a long banner, terminating in one or two points.

PIN RAIL. A rail, inside the bulwark, with holes to take belaying pins.

PINTLE. The pin fitted to a clamp on the leading edge of the rudder, point downward, which passes through the eye of the gudgeon on the sternpost.

POLEMAST. A mast formed by one single spar from keel to truck.

POOP. A deck above the open deck at the after end of a vessel. In warships it was above the quarterdeck and sometimes on really large vessels there was also a poop royal above the poop itself.

PORTS. Opening in the side of a ship for guns, oars, ballast or ventilation.

PORTHOLES. Glazed openings in a ship's side or the sides of a deck erection to allow light to enter.

PREVENTER. An additional rope used to support another when the latter is subjected to excessive strain: typical examples are preventer stays, preventer braces, much used in sailing men-of-war to lessen loss of masts and spars if the main rigging was damaged.

PUMP. The apparatus used to discharge water from a ship or to bring it on board for washing down decks, firefighting, etc. There are several different types of pump found on board.
(i) The chain pump, consisting of a series of receptacles attached to an endless chain which passes over a sprocket at deck level and another in the bottom of the ship, the chain and buckets being encased between the two, and operated by a pair of crank handles attached to the upper sprocket.
(ii) The hand pump, which consists of a metal chamber having a long tube of lesser diameter at its lower end extending down to the bottom of the ship. At the bottom of the chamber is a 'lower box', a wooden plug having a large hole in its centre covered on the top by a weighted flap. Sliding up and down within the chamber is a similar 'box', but this is attached to a long metal rod, or spear, the upper end of which hooks into an eye in the handle of the pump brake. This handle is supported by a metal stanchion or similar support. Pushing down on the handle draws the upper box to the top of the chamber, creating a vacuum which is immediately filled with water passing through the lower box. Raising the handle pushes the upper box down the chamber — the water therein passing through the hole to lie in the chamber above the upper box (this water being prevented from flowing back through either box by the weighted flap). On the next upward stroke the water above the upper box is discharged from the pump and the chamber immediately refilled by more water being drawn in through the lower box.

PURCHASE. An arrangement of blocks and falls which increases the lifting power of a rope.

QUARTER. (i) The part of a yard between the slings and the yardarm.
(ii) The part of a vessel's side towards the stern, usually about the quarter of its length measured from the stern.

QUARTERDECK. The deck above the upper deck, reaching forward from the stern. In the nineteenth century, when it was very short it was called the POOP.

QUARTER GALLERY. A small windowed cabin on the quarter of a vessel, usually acting as the officers' lavatories.

QUARTER NETTING. A form of netting stretching along the vessel's rails on the upper part of its quarter and supported by stanchions. To this at times were attached quarter cloths, on the outside, to keep out spray. In men-of-war this netting was double, and hammocks were stowed between the two lengths for protection purposes.

QUARTER RAILS. A rail running from the stern to the gangway, the length of the quarter deck, and acting as a guard rail.

QUOIN. The wedge shaped piece of wood placed under the breech of a carriage mounted gun to adjust the amount of elevation or depression.

RABBET. The groove cut longitudinally in a piece of timber to receive the edge or ends of a plank, or planks. Its depth is usually equal to the thickness of the plank.

RAILS. (i) the plank or planks forming the top of the bulwarks.
(ii) Fence-like structures dividing one part of the deck from another.
(iii) Short lengths of timber, suitably supported for specific purposes, such as fife rails, pin rails.
(iv) Strips of timber, sometimes moulded, fixed to various parts of the vessel's structure for longitudinal strength.
(v) See also HEAD RAILS.

RAKE. To incline from the horizontal or vertical; particularly the angle of inclination of the centre line of a mast from the perpendicular, frequently expressed as so many inches and fractions of an inch, measured horizontally from the centre line of the mast, per foot of length of the mast.

RATE. Warships, by virtue of their size, armament, tonnage were divided into various classes, designated rates, ie First Rate, Fifth Rate.

RATLINE. Small ropes attached transversely between the shrouds of a mast at intervals to form the steps of a rope ladder.

REEF. To reduce the area of a sail by tying part of it up to its yard or boom.

REEF BANDS. A piece of canvas sewn across a sail to strengthen it at the reef points.

REEF POINTS. Short pieces of rope which pass through eyelets in the reef band of the sail, and used for tying the reefed part of the sail to the yard or boom: they are of equal length on either side of the sail.

REEF TACKLE. The tackle attached to the reef cringle on a sail and used for hauling the sail to the yard to facilitate reefing.

REEVE. To pass the end of a rope through an opening.

RELIEVING TACKLE. (i) Another name for the training tackle of a gun.
(ii) Strong tackles attached to the tiller in bad weather.

RIBBAND. Long flexible pieces of timber fastened lengthwise to the outside of a vessel's timbers in specified positions, often connecting with the harpings.

RIBS. The word loosely used to refer to the timbers of a ship.

RINGBOLT. An eyebolt with a moveable ring through the eye.

RING TAIL. A sail sat abaft a gaff sail to increase its area.

ROYAL. The sail above the topgallant sail, on the royal mast.

ROYAL MAST. The mast above the topgallant mast. Often made as one single spar with the topgallant mast, but divided by the topgallant hounds.

RISING LINE. The line drawn on the sheer draught of a ship passing through the ends of all the floor timbers.

ROACH. The allowance made in cutting sail cloth to form the belly in the sail.

ROOM AND SPACE. The distance from the centre of one timber to the centre of the next timber: the space is the interval between the two timbers, the two halves of the timbers occupy the room.

ROVE. The small flat (copper) washer fitted over the end of the nails used in fastening the planks etc. of a boat before the end of the nail is burred over, or flattened against the rove to hold it in place against the plank etc.

RUDDER COATS. Pieces of canvas, well tarred, fitted round the rudder hole to prevent the entry of water into the ship.

RUDDER HEAD. The upper end of the rudder stock (post) to which the tiller is attached.

RUNNING RIGGING. The rigging used to handle the sails and spars of a vessel.

RUN. The aftermost part of a ship's bottom, where it becomes narrow as it approaches the sternpost.

RUNNING BOWSPRIT. A bowsprit which can be hauled inboard.

SAMPSON POST. A strong timber post — like a single bitt — well secured at the heel and passing through the deck just forward of the windlass, used as a seat for the windlass pawl. The heel of the bowsprit was often let into this post. Later it has come to refer rather loosely to any strong post to which mooring or other ropes can be belayed, and, in the case of modern steam or motor ships to the tall steel tubular post supporting some of the cargo handling derricks.

SAVEALL. The name given to the sail set below the foot of a sail to catch any wind which might escape.

SCANTLING. The name given to a piece of timber, or metal, to denote its size, principally breadth and thickness.

SCIATIC STAY. The rope (stay) led from the head of the mainmast to the head of the foremast. A tackle could be attached to the stay when working cargo out of or into a hatch.

SCORE. A groove, hollow, or notch cut in a piece of timber: the 'score of a deadeye' is the hole through which the rope passes.

SCUPPER. Channels cut through the waterways and sides of a vessel, at appropriate places, to carry the water away from the deck: often lined with lead in wooden vessels.

SCUTTLE. A small opening cut in the deck, or side, of a vessel for access to the space below and furnished with a tight-fitting removeable cover or lid.

SEAMS. The gap between the edges of the planks of a ship's side or deck, which are filled with oakum and sealed with hot pitch to prevent the entry of water.

SEIZE. To bind or fasten together two objects or ropes with a lashing of cord or small line, usually referred to as the seizing.

SERVING. Fine line, or spunyarn, wound round a rope to prevent chafe: usually performed with a special mallet.

SHACKLE. A bow, or U-shaped, metal link with the opening closed by a bolt or pin.

SHANK. The main 'stem' of an anchor.

SHEER. The longitudinal curve of a vessel's deck.

SHEERPOLE. Also called SHEER BATTEN; a batten fixed horizontally to the shrouds just above the upper deadeyes.

SHEERSTRAKE. The strake in a ship's topside below the gunwale.

SHEET. (i) The rope or tackle attached to the lower corners or clews of a square sail and led down to the deck: controls the angle at which the free part of the sail is set.
(ii) The rope or tackle from the clew of a jib or staysail to the deck.
(iii) The rope or tackle from the after end of the boom of a gaff sail to the deck.

SHELF. A heavy timber extending the length of a vessel and fitted to the inside of the timbers immediately below the deck beams, which it served to support.

SHELL. In modern usage the outer skin or plating of the hull of a vessel.

SHIP. A sailing vessel with three or more masts, square rigged on all masts.

SHROUDS. The standing rigging of a vessel leading from the mastheads to give lateral support to the masts. The lower masthead shrouds lead to the ship's side, the topmast shrouds lead to the extremities of the crosstrees on the top, and so on. Bowsprit shrouds are shrouds put over the head of the bowsprit and led back to the ship's bows. See also FUTTOCK SHROUDS.

SILLS. Pieces of timber fitted horizontally between the frames, or timbers, to form the upper and lower edges or framework of a port.

SKIDS. (i) Lengths of timber laid transversely across a vessel, and suitably supported, on which the lifeboats are stowed.
(ii) Vertical strips of timber fitted to a vessel's side to prevent damage being done to it when heavy objects are being raised or lowered.

SLING. (i) The rope or chain used to support a yard.
(ii) Special short ropes, etc, used for encircling or attaching to objects to facilitate the attachment of the lifting tackle.

SLINGS. That portion at the middle of a square yard to which the slings were attached.

SPAN. A length of rope secured at both ends, and with a thimble or block on it to which a tackle can be attached.

SPANKER. Another name for a vessel's DRIVER sail.

SPENCER. A fore and aft sail carried on the fore and main mast of a full-rigged ship, usually from a TRYSAIL MAST.

SPENCER MAST. A secondary or auxiliary mast fitted immediately abaft another mast and fitted, usually, between the deck and the trestletrees. The gaff carrying the fore and aft sail slides up and down this mast when being raised or lowered. Also called TRYSAIL MAST.

SPIDER BAND. A metal band set round a mast and fitted with belaying pins.

SPREADERS. Struts for the rigging, usually of wood or iron. Fitted to the crosstrees of large vessels to take the backstays, and at the head of the lower mast on small vessels.

SPRIT. The spar running diagonally across a spritsail to support the upper aftermost corner: the lower end is attached to the mast by a system of metal bands and links.

SPRITSAIL. (i) A large fore and aft sail, shaped like a gaff sail, but without gaff or boom, and supported by the sprit running diagonally across it.
(ii) The term used to designate the square sail carried on a yard below the bowsprit. The spritsail topsail was a square sail set ahead, and above, this spritsail, being attached to a yard slung below the jibboom. At one time this latter sail was set with its yard attached to the spritsail topmast — a short mast set perpendicularly above and on the end of the bowsprit.

STAFF. Light spars erected in various positions on a vessel to display the colours, such as the Ensign staff, the Jackstaff, the Flagstaff.

STANCHIONS. Small pillars of wood or metal used to support various items in a vessel — such as decks, rails, netting, awnings, etc.

STANDING PART. The fixed part of a rope or tackle.

STANDING RIGGING. The fixed rigging used to support the masts and spars, as opposed to the running rigging.

STARBOARD. The right-hand side of a vessel when looking to the bow from the stern.

STATION. The location of a frame or timber.

STAY. A rope used to support a mast in a fore and aft direction, and also in an athwartship direction — such as backstays.

STAYSAIL. A triangular sail set upon the fore and aft stays.

STEALER. A tapered plank worked into the planking at the ends of a vessel where otherwise the ends of the individual planks would become too narrow, or too wide.

STEM. The heavy piece of timber to which the sides of a ship are joined at the fore end.

STEP. (i) To erect a mast in its place.
(ii) The pieces of timber attached to the keels on to contain the heel of the mast.

STERN. The after end of a vessel.

STERN FRAME. The name given to the assemblage or frame of timber comprising the stern post, transoms and fashion pieces. In modern vessels it refers to the casting comprising sternpost and casting attached thereto to form the propeller aperture and bossing for the stern tube and propeller shaft bushes and bearings.

STERNPOST. The heavy timber set up vertically on the after end of the keel, and well secured thereto, upon which is hung the rudder, to which the ends of the lower planking of the vessel's hull are secured, and which carries the transoms, etc.

STERN SHEETS. In a boat the part between the stern and the aftermost seat of the rowers.

STIRRUPS. Short lengths of rope hanging from a yard, having an eye in the lower end through which the footrope is rove.

STOCK. The piece(s) of wood, or metal bar, fixed to the upper end of an anchor shank, and lying transversely to the arms.

STRAKE. A single breadth of planks of a vessel's hull or decks, running the full length of the vessel. Sometimes spelt STREAK.

STRAP. Sometimes STROP. The piece of metal, rope, wire passing round a block or deadeye, or round a yard. An endless loop of rope.

STUDDING SAILS. Light sails set outside the square sails on yards and booms. Always pronounced, and often spelt, STUNSAILS.

STUDDING SAIL BOOMS. The light spars which slide through boom irons fitted at the ends of the yards, and from the ship's side, to carry the studdingsails.

SWAY. To hoist, particularly yards and upper masts.

SWEEPS. The large oars used on board ships, particularly men of war.

SWEEP PORTS. Small openings, or ports, in a vessel's sides through which the sweeps are put when used to propel the vessel. Closed by hinged lids or covers when not in use.

SWIVEL. A small piece of artillery supported by a crutch, the stem of which is mounted in a socket on the vessel's bulwarks.

TABERNACLE. The casing which encloses the lower end of a mast and in which the mast is pivoted. The tabernacle is secured to the deck of the vessel, and allows the mast to be lowered when passing under bridges.

TABLING. On sails, the broad hem on that part of a sail to which the boltrope is sewn.

TACK. (i) The forward lower corner of a fore and aft sail.
(ii) The rope or tackle used to haul out or secure these corners, or that used to retain the clew of a course.

TACKLE. An assemblage of blocks and ropes used for hoisting and pulling.

TAFFRAIL. The rail round a vessel's stern. The carved work at the upper part of a ship's stern.

THIMBLE. A ring of metal, sometimes also heart-shaped, having a grooved outer edge which will fit within an eye or loop in a rope.

THOLES. Small wooden pins, set vertically into the gunwale of boats. Usually found in pairs, the oar being placed between the pins when rowing. Sometimes only one pin is fitted, in which case the oar has a short strip of wood attached to one side in the appropriate position, with a hole therein through which the thole pin is passed: alternatively the oar is secured to the thole pin by a strap or rope. The space between the pair of thole pins was called the row-lock. Nowadays the word rowlock is used to describe a U-shaped piece of metal into which the oar is placed: this U-shape is attached to a metal peg or stem which is inserted in a hole in the gunwale.

THROAT. The inner top corner of a gaff sail.

THWARTS. The seats or benches in a boat upon which the rowers sit.

TILLER. The piece of timber fitted to the head of a rudder, by which it is turned to steer the ship.

TIMBER. The general name given to all kinds of felled and seasoned wood.

TIMBERS. On a ship, the curved pieces of wood, branching out from the keel and rising vertically, forming the shape of the vessel, and often referred to as ribs or frames.

TOGGLE. A wooden pin, tapering at each end,

having a groove round the middle round which a rope can be spliced.

TOP. A platform round the head of a lower mast, resting on the trestle- and crosstrees; its principal function is to spread the topmast rigging.

TOPGALLANT MAST. The mast above the topmast.

TOPMAST. The mast above the lower mast.

TOPPING LIFT. The strong tackle used to suspend the outer end of a boom or gaff.

TOPSIDES. The part of the exterior of a vessel above the waterline.

TRAIL BOARD. The decorated board between the cheeks and fastened to the knee of the head.

TRANSOM. Beams or timbers fixed to and across the sternpost (transversely) to give shape and support to the stern structure. Usually named, starting from the uppermost and downwards, the Helmport transom, Wing transom, Deck transom, 1st, 2nd, 3rd, etc. transoms.

TRAVELLER. A ring, of rope or metal, sliding on a horse, stay, etc., to facilitate the movement of a sheet or sail.

TREENAIL. A wooden pin, or peg, used as a fastening in place of a nail. Usually pronounced TRUNNEL, and spelt in many ways.

TRESTLETREES. Strong timbers fitted fore and aft, horizontally, one on either side of the masthead to support the crosstrees, the frame of the top and the topmast. Usually rest on the top of the cheeks or at the hounds.

TRIATIC STAY. See SCIATIC STAY.

TRICE. To haul up or secure by a small rope or light-line.

TRUCK. (i) The small wooden cap fitted to the top of the uppermost mast: sometimes fitted with a small sheave to take the flag halliards.
(ii) The 'wheel' of wooden gun carriages.
(iii) The circular wooden balls set between the ribs of a parral.

TRUNNION. The short cylindrical metal projection on either side of a cannon, which support it in the carriage.

TRUSS. A rope used to hold or slacken a yard to or from its mast. Later, the metal device attaching a yard to the mast.

TUCK. The part of the after end of a ship where the ends of the bottom planks came together under the counter.

TRYSAIL MAST. See SPENCER MAST.

TUMBLEHOME. The part of a vessel's side above the maximum breadth which falls inward, thereby making the decks of the vessel narrower above this point. The amount by which the side has come inward at the upper (ie the principal deck) is sometimes expressed as a dimension, for example, 9″ tumblehome.

TYE. The part of a halliard which passes over a sheave at the masthead and down to the slings of the yard. Often made of chain, one end being shackled to the halliard to the other to the slings of the yard.

UPPERDECK. The uppermost continuous deck in a vessel running from stem to stern without a break. Often referred to as the strength deck.

VANGS. Braces which steady the outer end of a gaff or sprit being led, one each side, to the deck.

VOTIVE MODELS. Models of ships placed in churches as votive offerings.

WAIST. The part of the upperdeck of a vessel between the forecastle and the quarterdeck.

WAIST CLOTHS. Pieces of canvas stretched along the sides of the ship between the forecastle and quarterdeck, above the bulwark, to cover the stowed hammocks etc., and to keep out spray and wind.

WALES. The strong, thick strakes in a vessel's side planking, extending throughout the full length, giving added strength in way of decks and so on.

WATERWAYS. Long pieces of timber between the sides of a ship and the edge of the deck at one time used to connect the side to the deck, to carry off the water through scuppers. Sometimes found now more in the form of a covering board.

WHIP. (i) A small tackle.
(ii) To bind the end of a piece of rope with twine to prevent it from loosening or becoming untwisted.

WHELP. A batten on the barrel of a capstan or windlass to provide additional gripping power on the rope being hauled in.

WHEEL BOX. The casing or box over a vessel's steering gear or mechanism.

WOOLD. To wind a length of rope round a mast where it is spliced. The several turns thus made are known as WOOLDINGS.

WORMING. To wind spunyard round a rope to fill up the strands: it is laid spirally round the rope in the groove between the strands.

YARDS. Long pieces of timber, tapering from the centre to either extremity, secured to the mast and used to extend the sails.

YARDARM. The outer end of a yard, lying beyond the point where the brace pendant, lift-blocks etc., are secured.